PREVENTION'S

Quick and Healthy

LOW-FAT COOKING

1993

PREVENTION'S
Quick and Healthy
LOW-FAT COOKING
1993

FROM
ENTERTAINING TO
THE EVERYDAY,
OVER 200
DELICIOUS
RECIPES

EDITED BY JEAN ROGERS, FOOD EDITOR, *PREVENTION* MAGAZINE HEALTH BOOKS

RODALE PRESS, EMMAUS, PENNSYLVANIA

Copyright ©1993 by Rodale Press, Inc.

Prevention is a registered trademark of Rodale Press, Inc.

Printed in the United States of America on acid-free ∞, recycled ♲ paper

Recipe photograph on front cover: Blazing Shrimp (page 114)
Cover Photographer: Angelo Caggiano
Food Stylist: Mariann Sauvion

If you have any questions or comments concerning this book, please write:

Rodale Press
Book Readers' Service
33 East Minor Street
Emmaus, PA 18098

ISBN 0–87596–160–6 hardcover
ISSN 1064–7503

2 4 6 8 10 9 7 5 3 1 hardcover

OUR MISSION

We publish books that empower people's lives.

RODALE ❦ BOOKS

Prevention's Quick and Healthy Low-Fat Cooking 1993
Staff

Editor: Jean Rogers

Executive Editor: Debora Tkac

Writers: Dominick Bosco (Chapter 1), Mary Carroll (Chapter 2)

Book and Cover Designer: Debra Sfetsios

Illustrator: Barbara Fritz

Photographers: Angelo Caggiano, Michael Geiger, Rita Maas, Jerry Simpson

Photo Editor: Sabina Ineichen

Food Stylist: Mariann Sauvion

Recipe Development: Ali Barker, JoAnn Brader, Mary Carroll, Sharon Claessens,
Joanne D'Agostino, Barbara Fritz, Aliza Green, Mindy Heiferling,
Judith Benn Hurley, David Keh, Linny Largent-Mayer, Robert Levine,
Lori Longbotham, Emile Mooser, Jean-Claude Nédélec, Alex Panozzo,
Jean Rogers, Marie Simmons, Nancy Zelko

Home Economists, Rodale Food Center: JoAnn Brader,
Anita Hirsch, M.S., R.D.

Research Chief: Ann Yermish

Research Associates: Susan Burdick, Karen Lombardi Ingle

Production Editor: Jane Sherman

Copy Editor: Susan G. Berg

Editor in Chief: William Gottlieb

Editor, **Prevention** *Magazine:* Mark Bricklin

Contents

Menus

PRESTO PESTO
187

Angel Hair with Rosemary Pesto　　　*Tomatoes au Gratin*
Crusty Italian Bread　　　　　　　　*Pineapple Pound Cake*

MANDARIN MONDAY
190

Sweet and Sour Turkey Breast　　　*Apricot Parfaits*
Green Beans with Oyster Sauce

AN EVENING SOUTH OF THE BORDER
192

Bean Enchiladas　　　　　　　*Melon Balls with Lemon-Lime*
Salsa Cruda　　　　　　　　　*Sauce*
Steamed Rice

FRIDAY IN FLORENCE
194

Spaghetti and Meatballs　　　*Cucumber and Dill Salad*
Garlic Bread　　　　　　　　*Creamy Rice Pudding*

LET'S CELEBRATE
198

Peppered Lamb Loin　　　　*Honey-Glazed Carrots*
Squash Soufflé　　　　　　*Cheese Blintzes*

FISHING FOR COMPLIMENTS
202

Lemon Halibut　　　　　*Gingersnaps with Frozen Vanilla*
Potato Crisps　　　　　*Yogurt*
Colorful Pepper Salad

SOUTHERN HOSPITALITY
205

Cheese Grits　　　　　　　　*Spicy Turkey Links*
Scrambled Eggs with Toast　　*Hot Apples with Oat Topping*

FISH 'N' CHIPS
210

Stuffed Cherry Tomatoes　　　*Two-Cabbage Cole Slaw*
Light and Luscious Fish Fry　　*Steamed Snow Peas*
Dill Sauce　　　　　　　　　*Festive Angel Food Cake with Berries*
Oven Fries

GRILLED TO PERFECTION
214

Gazpacho on the Rocks
Pita Chips
Ginger Bass in Foil

Grilled Summer Salad
Herb-Flavored Corn on the Cob
Seared Pineapple and Peaches

THAT'S ITALIAN!
219

Chilled Honeydew Soup
Chicken Cacciatore with Spaghetti
Broiled Vegetables Diablo

Green and Orange Salad
Peach Crisp

FOR MEAT-LOVERS
224

Asparagus Soup
London Broil
Lean Gravy

Cheese-Stuffed Potatoes
Orange-Glazed Carrots
Apple Crumb Pie

A PIZZA PARTY
228

Raspberry Juleps
Smoked Chicken Appetizers
Broccoli Pizza

Turkey and Mushroom Pizza
Easy Pea Salad
Summer Sundaes

SOME LIKE IT HOT
233

Lime-Scented Fruit Wedges
Curried Lamb
Rice Pilaf with Indian Spices

Cucumber Raita
Fresh Pineapple Chutney
Figs and Dates with Whipped Yogurt

THE ORIENT EXPRESS
237

Vegetable Rolls
Stir-Fried Broccoli Medley
Sizzling Beans with Peanuts

Frozen Yogurt with Sweet Peach
Sauce

Introduction

*I*t's hard to believe, but low-fat cooking is now as American as apple pie. And apple pie is just one of the foods you *can* enjoy and still have a healthy diet. All it takes is a little ingenuity to cut unwanted fat from family-favorite recipes—without sacrificing old-time flavor and without depriving yourself.

Just imagine feasting on fun foods such as nachos, chili, burgers, pizza, chicken cacciatore. How about London broil with gravy? Chocolate sorbet? Pineapple blintzes? Whoever thought low fat could taste this good?

But why is it so important to slash the fat in your diet? Because heart disease and cancer, our nation's top two killers, often have a direct link to a high-fat diet. What's more, diabetes, obesity, gallstones and osteoarthritis also have a proven diet connection. Clearly, we need to eat smart if we want to safeguard our health.

These days, however, it's not enough for recipes to be healthy. They've also got to be *quick*. Our busy lifestyles just don't leave much room for lengthy meal preparation.

To get an idea of just what kind of recipes home cooks want in 1993, we went out and talked to many of you. *Prevention's Quick and Healthy Low-Fat Cooking* reflects what you told us: that you want simple, nutritious and delicious recipes—in about the same time it takes to heat up a TV dinner. That you want *your* individual needs met, no matter what the occasion—weeknight meals, company dinners, home-alone dining, parties and more.

To make things really easy for you, we accompany each recipe with guidelines that let you see how much time to allow for up-front prep work and how long the dish takes to cook or bake. And we let you know which recipes can be made ahead so you can get a jump on meal preparation; just look for this symbol. ▶

Think of this book as more than a collection of mouth-watering, kitchen-tested recipes. Let it be your inspiration for making 1993 the year when you finally start living the low-fat life—without turning your life upside down.

Jean Rogers

JEAN ROGERS
Food Editor, *Prevention* Magazine Health Books

CHAPTER 1

WHAT
A LEAN
DIET
CAN DO
FOR YOU

COOKING FOR THE HEALTH OF IT

t wasn't so long ago that if you announced you were serving a low-fat dinner, people would get an uneasy look in their eyes and suddenly remember previous engagements that required their immediate attendance. What they were really remembering was low-fat meals they'd eaten in the past—ones that delivered low taste and little or no eating satisfaction. What's more, they didn't make a connection between what they ate and the state of their health.

Those days are gone for good. At the same time that new and exciting medical research is forging the link between a low-fat diet and a healthier life, people are discovering just how delicious and satisfying this lean cuisine really is.

We recognize now that low-fat cooks have always been solidly on the road to better health. And as their cooking skills sharpen and the ingredients available to them expand beyond plain brown rice and a limited array of produce, we're able to really savor the culinary creations they whip up. Even top-rated chefs are featuring light and lean entrées, side dishes and desserts on their star-studded menus. More to the point, fast-food establishments are acknowledging the low-fat movement and bringing lighter fare to their patrons.

The National Institutes of Health, the largest research-supporting body in the world, would like to see more Americans take up the low-fat lifestyle. "It's prudent to reduce the fat content of your recipes and your diet," says Carolyn Clifford, Ph.D., chief of the Diet and Cancer Branch of the National Cancer Institute, one of the National Institutes of Health. "Eating a well-balanced, low-fat diet that includes a variety of fruits, vegetables and grains is no longer a radical idea."

In the next few pages, we'll give you all the latest research showing just how a low-fat diet can make a big difference in your life, whether you're waging a war with the bathroom scale, hoping to prevent serious illnesses such as heart disease and cancer or just trying to live the healthiest way possible.

And in the remainder of the book, we'll give you delicious recipes that your friends and family will love. These dishes will ensure that low-fat meals at your house are well attended—even eagerly awaited.

EATING LIGHT TIPS THE SCALES

Attention, all you perennial dieters: The medical community has good news—low-fat cooking will help you lose weight and keep it off. Actually, that's not one of the most closely guarded scientific secrets of the universe. But it is basically all you need to know to get off your diet and on with a normal life.

The weight-loss benefits of a low-fat diet have been recognized for almost half a century, says Jay Kenney, Ph.D., R.D., nutrition research specialist at the Pritikin Longevity Center in Santa Monica. "Back in the late 1940s and early 1950s, Walter Kempner, a doctor from Duke University, developed a diet that was basically fruit, rice and a little bit of fish and poultry," says Dr. Kenney. "The idea was to use a low-fat and very-low-salt diet to treat high blood pressure. But it soon became apparent that this diet was an excellent treatment for obesity. More people now go to Duke to be put on that weight-loss diet than for anything else."

Fortunately, you don't have to travel to Duke, or anywhere else, to lose weight on a low-fat diet. Just learning how to cook the low-fat way may be enough to trim those unwanted pounds. And that's where this book can help. The tips, techniques and recipes in it will give you ammunition to win the battle of the bulge.

And you won't even have to count calories! In one study, simply learning low-fat cooking techniques helped a group of essentially normal-weight women to lose a few additional pounds—without restricting their calorie intake. Researchers divided more than 300 women into two groups. One group was taught enough about low-fat cooking and food choices that they could slash the proportion of fat in their diet to a lean 21 percent. The other group received no such instruction and continued to follow a typical American diet in which about 40 percent of their calories came from fat.

None of the women were instructed to lose weight, nor were they subject to any restrictions on how much they could eat. Nevertheless, the women in the low-fat group lost an average of nearly seven pounds in the first six months of the experiment. And they *kept the pounds off* for at least another six months. Women in the higher-fat group lost no weight.

Why does cutting fat in the diet help trim your weight? Scientists believe extra dietary fat is easily *stored* as body fat, whereas excess amounts of protein and carbohydrates must first be *converted* to fat before they can become a permanent part of your hips (or any other part of your body). Apparently, the extra metabolic step needed for the conversion is enough to make the difference.

DON'T DEPRIVE YOURSELF!

We hope you noticed one really important point about that experiment: The women did not restrict how much they ate. This appears to be one of the hallmarks of the low-fat diet, one that comes up again and again in the scientific research: A low-fat diet helps you lose weight without putting a padlock on the refrigerator—or on your appetite.

"As long as people eat low-fat versions of the foods they like, they'll lose weight without dieting," says David Levitsky, Ph.D.,

(continued on page 7)

YOUR FAT BUDGET

*T*here's a lot of talk these days about the best diet for good health. And prominent in most discussions is the mysterious phrase "percent of calories from fat." Doctors say the average American gets approximately 40 percent of his calories from fat. And they say that's far too high.

The American Heart Association strongly recommends reducing that number to 30 percent or less. The Pritikin Longevity Center and heart disease specialist Dean Ornish, M.D., take a harder line. They've gotten excellent results, including reversal of heart disease, with levels of 10 percent or less. The National Cancer Institute is currently conducting a long-term study on the effect of a 20 percent diet.

Numbers! What do they all mean? And do you need a degree in higher mathematics to figure out the percentage of calories from fat in *your* diet?

It's not so difficult. First, if you're eating a typical American diet, you probably need to give your food choices a little more thought. And second, you don't need Einstein's IQ to do the math involved in calculating your current percentage—and then in figuring how to lower it to a level that will do you the most good.

In its most simplified form, the percentage is calculated this way: Total up the grams of fat you consume in a day. Multiply them by nine. Divide that number by your total calorie intake.

If most of your meals are from take-out joints, coming up with those figures might not be so easy—although many of the national fast-food chains do have nutritional analyses available for the asking. If most of your food comes from the supermarket, a little label reading will go a long way toward making the math easier. More and more manufacturers are providing the pertinent information on their labels.

The best way to improve your diet is to aim for a level of 30 percent and then gradually lower that to whatever level you and your doctor deem best as you become more comfortable with your new eating style.

Here's how to figure out where you stand.

1. Start by honestly assessing your ideal weight. There are all sorts of height and weight charts available that can help you determine what that is. From there, you can use the following table to calculate your maximum calorie intake. To use the table, first determine how active you are, then write your ideal weight in the corresponding space in the second column. Do the math, and you've got your daily calorie limit.

IF YOU ARE…	AND WANT TO WEIGH…	MULTIPLY…	FOR YOUR DAILY CALORIE LIMIT
A sedentary woman	_____	× 12 =	_____
A sedentary man	_____	× 14 =	_____
A moderately active woman	_____	× 15 =	_____
A moderately active man	_____	× 17 =	_____
A very active woman	_____	× 18 =	_____
A very active man	_____	× 20 =	_____

2. Once you know your daily calorie goal, it's easy to figure out how many grams of fat you're allowed per day—and that will depend on what percentage of calories from fat you're aiming for. Here's the basic math, followed by another table that will make your calculations even easier.

- Multiply your calorie allotment by the percentage you're aiming for (say, 1,800 calories a day × 25 percent of calories—0.25—from fat). That gives the total number of fat calories you can consume each day. In our example, that's 450 fat calories.

- Now all you have to do is convert *fat calories* to *fat grams*, and that's easy: Divide by 9 (there are 9 calories in 1 gram of fat). So 450 ÷ 9 = 50. You're allowed 50 grams of fat a day.

On the next page is a table that has done all the math for you.

(continued on page 6)

CALORIE LIMIT	FAT GRAMS (20% GOAL)	FAT GRAMS (25% GOAL)	FAT GRAMS (30% GOAL)
1,200	27	33	40
1,300	29	36	43
1,400	31	39	47
1,500	33	42	50
1,600	36	44	53
1,700	38	47	57
1,800	40	50	60
1,900	42	53	63
2,000	44	56	67
2,100	47	58	70
2,200	49	61	73
2,300	51	64	77
2,400	53	67	80
2,500	56	69	83
2,600	58	72	87
2,700	60	75	90

If you memorize your individual number and keep a running total of the fat grams you consume each day, you'll be all set. You won't have to count calories. And you won't bog yourself down with complicated calculations.

Again, look to supermarket labels and recipe nutrient analyses, like the ones in this book, to find out how many grams of fat there are in the foods you eat. You can also buy little booklets that list the grams of fat in many common foods. Carry one with you for easy reference.

Sometimes you'll come across foods and recipes in which more than 30 percent (or 25 percent or 20 percent, depending on what your goal is) of the calories come from fat. Even some of the recipes in this book may be higher than what you're looking for. Does that mean you can't eat them? No!

It's your day-to-day diet that counts, not the percent figure for any single food. If your diet contains a sensible mix of healthy foods—and doesn't lean heavily toward fatty snacks and desserts—the figures will balance out.

professor of nutrition at Cornell University in Ithaca, New York. And that's another reason this book can be invaluable to your weight-loss efforts. Included among the 200-plus low-fat recipes, which range from appetizers to desserts, are party fare, picnic foods, family dinners, elegant fit-for-company meals and mouth-watering sweets. When you've got lean versions of pizza, deviled eggs, spaghetti with meatballs, steak dinners, fish 'n' chips, apple pie and more to choose from, losing weight will just come naturally.

One study that bore this out put women on either a high-fat diet (37 percent of calories from fat) or a low-fat diet (no more than 25 percent of calories from fat). The low-fat diet was by no means "diet food." Similar to the recipes offered here, it included low-fat versions of chicken stir-fry, casseroles, pasta, ice cream, pudding and cookies. Yet the women eating this luscious food lost an average of ½ pound per week. Think about how many pounds *you* could lose if all your meals contained no more than 25 percent of calories from fat!

Of course, *Prevention* readers already know the benefits of low-fat cooking. In our 1991 Home-Remedy Survey of more than 5,000 subscribers, 82 percent of them reported trying a low-fat diet to lose weight *and* having good results.

When we say that a low-fat diet will improve your profile, we aren't just tossing around words. In fact, doctors contend that a low-fat diet not only melts the fat off your body but also replaces a portion of that fat with muscle.

Researchers from the department of nutrition and medical dietetics at the University of Illinois at Chicago measured the effects of both a high-fat diet and a low-fat diet on premenopausal women. After 20 weeks on the low-fat diet, the women experienced a welcome 11.3 percent decrease (by weight) in the fat on their bodies. Even better, their lean muscle mass *increased* an average of 2.2 percent—without the exercise that is normally required for adults to build up muscle.

Amazingly, the women *ate more calories* on the low-fat segment of the experiment than they did on the high-fat portion.

TAKE IT OFF—AND KEEP IT OFF

The true test of a financial strategy is not how much you earn, it's what you *keep*. Well, the true test of a weight-loss strategy is not what you take off but what you *keep off*. And the low-fat diet scores heavily over the low-calorie regimen. In one study pitting the two approaches against each other, overweight men and women were randomly assigned to either a strict low-cal diet (1,200 calories per day for women, 1,500 for men) or a restricted-fat diet (one ounce or less a day). The second group had no calorie restrictions.

After about five months, the low-calorie group had indeed lost more weight than the low-fat group—an average of 21.6 pounds versus an average of 12.3 pounds. But nine months to a year later, the low-calorie group had gained back an average of 13 pounds apiece. The low-fat group, on the other hand, had regained about 3.3 pounds each.

Now if you do a little figuring, you'll see that in the final analysis, both groups had a net loss of the same amount—about nine pounds—at the end of the experiment. But then you should consider what the low-calorie group had to endure for that nine-pound loss: four to five months of sheer deprivation.

And the low-fat group? Were they deprived? Hardly! An ounce of fat per day translates to 28 grams. If you check the nutritional analyses that accompany the recipes in this book, you'll see that you can dine quite nicely on 28 grams of fat. You could have, for instance, a dinner of lemon chicken with noodles, broccoli Parmesan and baked bananas (served with nonfat frozen yogurt) and use up only about 8 of those grams. Or you could enjoy an elegant dinner of peppered lamb loin, pasta, squash soufflé and honey-glazed carrots—topped off with fruity cheese blintzes—for about 15 grams of fat. And you'd have enough of your fat allowance left over for a breakfast of Spanish omelet, juice, toast and turkey links *and* a lunch of chicken noodle soup, a tossed salad with green goddess dressing and nonfat yogurt with berries. Some diet!

Diet for a Happy, Healthy Heart

Although weight loss may be uppermost in many of our minds, it is not the most important benefit of a low-fat diet. In fact, health benefits of this diet that were only controversial conjecture a few years ago have become firmly established. For one thing, the low-fat diet is now recommended by the National Heart, Lung and Blood Institute, another of the federal government's National Institutes of Health, to help prevent and treat cardiovascular disease, the nation's major cause of death.

"Half the people in the United States die because their arteries clog up," says Dr. Kenney. "And yet we've known for more than 30 years that a low-fat and low-cholesterol diet can reduce the risk of death from cardiovascular disease. In the early 1960s, Lester Morrison, M.D., published the results of his 12-year study on the effects of a low-fat diet on heart patients. He put one group of people, all of whom had suffered a heart attack, on a diet that supplied 12 percent of its calories from fat and less than 100 milligrams of cholesterol a day. He also taught them how to reduce the fat in their diet to that level so they could continue the treatment at home. Another group was allowed to eat the regular high-fat American diet.

"Twelve years later, everyone in the second group had died, but 40 percent of the low-fat group were still living," continues Dr. Kenney. "And all of them had started out with rather serious atherosclerosis—clogged arteries. It was a very remarkable study. But few people paid attention to diet as the key to heart disease back then."

That was then; this is now. And since the 1960s, we've come a long way. A recent part of the famous Framingham Heart Study spanning 16 years found that as the amount of fat in the diet rose, so did the incidence of heart disease among men aged 45 to 55. And people are sitting up and listening to that kind of news.

In addition, more than 30 years of research have convinced the National Cholesterol Education Program that saturated fats are the most potent dietary factor in raising blood levels of cholesterol—a major risk factor in heart disease.

Low-Fat Food Keeps Arteries Clear

A low-fat diet helps prevent cardiovascular disease where it counts: on the very walls of the arteries. A study performed at the Atherosclerosis Research Institute of the University of Southern California School of Medicine, Los Angeles, found that a low-fat diet can prevent new deposits of cholesterol-laden plaque from forming on artery walls.

The study focused on 162 men who had just had coronary bypass surgery—men who were known to be at very high risk of new plaque formation. They were asked to keep the fat in their diet to 26 percent or lower. Researchers did tests at the beginning of the study to determine the degree of blockage in the men's arteries. Two years later, they repeated the tests. What they discovered was that the men who succeeded in keeping the fat in their diet very low—below 23 percent—had almost no risk of developing new blockages. Out of the 20 men who did keep their diet that low, 19 had *no new plaque at all.*

A really-low-fat diet can take you even further: It can actually *reverse* the progress of heart disease. Dean Ornish, M.D., assistant clinical professor of medicine at the University of California, San Francisco, tested the effects of a vegetarian diet in which fewer than 10 percent of the calories came from fat. The 28 heart patients he put on the diet also performed moderate exercise, such as walking, along with some yoga and meditation to reduce stress. After the men were on the program for one year, Dr. Ornish again measured the degree of blockage in their arteries. And in that relatively short period of time, the degree of blockage *was actually reversed in 82 percent of the patients.* Arteries began to clear even in those with severe coronary blockages.

Elsewhere, Stephen B. Inkeles, M.D., typically sees several beneficial changes due to a low-fat diet in the men and women who come to the Pritikin Center, where he is a staff physician and director of clinical nutrition: "After as little as one week on the Pritikin diet, which supplies about 10 percent of calories from fat, we see a predictable drop in serum cholesterol, a drop in dangerous triglyceride levels, a drop in blood pressure and weight and frequently a normalization of blood sugar."

You might not think a low-fat diet would affect blood pressure one way or the other, but it does. And in fact, high blood pressure is a danger on several fronts. It's a leading cause of strokes. And it's also a potent risk factor for heart disease. The connection with heart disease occurs because a high-fat diet, which is often loaded with saturated fat, raises blood pressure.

Two Finnish studies looked into this relationship. One study of more than 700 men found that saturated fats in the diet tended to raise blood pressure, especially systolic pressure (which is the higher number in a blood pressure reading and gives an indication of how hard your heart is pumping out blood). The other study tested the effects of a low-fat diet on blood pressure in 57 rural couples. A diet that supplied no more than 23 percent of its calories from fat lowered the participants' average systolic blood pressure from 138 to 130 and reduced their diastolic blood pressure from 89 to 81. Such reductions can help bring elevated blood pressure down to more normal levels.

The Link between Food and Cancer

A low-fat diet can also help lower your risk of cancer. A number of studies have linked high fat intake with high incidences of various deadly cancers, particularly cancers of the colon, breast, prostate and endometrium. According to Dr. Clifford of the National Cancer Institute, "We know that diet plays a role. What we don't know is precisely how much of a role that is."

The institute is supporting several studies to find out. "Most of these are clinical trials," says Dr. Clifford. "That means one group will remain on their usual diet, while another will be provided with counseling and nutrition education on how to reduce their fat intake to 20 percent of calories from fat. They'll also learn to increase the amounts of vegetables, fruits and grains in their diet and to increase their fiber intake in general. These studies will take five to ten years."

In the meantime, Dr. Clifford acknowledges that the available research to date should be enough to convince most people to reduce the level of fat in their diets. "There is already a lot of evidence that a low-fat diet may reduce the risk of several types of cancer," she says.

Colon cancer is the second most lethal form of cancer. Only lung cancer kills more Americans every year. Many colon cancer deaths are preventable, say researchers. And reducing the amount of fat in the diet is emerging as the prevention method of choice, according to the latest research.

In one study, scientists compared the incidence of colorectal adenomas (which precede and often lead to cancer) with the amount of saturated fat in the diet. What they found is just part of the convincing case for a low-fat diet: As saturated fat increases in the diet, the risk of colorectal adenomas rises right along with it.

If you know a little about what goes on in the digestive system when you eat fat, it might help you understand why decreasing dietary fat is so important. Though fat itself is not carcinogenic, it does set off a chain reaction in the body that can lead to the production of cancer-causing substances. When fat is digested, the gallbladder releases bile acids. These bile acids then wind up in the colon, where bacteria convert them into *secondary* bile acids. It's these secondary bile acids that can produce certain changes in the intestinal walls that, over time, may lead to cancer.

A low-fat diet weakens this chain reaction. With smaller amounts of fat to digest, less bile acid is secreted, and less secondary bile acid is produced. Furthermore, on a low-fat diet, fewer of the bacteria that convert bile acids to cancer promoters are produced. This is one currently popular theory as to how a high-fat diet promotes colon cancer, although the mechanism is still unknown.

BIND UP THOSE FREE RADICALS!

Researchers believe there are other ways in which a low-fat diet helps protect against cancer. When fat breaks down in the body, chemically unstable molecules called *free radicals* are created. Although they sound like bail-jumping terrorists, free radicals are actually more dangerous to your personal health. They damage the cells and tissues they touch. And when they come in contact with DNA—the very building block of your cells—tumor growth can result.

One National Cancer Institute study found that a low-fat diet dramatically decreased the amount of free radical damage in women with an elevated risk of breast cancer. Women on a 15 percent calories from fat diet for as long as two years had only one-third as much free radical damage to the genetic material in their blood as did other women on a 30 percent or higher diet.

Concentrations of hormones in a woman's body can also affect cancer risk, particularly for breast cancer. Research has shown that a low-fat diet can reduce such dangerous concentrations. After a group of postmenopausal women spent from 10 to 22 weeks on a diet that reduced the amount of fat in their diet from 40 percent of calories to 20 percent of calories, the amount of a hormone believed to increase risk of breast cancer was reduced by 17 percent. That may not sound like a dramatic reduction, but the researchers involved note that it could eventually account for a fourfold to fivefold reduction in breast cancer risk. And that is significant.

As for lung cancer, the most deadly cancer in America, Dr. Kenney says that fat appears to be a powerful factor there, too—perhaps as powerful as cigarette smoking: "The Japanese have twice as many men who smoke as Americans, but they have a lower incidence of lung cancer. That wouldn't make sense if cigarettes were the only cause of lung cancer. By that measure, the Japanese should have twice as much. But they also eat far less fat than Americans."

In the same vein, says Dr. Kenney, southern European smokers have far less cancer than northern European smokers. Guess which group eats more fat. The northern Europeans consume a lot more saturated fat and cholesterol, while the southerners take in considerably less. Of course, other factors may be involved, such as the increased intake of fruits and vegetables that's typical of a low-fat diet.

"In Hawaii," continues Dr. Kenney, "they compared how much cholesterol different groups of smokers consumed and found a high correlation between eating more cholesterol and having lung cancer. Cholesterol consumption tends to go up as fat—especially saturated fat—in the diet increases. So a high-fat diet may put smokers at a greater risk for lung cancer."

SUPERCHARGE YOUR IMMUNE POWER

A low-fat diet may also help protect against cancer by giving a boost to the body's own immunity defenses. "A lot of research—on both animals and people—indicates that a high-fat diet causes changes in the immune system that adversely affect its function," says Dr. Kenney.

In fact, research seems to indicate that a low-fat diet can actually strengthen the body's first line of defense against cancer: natural killer cells. These fierce cells are the body's superheroes. They attack and kill malignant cells before the immune system's other soldiers, the T-cells and the macrophages, are even mobilized. Think of killer cells as the A-team.

When scientists put a group of men in their twenties and thirties on a lowered-fat diet, they found something startling: For every 1 percent decrease in dietary fat, the activity of natural killer cells increased significantly. In other words, the lower the percentage of calories from fat in the men's diets, the more lean and mean their cancer-fighting killer cells became.

A low-fat diet can help prevent cancer in one other way: by encouraging you to eat better, healthier foods. One study at the National Cancer Institute found that as the percentage of fat in the diet fell, the intake of vegetables, fruits and cereals—which contain fiber and vital nutrients such as vitamin C, carotene and vitamin A—increased. Conversely, as the percentage of fat in the diet rose, so did the consumption of less healthy foods such as high-fat red meats, processed meats, whole milk, fatty cheeses, whole eggs and rich desserts. Those are the very foods that tote hefty amounts of saturated fat, cholesterol and sodium. And they're not just undesirable in their own right—they crowd more healthy foods right out of the diet.

All of that is especially significant in light of another study that demonstrated food choice *patterns* can also determine cancer risk. Researchers at the State University of New York at Buffalo looked at the food choice patterns of more than 2,200 men and women.

They found that high-fat diet patterns significantly increased the risk of colon cancer.

As Dr. Clifford points out, "If you reduce the fat content of your diet, you're also changing other components. Fat is a dense source of calories. If you reduce your fat intake, you must replace at least part of it with fruits, vegetables and grains—which are low in fat and high in beneficial fiber."

The recipes in this book can show you how to cut back on fatty foods and replace them with fiber-rich, nutrient-dense ones. Our low-fat, no-cholesterol omelets and frittatas, for instance, include high-fiber vegetables. Most of our main-course meat dishes combine a modest amount of meat with filling low-fat pasta, rice or other grains. All of our full-meal menus are designed to balance meat, fish and poultry with healthy appetizers, vegetable side dishes and satisfying low-fat desserts.

THE DIABETES CONNECTION

A low-fat diet also will dramatically reduce your risk of diabetes—in two ways. First, excess fat in the diet has been directly linked with an increased risk of diabetes. Scientific research suggests that for every extra 40 grams of fat in the diet per day, the risk for adult-onset, non-insulin-dependent diabetes (Type II) may rise threefold. How much fat is 40 grams? Well, a quarter-pound fast-food hamburger with a large order of fries has that alarmingly high amount. Even a three-scoop ice cream sundae can cost you that much.

The second way a low-fat diet can reduce diabetes risk has to do with food choices. Remember those studies that demonstrated high-fat foods tend to crowd out healthier ones? Well, in this case, if you allow fatty foods to nudge out of your diet just 90 grams of carbohydrates—equal to one apple, one banana and a baked potato—your risk of impaired glucose tolerance could rise by more than half.

"What promotes diabetes more than anything else, other than genetics, is being fat and inactive," says Dr. Kenney. "It's no wonder Americans have a high rate of diabetes. Insulin resistance seems to develop in people who are overweight and inactive and who eat a lot of foods high in fat and sugar or refined carbohydrates—junk food like potato chips, candy and pastries." Low-fat, no-sugar recipes like the ones in this book can go a long way toward satisfying anyone on a diabetic diet.

There are other health problems you may be able to avoid by adopting a low-fat diet. They include:

Arthritis. According to Dr. Inkeles, "A high-fat diet tends to produce obesity, and obesity is a major cause of the most prevalent type of arthritis, osteoarthritis." So eating low-fat foods will help keep your weight down and thereby possibly help prevent osteoarthritis.

Gallstones. "You tend to see gallstones in overweight people," says Dr. Kenney. "If you eat a high-fat diet, you become obese and are more likely to get gallstones. Whether it's a direct effect or not is debatable, but we do know that the normal, high-fat American diet encourages the development of gallstones." One more reason to keep your diet on the lean side.

There's another potential benefit of the low-fat lifestyle: **a better sex life.** Researchers at the University of Utah have discovered that high-fat meals reduce the production of testosterone, the hormone that fuels sex drive. Exactly why this occurs is still a mystery, but the theory is that fat somehow inhibits the very cells that produce testosterone. Furthermore, men with the most fat on their bodies tend to have the lowest testosterone levels. So it could be that a low-fat diet makes you not only look sexy but also feel sexy!

The time has never been better to become a low-fat cook. As Dr. Kenney says, "It's a lot easier today to eat a low-fat diet than it was in the 1950s. But if it could be done back then, by the people Dr. Kempner and Dr. Morrison trained, it certainly can be done today with all the interest in the subject and so many of the nation's favorite foods available in low-fat versions. Food companies are falling all over themselves to produce low-fat and fat-free foods. It's quite a change from the 1950s!"

We agree with Dr. Kenney. And with Dr. Clifford, who says, "It's easier to reduce the fat content of your diet if you know how to do it."

That's what this book is all about. We'll give you all the tools—from a rundown of the kitchen equipment and pantry supplies vital for low-fat cuisine to recipes you'll really use and love—to live happily ever after on the low-fat lifestyle. Following the tips, techniques and recipes, you'll never have to say "diet" again. And you just may avoid or help lessen the impact of some very serious health problems. Here's to your health!

CHAPTER 2

STOCKING
THE
HEALTHY
KITCHEN

PANTRY PRIDE

If you're like most busy people, you may think there aren't enough hours in the day to get your work done, much less plan healthy, low-fat meals. How can you create satisfying menus for yourself and your family with a minimum of fuss and a maximum of flavor?

The most important ways are to shop smart—choosing healthy ingredients that cook fast—and to use timesaving equipment when preparing those foods. In this chapter, we'll show you how to stock your pantry with nutritious, quick-cooking ingredients and what to do with them once you have them in the house. We'll also give you a rundown of which kitchen tools are best for making healthy meals fast. In addition, we'll share cooking tips from health-conscious chefs.

Smart Shopping

Some healthy items take forever to cook—you might buy them once, but it's practically guaranteed they won't make their way into your everyday meals. Luckily, quicker-cooking low-fat foods abound in today's health-conscious marketplace. The detailed list starting on page 18 will tell you what to look for.

But smart shopping starts at home. Your first item of business should be to draw up a plan before you leave the house. It'll save you time and reduce your chances of bringing home impulse buys—especially high-fat and sugary ones.

You can get as detailed as Mark, a banker in San Francisco, who obtained a map of his local supermarket from the manager. Mark photocopied the map and tapes one to his refrigerator door each week. On it he marks his shopping list by writing foods right on the aisles where they are shelved. Following his map, Mark can skip whole aisles of foods that aren't on his healthy eating plan. He's usually in and out of the store within 30 minutes.

Nancy, a dietitian from Minneapolis, recommends shopping on a full stomach. Hungry shoppers tend to buy more than they can use, she says, and that usually translates to an excess of junk food. Before leaving home, she eats lightly, even if it's only a piece of fresh fruit. That way, she has an easier time resisting the urge to buy fatty foods. She also tries to avoid peak store hours, shopping in her neighborhood supermarket before work. Setting her alarm 30 minutes earlier on Wednesdays, Nancy dresses for work, then heads to the store. At that hour, she has the place to herself. She's less apt to feel frantic—which often results in impulse purchases—and gets home with plenty of time to put groceries away before work.

Look Out for Labels

Since even so-called health foods can be high in fat, careful label reading is essential to smart shopping. Ingredients are listed on labels in descending order of quantity. Ideally, choose products with no fats or oils. When that's not possible, opt for ones where fats and oils are low on the list.

Remember that many prepared foods such as canned soups,

baked goods, sauces and frozen dinners contain astonishingly high amounts of fat. If you're confused, ignore any nutritional claims on the package front, since they are often misleading. Read the back first. In general, you'll do best to choose fresh food over frozen and frozen over canned.

Remember that changing eating and shopping habits is a long-term process. Start by trying new foods each time you shop. The produce section makes an ideal testing ground. Due largely to the efforts of distributors such as Freida's of California, more and more exotic produce is showing up in supermarkets. Make it a goal to select one new item every week to try in a recipe. Remember that fresh fruits and vegetables are usually low in fat and high in fiber—so they're safe bets for experimenting.

THE LOWDOWN ON LOW-FAT INGREDIENTS

The real secret to eating healthy without spending all your time in the kitchen is choosing the finest easy-to-prepare ingredients. The list below gives our favorite fast, low-fat foods. Try them and transform your cooking!

Berries. Fresh, summer-ripened berries are the height of low-fat luxury. The most succulent berries are brightly colored, uniform in size and fragrant. Whenever possible, buy locally and in season. Check the fruit when you get it home for any bruised or moldy pieces. Store the fruit in the refrigerator and use it within a few days. For longer storage, place unwashed berries on a cookie sheet and freeze until solid, then pack into self-sealing bags. To use, rinse while still frozen—the water will clean and partially defrost the berries.

Naturally, berries are best eaten out of hand. But you can make great low-fat desserts by using pureed berries on top of pudding or sliced ones over angel food cake (a smart alternative to shortcake). And don't forget fat-free sorbets—mash fresh berries with fruit juice or sweetener, freeze in ice-cube trays, then puree briefly in a food processor.

Bran and wheat germ. Bran is the outer coating of grains, and there are a variety of brans on the market: wheat, oat, corn and rice, for example. Wheat germ is the inner kernel of wheat berries. Both products add essential fiber to your diet. You can easily incorporate them into everyday dishes such as meat loaf, casseroles, muffins, chili, stews, sandwich fillings and thick beverages. You can also use toasted bran or wheat germ as breading for fish and chicken or as a replacement for buttered crumbs atop a casserole. Or take a tip from Chef Jacques Pepin, who likes to enrich regular white flour with bran when making bread.

Butter-flavored sprinkles. When you want the taste of butter without a lot of fat and calories, turn to this flavorful powder. Use it straight from the jar over cooked vegetables, omelets, pasta, warm toast and all sorts of other foods. Or dilute it with water and use the liquid to baste cooking foods or to steam-sauté them without added fat. Two popular brands are Butter Buds Sprinkles and Molly McButter. Do be aware, however, that sprinkles contain a fair amount of sodium. If you're on a salt-restricted diet, you'll want to go easy on them.

Canned tomato puree and tomato paste. Look for low-sodium versions. Add the puree to soups as a thickener, or whir it in the blender with garlic and spices for an instant low-fat spaghetti sauce or pizza topping. Add a dab of tomato paste to soups and cooking grains, such as rice or couscous, for added color and flavor.

Chili peppers. At least 200 types of chili peppers exist. The rule of thumb is that the larger and greener the pepper, the milder it is; conversely, the smaller and redder, the hotter. Either type will add robust flavor to foods, so you can forgo fatty ingredients and even cut back on salt.

When cutting fresh chili peppers, wear rubber gloves to avoid contact with oils in the seeds and membranes that can irritate skin. A few ways to use the peppers: Add one or two whole peppers to simmering soups and stews for extra spiciness. Use chopped peppers in salsas and casseroles. Roast whole, large green chilis to soften them and so that you can remove the skin. Then stuff the peppers with low-fat cheese or even something as unusual as chicken salad. No matter what type you choose, they'll add vitamins A and C to your meals.

Citrus. Whether it's lemon, lime, orange, grapefruit or one of the myriad other types, citrus fruits add great flavor to low-fat cooking. Lydia Shire, chef at the celebrated Biba restaurant in Boston, uses lemon juice as a quick seasoning. "It's amazing what a squeeze of lemon can do for a dish," she says. "Most of the time you don't even realize it's there, but citric acid in the juice heightens other flavors naturally."

If you have extra citrus fruit that you need to use up, squeeze the juice and freeze it in ice-cube trays. Then store the cubes in a plastic bag. Either thaw before using or toss frozen cubes into soups, stews, simmering grains or other dishes.

Cruciferous vegetables. Broccoli, cabbage, cauliflower and other members of this vegetable family are great low-fat sources of vitamin C and beta-carotene. They've also been shown to have some protective effects against certain types of cancer. They're certainly quick cooking, so you should eat them often. (For that matter, most types are delicious raw; use them in salads and as crudités for low-fat dips.) All are delicious steamed and sprinkled with balsamic vinegar or fresh lemon juice—serve as a side dish with grilled or baked foods.

Besides the usual varieties, try the new broccoflower, a bright-green hybrid that looks like cauliflower but tastes like mild broccoli.

Defatted stock. For the quickest low-fat stock to use in soups, casseroles, pilafs and other dishes, buy canned chicken or vegetable broth—low sodium is best. When using the chicken stock, be sure to skim off the globules of fat that are on the surface. (In winter, they'll congeal on their own for easy removal. But in summer, they'll tend to liquefy—store the cans in the refrigerator so that the fat will harden.)

When you have a little extra time, make your own low-fat stock and freeze it for future use. A quick way is in the microwave. Take about 12 ounces of boneless, skinless chicken meat and cut it into small cubes. Combine in a casserole with about four cups of water and some finely chopped vegetables, such as carrots, onions, garlic and celery. Microwave on high for 20 minutes, stirring occasionally. Let stand for another 20 minutes before straining. (Reserve the meat and vegetables for another use.) Skim any visible fat from the surface.

Fish and shellfish. Fish and shellfish should play a big role in a healthy diet because they're low in calories and saturated fat. And they're doubly appealing because they take less time to prepare than many cuts of meat and bone-in poultry. Whenever possible, buy fresh fish. For less work in the kitchen, choose fillets and steaks rather than whole fish, preshelled shrimp, shucked oysters and clams and containers of ready-to-eat crabmeat. When purchasing canned tuna, choose water-packed for the lowest fat.

When buying frozen fish, look for the new flash-frozen ones sold in vacuum packs. This freezing technique gives you fish that tastes ocean-fresh and is an improvement over old freezing methods. And fish packaged in a single layer thaws more quickly than that sold in a solid block.

Flour. Many varieties of flour are available for nutritious desserts and breads. Among the types you might want to keep on hand are regular whole-wheat, whole-wheat pastry, unbleached and specialty items like buckwheat. Store whole-grain flour in the freezer so that its oils won't turn rancid. But bring the flour to room temperature before using in any yeast-risen recipe. Choose lighter-textured flours for pastry and quick breads. Flours with coarser texture and more gluten are best for yeast breads.

Fresh ginger. Grated fresh ginger adds sparkle to stir-fries, sautés, salad dressings and marinades. It's got a fresh flavor that powdered ginger just can't match. Leo Goto, chef/owner of the Wellshire Inn in Denver, likes to combine ginger with low-sodium soy sauce to use as a no-fat flavor enhancer for soups, sauces, dressings and casseroles.

Because fresh ginger is perishable, some chefs like to grate it and freeze the shreds for quick future use. Just pack the ginger in self-sealing bags or small containers—the pieces will stay loose, so you can measure out what you need for a recipe. It will last for up to six months.

Fruit. Whether fresh or dried, fruit adds dietary fiber, vitamins and minerals to a low-fat diet. And there are lots more ways to use fruit than just in fruit salad. Add small amounts of raisins or chopped bananas, for instance, to stews for Caribbean-style flavor. Substitute part of the meat in burrito and enchilada fillings with chopped apples, pears or dried apricots. Add slices of fresh strawberries and oranges to green salads.

You can also bake apple or pear halves along with winter squash, then puree the cooked fruit as a fat-free topping for the squash. Or take a tip from Robin O'Neill, senior general manager at Kincaid's Restaurant in Minneapolis: Make a quick glaze for fish by pureeing fresh peaches or apricots with spices and a touch of sweetener.

Fruit also makes fast dessert—whether eaten out of hand, poached or simply sliced and served over low-fat cake or sorbet. For something different, freeze whole grapes, pineapple chunks, peach slices and strawberries. Eat as is or puree for summer smoothies. Tropical fruits are an exotic way to splurge without added calories or fat. Try sliced ripe melons, such as cantaloupe, honeydew and crenshaw, topped with a puree of dates, orange sections and lemon juice. Chop fresh figs to top low-fat frozen vanilla yogurt. Or slice the figs and serve in a pool of pureed raspberries. The possibilities are endless.

Greens. Make a big, fresh salad part of your daily meals—

nothing could be easier. And as long as you use low-fat dressing, salads can be very lean indeed. For extra flavor and eye appeal, stock up on different kinds of greens, such as endive, arugula and radicchio and Bibb, romaine and red leaf lettuces. Don't forget raw spinach—it's packed with vitamins. To make salads a snap to throw together, wash the leaves as soon as you get home from the store. Shake off excess water and roll up the greens in paper towels or kitchen towels; place in a plastic bag and refrigerate.

Learn to love your greens minus heavy dressings. Purchase fat-free varieties or make your own with nonfat mayonnaise, yogurt or buttermilk and fresh herbs. For something a little different, sprinkle the greens with balsamic vinegar or a generous squeeze of fresh lemon juice.

Herbs. Nothing compares with the flavor of fresh herbs in salads, soups and dressings. Supermarkets are beginning to carry a nice variety of fresh herbs in the produce section. And herbs are easy to grow, so you can have your own supply in summer. Cookbook author Martha Stewart recommends potting up your favorite varieties and growing them on the windowsill during the winter. They take little care and repay you with a burst of flavor.

Most chefs use fresh herbs in marinades. California restaurateur Wolfgang Puck, owner of Spago, Chinois on Main and other popular establishments, makes his own herb basting sauce to bring out the flavor of grilled foods. "I use chopped tomatoes, vinegar, some fresh basil and lime juice," he says.

If you simply can't get fresh herbs, use about one-third as much dried. Crush the dried herbs in the palm of your hand and take a whiff to check their pungency. Dried herbs will keep about six months if they're stored in well-sealed jars away from light and heat.

Lean meats. Smart consumers are demanding lower-fat cuts of meat, so many butchers and supermarkets now offer the very leanest selections. Beef reigns supreme when it comes to iron—it's got about 1½ times more of this blood-building mineral than equivalent servings of chicken and fish. Lamb and pork also contain good quantities of this nutrient.

Eaten in moderation, lean red meats won't blow your fat budget. When you buy meat, choose trimmed cuts without visible marbling. Cuts that make the grade for leanness include beef eye of round, top round, tip round, top sirloin, top loin, tenderloin and flank steak; pork tenderloin or center loin; and lamb leg, sirloin or loin.

Because the lean cuts are typically tougher than fatty ones, it's often a good idea to marinate them before cooking. See page 136 for some marinade suggestions.

Legumes. Doctors say that a high-fiber diet can reduce your cancer risk and help lower serum cholesterol. Dried beans and peas are an important source of dietary fiber. They're a protein staple for many Third World cultures, and some nutritionists recommend that we Americans replace half our daily meat intake with cooked beans as a low-fat alternative.

Although dried beans require lengthy soaking and cooking, you can save time—and still get plenty of fiber—by using canned beans. Simply spoon them into a strainer and rinse under cold water to remove excess sodium and the thick liquid they're packed in. Use in salads, soups, casseroles, dips and spreads. Dried lentils and split peas cook quickly, so they need no presoaking—use them for quick soups, taco fillings and such.

For times when you do want to cook your own dried beans, cut time by using a pressure cooker. (It works for any variety except chick-peas, lentils and split peas—their skins float to the top of the cooker and can clog the vent.) Pressure cooking can cut total time from several hours to 30 to 45 minutes if the beans are presoaked. Quick-soak the beans by covering them with about one inch of water and microwaving them on high for 15 minutes. Let stand for 15 minutes, or until the beans have swelled up.

Some of the most versatile beans are:

Black beans. Latin-American cooks mix them with chili peppers for stews, chili and burrito fillings. Black beans have a rich, meaty flavor. They're often served with rice.

Chick-peas. Also known as garbanzo beans, chick-peas lend a delicious flavor to soups, especially minestrone, and are great marinated for a quick antipasto.

Lentils and split peas. The quickest-cooking legumes, both add a buttery flavor to soups, stews and vegetable pâtés. Lentils hold their shape when cooked and marinated for summer salads. Indian cooks use red lentils in dahl, a pureed bean condiment for curry dishes.

Lima beans. Limas have a naturally rich flavor that makes most dishes taste like they contain olive oil. They also thicken soups quickly. Puree them with garlic and spices for a quick sandwich spread or party dip.

Pea beans. These tiny white beans hold their shape when cooked. They're a low-fat choice for bean salads, minestrone and bean stew; they're also delicious pureed for sandwich spreads and party dips.

Pinto and kidney beans. These Southwest standbys are naturals for burritos, tacos, enchiladas and chili. Kidney beans are also a staple in three-bean salad. Puree and season them for low-fat refried beans or as a dip for tortilla chips.

Low-fat cheeses. If you use low-fat cheeses in moderation for flavoring, they can be a healthy addition to a low-fat diet. The selection has grown in recent years and includes Cheddar, Swiss, Colby and others.

Hard cheeses are generally higher in fat than soft ones. A notable exception is sapsago, a light-green low-fat cheese from Switzerland. It's worth seeking out in cheese shops and large supermarkets. Very soft types, like cottage cheese and ricotta, tend to be the lowest in fat and calories, with fat-free varieties of both widely available.

Some chefs use pureed soft cheeses in place of oil in salad dressings, sauces and spreads. Caprial Pence, co-owner/chef of the Westmoreland Bistro in Portland, Oregon, purees cottage cheese with lots of garlic, shallots, Dijon mustard and fresh herbs for a deliciously creamy dressing.

Low-fat milk products. Other low-fat dairy products include buttermilk and nonfat versions of sour cream, milk and yogurt. You may substitute equal quantities of the lean varieties in recipes that call for the full-fat versions. Try nonfat yogurt or sour cream on baked potatoes; add low-fat buttermilk to muffin recipes and salad dressings. Chef Pence replaces most of the cream in many of her restaurant's cream soups with condensed skim milk and pureed potatoes.

When cooking with yogurt or nonfat sour cream, add them to cooked dishes after removing the food from the heat. That keeps these cultured dairy products from separating.

Mustard. Don't overlook this piquant condiment in sandwiches and salad dressings. And use both creamy Dijon and coarse stone-ground mustards as low-fat flavorings for meats, fish and poultry before—and after—grilling or baking.

Nonfat mayonnaise. Mayonnaise has slimmed down a lot in recent years and now can be part of the low-fat diet. Although slightly paler in color and stiffer in texture than full-fat mayonnaise, most nonfat brands work as well in recipes as their traditional counterparts.

Oils. Oils are pure fat, so it's important to use a light hand. But small amounts of extra-flavorful oils can magically enhance low-fat recipes. That's because oils serve to transport flavor to the taste buds. Even a tiny amount of olive, walnut, toasted sesame or hazelnut oil gives extraordinary flavor to marinades and stir-fried dishes. For everyday sautéing, use small amounts of canola, a bland oil that's high in heart-healthy monounsaturated fat.

For best flavor, store oils in the refrigerator. If they thicken from the cold, let them stand at room temperature for a few minutes before using. Try not to use too high a heat when cooking with oil, says Wolfgang Puck. "High heat brings out the acids in the oil and spoils the flavor."

Onion-family vegetables. The onion family includes aromatics such as garlic, leeks, onions, scallions and shallots. All onions have the ability to heighten the flavor of meats, grains and vegetables. They are an important ingredient in the low-fat kitchen. As with many ingredients, fresh types rate much higher than dried or powdered ones. In fact, dried onions and garlic powder can be bitter.

For a delicious low-fat sauce, roast any onion-family vegetables on the grill or in the oven, then puree them, says Chef Brenda Langton. She uses onion and garlic sauces over croquettes, vegetable loaves and casseroles at Cafe Brenda, her popular Minneapolis restaurant. They substitute for traditional cream sauces without any loss of flavor, she says.

Pasta. In all its shapes and sizes, pasta is a number one quick-cooking food. And it's a natural for low-fat menus. Just make sure to top it with fresh tomato, herb and vegetables sauces rather than fatty cream ones. For an extra bit of variety, choose a flavored pasta. Artichoke, spinach, beet and tomato are just a few of the savory choices available.

Although pasta cooks quickly, you might consider making extra while you've got the pot boiling. Leftovers keep up to five days in the refrigerator. Use them cold in salads, or reheat them briefly in the microwave for hot meals.

Poultry. Chicken and turkey are lean and light, but only if you remove all visible fat and don't eat the skin—the skin contains a large percentage of poultry's fat. The very leanest cuts are boneless, skinless chicken and turkey breasts. Ground turkey is a lower-fat substitute for ground beef, but be aware that most brands aren't nearly as lean as turkey breast that you grind yourself (cut the meat into cubes and grind with on/off turns in the food processor).

You can poach skinless turkey or chicken breasts in defatted broth, then top them with fresh or canned salsa to make a low-fat Mexican entrée. Or brown turkey cutlets for two to three minutes per side in a no-stick pan, then cut the cooked meat into strips for salads. You can also shred cooked poultry for use in casseroles or as a topping for pasta.

Quick-cooking grains. These indispensable foods are high in hunger-appeasing carbohydrates but very low in fat. And the ones listed below cook very quickly, so you can incorporate them into everyday meals. If you prepare extras, you can reheat the leftovers in a minute in the microwave.

Barley. A great fiber source, quick-cooking barley gives soups and stews a chewy texture and rich flavor. You can also use it as the base for pilafs and casseroles. Or mix cooked barley into bread dough. For unusual muffins, grind raw barley into flour and substitute it for part of the flour in your favorite recipes.

Bulgur. This parboiled and dried form of whole wheat needs only to be rehydrated with boiling liquid, which takes about 15 minutes. It's a favorite for tabbouleh and other Middle Eastern dishes. If you toast the bulgur over low heat before adding your liquid, you'll get a pleasantly nutty flavor. Besides eating bulgur as a side dish, you can add a cupful of the cooked grain to vegetable soups or green salads for extra protein.

Couscous. Another Middle Eastern offering, couscous is a granular product made from semolina flour. It's ready even faster than bulgur (but because it's a refined wheat product, it's lower in fiber). Serve as a side dish with skewered lean meat, broiled chicken, stir-fried seafood or sautéed vegetables.

Millet. Pearly yellow millet is a common ingredient of birdseed, but it's also good people food—nutty and delicious in soups, salads and stews. It cooks in about half an hour. For a delicious and easy pilaf, mix with cooked brown rice. When making quick breads, add some uncooked millet directly to the batter.

Oats. Because the bran is retained during milling, oats are an exceptional source of fiber. Quick-cooking oats are the fastest to prepare, but even old-fashioned oats are ready in a short time. Add either type to meat loaves and pilafs. Use them in stews and soups as a thickener. Or grind the oats into flour (use your blender) to use in muffin, pancake and waffle batters.

Rice. White rice cooks a lot faster than regular brown—taking about 20 minutes instead of 45 or more. But the new quick-cooking brown rice is ready in a mere 10 minutes, making it so easy to include this fiber-rich grain in your diet. Use rice as a casserole filler or as the base for stir-fried vegetables. For extra color and flavor, add finely chopped peppers, onions and carrots. Make exotic pilafs by incorporating minced dried apricots or unsweetened pineapple.

Spices. Like herbs, spices add incomparable flavor to low-fat dishes. Defined as the bark, seeds or roots of aromatic plants, they're available whole or already ground. To bring out their full flavor, try toasting them in an ungreased skillet over low heat until fragrant, about five minutes. For the longest shelf life, store spices as you do dried herbs—away from light and heat.

Skillful use of certain spices can help the cook cut way back on fat. One of Chef Lydia Shire's favorite quick tricks is to sprinkle curry powder on chicken breasts before baking them.

Sprouts. These fledgling plants are a common sight in supermarkets. Sprouts from alfalfa seeds, radish seeds, sunflower seeds and mung beans add crunch to salads, sandwiches and stir-fries. Because you buy them ready to eat, they're really convenient to use; they don't even need rinsing. The smaller, more delicate sprouts (such as alfalfa and radish) are best as salad and sandwich toppers; hardier sprouts (bean or sunflower) are great chopped for stir-fries or as sprinkles on soup instead of high-fat croutons.

Tofu. Made from soybean milk in the same way cheese is made from cow's milk, tofu is a main protein source in Asian cooking. Straight from the package, tofu is bland, but it takes on a whole new taste when marinated.

Look for it in the produce section of most supermarkets. Tofu comes in both firm and soft varieties. Firm is best to slice and marinate or to crumble with sautéed vegetables for a tofu scramble. Soft tofu is easily mashed; you can also puree it for a satiny sour cream substitute.

Tortillas. Both corn and flour tortillas provide a low-fat, no-fuss way to wrap a sandwich filling fast. They're also great for homemade chips for dips—just cut them into wedges and bake at 350° for ten minutes. Or you can create an easy pizza by topping a tortilla with sliced vegetables, tomato sauce or salsa and shredded low-fat cheese.

Vegetables. Eat your vegetables! The National Academy of Sciences recommends that you get at least five servings a day of vegetables and fruits for optimum health. That's because produce is high in fiber and low in fat and calories. What's more, most types of fresh vegetables are really quick to cook. In fact, the quicker you cook them, the more vitamins they retain.

Look for vegetables with rich color—deep red peppers and tomatoes, bright green lettuces, vivid orange carrots. Leave the peels on whenever possible for more nutrition—but be sure to peel waxed vegetables, such as cucumbers. Try your vegetables stir-fried, steamed or microwaved. For an easy stir-fry, chop about one cup of vegetables per person and cook in a wok or no-stick skillet for five minutes.

Small new potatoes, scrubbed but unpeeled, are filling and cook fast in the microwave. Larger bakers can be microwaved, then stuffed with cooked, chopped broccoli and low-fat cottage cheese for a quick lunch.

For color and beta-carotene, steam squash or carrots, then puree them with ground cardamom, grated fresh ginger and honey to taste. Chefs often swirl a colorful spoonful of such a puree into creamy soups as garnish.

Another new restaurant trend: fresh vegetables juiced or pureed into low-fat sauces. Doug Flicker, chef at D'Amico Cucina in Minneapolis, juices carrots and other vegetables, then cooks the juice into a thick sauce. He seasons the sauce with herbs and spices to create a satisfying low-fat topping for roasted chicken, poached fish or pasta. He says that roasting the vegetables before juicing makes them even tastier.

Vinegar. This pungent ingredient is basic to many marinades and salad dressings. Keep a variety of vinegars on hand to perk up all types of low-fat dishes. Among the types available are apple cider, red wine, white wine, herb, rice, fruit and balsamic vinegars. Drizzle a little over salads and cooked vegetables; use a generous splash to deglaze the pan after sautéing chicken or pork cutlets; sprinkle mellow balsamic vinegar over fresh berries for a sophisticated dessert. Don't worry about overstocking your pantry—vinegar keeps a long time.

Winter squash. These hard-shelled squash contribute few calories and barely any fat to your diet, but they add plenty of vitamins, fiber and flavor. Although they're traditionally long cooking, you can speed up the process by cutting the squash and either microwaving or steaming the pieces. Squash is easier to peel after it's cooked, so don't waste time doing it beforehand. There are so many varieties available that you can enjoy squash often without getting bored.

What chef would be without trusty knives or an assortment of pots and pans? Fast, efficient cooking relies on good kitchen equipment. Take advantage of the newest tools to make the most of your time and to yield the most nutritious food possible. Here's some equipment that's virtually indispensable for quick and healthy cooking.

Blender. This tried-and-true appliance is great for pureeing soups and creating breakfast beverages. But a blender can do so much more. It can let you make creamy low-fat sauces from ingredients such as nonfat cottage cheese, fruits and vegetables. For the most versatility, get a blender that has several speeds. And check that it's got a tight-fitting lid.

You can follow the lead of Chef Robert Del Grande of Houston's popular Cafe Annie, who says, "We puree simmered vegetables, such as tomatoes, onions, garlic and chili peppers, with a little broth to create virtually fat-free sauces. They taste as good as fat-based sauces made with butter or cream."

Hand-held blenders, also known as immersion blenders, allow you to puree foods right in their bowl or saucepan. They may be the perfect choice if you're on a budget or if your kitchen is small, because they're less expensive than standard blenders and also take up less space.

Broiling racks. Use these in your conventional oven to let fat drip harmlessly away from cooking meats. Those with no-stick surfaces are particularly easy to clean. Folding poultry racks are ideal for roasting whole chickens—set them in a baking pan to catch the dripping fat. Or get a vertical poultry roaster, which holds the bird upright so that the maximum amount of fat can drip away.

Fat removers. The easiest way to remove fat from stocks, soups and stews is to refrigerate them until the fat congeals on the surface. Then you just lift it off with a spoon. But when you're in a hurry, try one of these gadgets. Specially slotted ladles can scoop fat off soups and stews in a jiffy. When you lower the ladle into the liquid, the fat runs in through side slots and is easily removed.

For larger quantities of liquid, such as stock, you'll find a fat separator handy. This special cup has a pouring spout that reaches to the bottom of the container. The design allows you to pour off the fat-free liquid and leave behind fat that floats on the surface.

Food processor. This is the busy cook's essential kitchen tool. Food processors come in several sizes and do everything from julienning vegetables and grinding turkey breast to mixing bread dough and pureeing cottage cheese—all in minutes. The new miniature models are even easier to clean than the full-size machines and take up less counter space.

Gadgets. Equip your kitchen with a range of gadgets. Among the ones to consider: a zester (for easily grating the flavorful outer rind of citrus fruit), a sturdy vegetable peeler, a stainless steel grater, a pastry brush, wire whisks and at least three high-quality knives. Don't forget a knife sharpener—finely honed blades are a must for trimming fat from meat and poultry and for slicing lots of low-fat vegetables and fruits quickly.

Hot-air popcorn popper. Popcorn—without added butter and salt, of course—is a very healthy snack. This machine turns out bowlfuls of fluffy popcorn in minutes with no added oil and no risk of scorched kernels. To season the popped corn, simply spritz it with a little water, then sprinkle it with herbal salt substitute or another seasoning (the water makes the seasoning stick).

Kitchen parchment. Cooking foods in parchment (known as cooking *en papillote*) is an easy, low-fat method for sealing moisture and flavor in delicate foods. "It's a nice way to gently steam vegetables," says Chef Del Grande.

Look for rolls of parchment near the plastic wrap in your supermarket. To use, just place boneless, skinless chicken breasts, fish fillets, pieces of seafood or thin pieces of low-fat meat in the center of a piece of parchment. Add some julienned vegetables, herbs, lemon juice or other flavorings. Fold up the sides to form a sealed pouch, and pop it into a very hot oven for about 15 or 20 minutes.

You can also poach sliced fruit in parchment packets—sprinkle the fruit with cinnamon and a drizzle of fruit juice, wrap, and bake.

Kitchen scale. Check your portion sizes with a small countertop scale. It's an essential kitchen tool when you're watching calories and fat.

Microwave oven. This has become an indispensable appliance for those committed to quick and healthy cooking. Foods cook very fast in a microwave, so they retain nutrients that might be lost by longer cooking techniques. And they can be cooked with little or no added fat.

Many of the recipes in this book use the microwave to save time. They were created using a 650- to 700-watt oven. Because microwave ovens vary in wattage and power output, you may need to adjust the cooking times. Remember also to allow a few extra minutes for standing time—most foods continue to cook after they've been removed from the microwave.

Always follow the manufacturer's guidelines for appropriate cooking utensils. Glass bowls and pans are generally good bets. Look for plastics labeled microwave-safe. Check your owner's manual for directions on testing questionable cookware.

Mortar and pestle (or electric spice grinder). Freshly ground spices have incredibly more flavor than preground ones, so they really give low-fat foods a flavor lift. For even more zip, lightly toast the spices in a dry skillet before grinding. An old-fashioned mortar and pestle lets you crush spices with ease—and without having them roll all over the kitchen counter. An electric grinder has the added advantage of allowing you to mince fresh herbs in seconds. Although you can buy electric grinders specifically targeted for spices, an inexpensive electric coffee mill will do just as well. But reserve it only for herbs and spices—if you grind coffee in it, the bitter coffee-bean oils will taint your spices.

No-stick pans. These pans let you sauté and bake foods with absolutely no added fat. They come in all shapes and sizes—among the most useful are 9- and 11-inch skillets. Get the best quality you can—the coated surface of inexpensive no-stick cookware tends to chip or flake as the years go by. Wooden or plastic utensils will be kinder to the surface than metal and less likely to scratch your no-stick pans.

Pressure cooker. Pressure cooking is modern, safe and very fast. It's great for preparing traditionally long-cooking foods such as dried beans, brown rice, winter squash, potatoes and meat stews. A pressure cooker has another benefit: It lets you cook the leanest cuts of meats without added fat. Simply follow the manufacturer's directions for perfect results every time.

Steamer. Steaming is much faster than boiling, and it safeguards more of the color, flavor and nutrients in foods. For a steamer that you simply insert in a larger pan, choose either a stacking bamboo model or a collapsible metal one. For a self-contained steamer, you can buy a glass model that lets you watch the food as it cooks—to really ensure that it doesn't overcook.

Stove-top grills. There are a few types to choose from, and they're quicker than heating up an outdoor charcoal grill. One type is a preseasoned cast-iron pan whose raised ridges capture the fat that runs off meat and poultry. It's a favorite with Chef Lydia Shire: "You can sear lean beef, chicken breasts, scallops or swordfish with very little oil, yet the food takes on beautiful markings. It's best to use firmer fish that doesn't flake easily." For extra flavor, Shire rubs the food with a mixture of spices before grilling it.

Equally popular is the kind of stove-top grill with a bottom rim that you fill with water. It serves two purposes: As the water heats, steam cooks your meat or vegetables. At the same time, the rim catches fat drippings, so your food turns out lean, and your stove top stays clean. Lightly coat the grill surface with no-stick spray before using to keep foods from sticking.

Wok. Stir-frying is a really quick and easy way to cook all types of meat, seafood and vegetables. And it requires just a minimum of oil. A large frying pan will do the job. But if you do a lot of stir-frying, you might opt to purchase a wok. Electric woks are handy, but they are difficult to cool down quickly (add ¼ cup cold water in a pinch). Regular no-stick and cast-iron surfaces tend to distribute heat unevenly. Carbon steel is the favorite of many chefs; it must be seasoned to prevent rusting, so follow the manufacturer's instructions.

Fresh vegetables really shine in stir-fries; they stay colorful and crisp and retain valuable nutrients. For extra flavor, Chef Brenda Langton stir-fries the vegetables with tofu, tempeh, eggplant, seafood or other foods that she's marinated in a low-fat mixture of garlic, ginger and soy sauce. She often reduces and thickens the leftover marinade for a quick low-fat sauce.

Yogurt cheese funnel. This handy gadget lets you make nonfat yogurt cheese whenever you want. Although you can achieve the same results with a cheesecloth-lined sieve or strainer, the inexpensive funnel is easy to wash and snaps apart for convenient storage.

BASIC TIPS FOR LOW-FAT COOKING

Now you have an idea of which ingredients to buy and what appliances will make quick and healthy cooking a breeze. Here are some extra tips for getting the most flavor from your food with the least amount of fat.

- Use cooking techniques that require little or no added fat, such as steaming, grilling, broiling, baking and light sautéing. When needed to keep food from sticking, use a spritz of no-stick spray.
- Baste meats and poultry with defatted stock instead of butter.

- Try the French reduction method when making sauces: Skim any fat from pan juices, then add defatted stock to them and thicken the liquid by boiling it rapidly. Season it with herbs, low-sodium soy sauce, ginger or garlic.
- Baste grilled foods with lemon juice or flavored vinegar instead of oil.
- Use your microwave to reheat leftovers—it's a fast method that requires no added fat.
- Flavor foods with low-fat aromatics and condiments—herbs, spices, mustard, vinegar, garlic, lemon juice and rind, ginger or onion—instead of butter or oil.
- Use nonfat or low-fat dairy products instead of whole-milk products. To add richness and body to skim milk, puree it in a blender with powdered dry milk (¼ cup powder for each 1 cup liquid).
- To slim down lasagna, casseroles and meat loaves, replace one-fourth or more of the ground beef with cooked brown rice, whole-wheat bread crumbs or ground turkey breast.
- Automatically replace one-third of the oil in salad dressings with water. You'll never know the difference, especially in pureed dressings. Other good oil substitutes: canned no-salt tomato juice, fresh lemon juice, flavored vinegar and nonfat plain yogurt.
- Make homemade low-fat whipped cream: Whip well-chilled evaporated skim milk with an electric mixer. Flavor it with vanilla extract and a dusting of cinnamon. Use quickly—this version will not hold as long as regular whipped cream.

CHAPTER 3

FESTIVE
FARE FOR
SPECIAL
OCCASIONS

LET'S PARTY

ood food and good friends—they're the ideal recipe for a successful party. So when it's your turn to play host, treat your guests to the very best. And by that we mean delicious low-fat fare that will help them maintain their good health. Serve creamy dips, like Sweet and Spicy Curry Dip, that *taste* fattening but are light on fat and calories. Whip up festive nonalcoholic beverages, such as Kiwi Coolers, to keep guests bright-eyed and alert. Prepare slimmed versions of perennial favorites such as nachos, deviled eggs and burgers. And do it all with ease, so you can enjoy your own party. The following recipes will make any get-together special.

NO-FUSS NIBBLES

Finger foods are the backbone of any informal get-together. Make sure the ones you serve offer your guests a healthy alternative to fatty chips, salty nuts and neon-colored cheese curls.

Platters of crisp, colorful vegetables, for example, are low in calories, low in fat, high in vitamins and easy to prepare. Choose vegetables that will give an interesting mix of colors and textures. Carrot and celery sticks are always welcome, but flesh out the platters with cauliflower and broccoflower florets, strips of peppers, small mushrooms, thinly sliced sweet potatoes, jícama sticks and a variety of radishes. Add some lightly blanched vegetables, such as asparagus spears, snap peas and halved brussels sprouts.

Here are some other quick and easy little snacks.

TANGY ZUCCHINI SPEARS

SERVES 8

*T*hese sweet-and-sour tidbits are a snap to prepare. They also make fine accompaniments to sandwiches.

1½	*pounds small zucchini*
1	*cup apple cider vinegar*
2	*tablespoons honey*
½	*teaspoon celery seeds*
½	*teaspoon mustard seeds*
½	*teaspoon turmeric*
¼	*teaspoon dry mustard*

Cut the zucchini into finger-size spears. Place in a shallow bowl.

In a 1-quart saucepan, combine the vinegar, honey, celery seeds, mustard seeds, turmeric and dry mustard. Bring to a boil, then reduce the heat and simmer for 5 minutes. Pour over the zucchini.

Cover and refrigerate until chilled. Drain before serving.

(continued)

Preparation time: 10 minutes plus chilling time
Cooking time: 5 minutes

Per serving: 32 calories, 0.1 g. fat (3% of calories), 1 g. dietary fiber, no cholesterol, 3 mg. sodium.

LIGHT 'N' LEAN NACHOS

SERVES 8

*N*achos are a perennial party favorite, but they're generally loaded with fat, sodium and calories. This version gives nachos a health boost—and some international flavor—by replacing the chips with potatoes, an Irish staple. And the potatoes add a welcome bonus of dietary fiber.

1½	*pounds large potatoes, scrubbed and sliced ⅜" thick*
½	*cup defatted chicken stock*
1⅓	*cups salsa*
1	*cup rinsed and drained canned pinto or white beans*
½	*teaspoon hot-pepper sauce*
⅔	*cup shredded low-fat Monterey Jack cheese*

In a 4-cup glass measuring cup, combine half of the potatoes and ¼ cup stock. Cover with vented plastic wrap and microwave on high for 5 to 7 minutes, or until the potatoes are just tender.

Let stand for 5 minutes, or until cool enough to handle. Drain the potatoes and pat them dry with paper towels. Layer the potatoes on a large microwave-safe serving plate.

In a small bowl, mix the salsa, beans and pepper sauce. Spoon half of the mixture over the potatoes. Sprinkle with ⅓ cup Monterey Jack. Loosely cover with wax paper.

Microwave on medium (50% power) for 2 minutes, or until the cheese has melted. Serve immediately.

Repeat with the remaining potatoes, ¼ cup stock, salsa mixture and ⅓ cup Monterey Jack.

Preparation time: 10 minutes
Cooking time: 15 minutes

Chef's Notes: Microwaving cheese on medium power prevents it from turning rubbery.

If you don't have a microwave, steam the potato slices until tender, about 10 minutes. Then layer on ovenproof platters as directed above and bake at 350° for about 15 minutes.

Per serving: 146 calories, 3.2 g. fat (18% of calories), 2.4 g. dietary fiber, 7 mg. cholesterol, 215 mg. sodium.

STUFFED SPINACH BUNDLES

Make easy appetizers from fresh spinach. Take large leaves, remove the stems, and wash the spinach well in cold water to remove any grit. Blanch the leaves for about 5 seconds in boiling water. Drain and run under cold water to stop the cooking. Pat dry with paper towels.

Then place a dab of stuffing near the stem edge of each leaf. Roll up the leaf to enclose the filling. Secure with a food pick.

For variety, you may also use chard, bok choy, turnip or beet leaves.

Here are some excellent low-fat stuffings.

■ Cooked barley, minced apples, raisins and allspice
■ Cooked bulgur, minced tomatoes, basil and shredded part-skim mozzarella cheese
■ Corn, mashed pinto beans, minced green chili peppers and oregano
■ Finely diced poached chicken, shredded spinach, minced water chestnuts, garlic and ginger
■ Mashed potatoes, dill and parsley
■ Cooked rice, chopped toasted almonds, sautéed chopped mushrooms and minced scallions

FESTIVE KABOBS

SERVES 8

*Y*our guests will relish these beautiful tortellini skewers.

16	*cheese-filled spinach tortellini*
8	*cheese-filled white tortellini*
⅔	*cup fat-free Italian dressing*
¼	*cup water*
16	*small cherry tomatoes*
8	*small mushrooms*
16	*pieces (1″ × 1″) yellow peppers*
16	*pieces (1″ × 1″) sweet red peppers*
8	*pieces (1″ × 1″) green peppers*
¼	*teaspoon olive oil*

Cook the tortellini in a large pot of boiling water according to package directions. Drain and place in a large shallow baking dish.

In a small bowl, whisk together the dressing and water. Pour over the tortellini. Add the tomatoes and mushrooms. Stir to coat.

In a 1-quart microwave-safe casserole, combine the yellow peppers, red peppers and green peppers with the oil. Cover with vented plastic wrap and microwave on high for 2 to 4 minutes, or until the peppers are crisp-tender. Add to the baking dish. Toss gently. Chill.

Evenly divide the ingredients among 8 wooden skewers.

Preparation time: 5 minutes plus chilling time
Cooking time: 10 minutes

Chef's Note: If you don't have a microwave, sauté the peppers in the oil until crisp-tender, about 10 minutes.

Per serving: 117 calories, 2.4 g. fat (18% of calories), 0.8 g. dietary fiber, 10 mg. cholesterol, 110 mg. sodium.

38

LET'S PARTY

STUFFED BABY SPUDS

SERVES 8

*H*ere's a light alternative to greasy potato skins. You can easily vary the filling by using different herbs. Or you may replace the horseradish with about ¼ cup minced pimentos, pesto sauce, salsa or chopped cooked spinach.

1	*pound small red potatoes, scrubbed and halved*
1	*cup low-fat cottage cheese*
2	*teaspoons prepared horseradish*
1	*tablespoon minced chives*
½	*teaspoon dried dill*
¼	*teaspoon ground black pepper*

Prick the potato skins in several places with a fork. Arrange half of the potatoes in a ring pan. Microwave on high for 3 to 4 minutes, or until fork-tender. Transfer to a plate.

Repeat with the remaining potatoes. Let stand until cool enough to handle.

Using a tiny melon scoop or spoon, hollow out each potato, leaving a sturdy shell.

Puree the cottage cheese in a food processor until smooth. Transfer to a small bowl. Stir in the horseradish, chives, dill and pepper. Spoon into the potato shells. Serve warm or chilled.

Preparation time: 10 minutes
Cooking time: 10 minutes

Chef's Note: If you don't have a microwave, steam the potatoes until tender, about 20 minutes.

Per serving: 37 calories, 0.3 g. fat (8% of calories), 0.3 g. dietary fiber, 1 mg. cholesterol, 117 mg. sodium.

SKINNY DIPS AND SIMPLE SPREADS

Party dips and spreads are the downfall of many a weight-watcher. Fortunately, the appearance in supermarkets of nonfat mayonnaise, light sour cream and low-fat cream cheese makes it easier than ever to slim down these party standards. Just make the appropriate substitutions in your favorite recipes.

Another alternative to full-fat dairy products in dips and spreads is yogurt cheese, which has a creamy texture but few calories and no fat. And it's a breeze to make at home: Spoon nonfat yogurt into a yogurt cheese funnel or a sieve lined with cheesecloth. Cover with plastic wrap, set over a bowl, and place in the refrigerator to drain. For use in dips, drain for only an hour. For a thicker product, suitable in spreads and as a replacement for cream cheese, drain overnight.

CREAMY SALSA DIP

MAKES ABOUT 1 CUP

*Y*ou couldn't ask for a more effortless dip to make for spur-of-the-moment entertaining.

½ *cup nonfat yogurt cheese*
½ *cup salsa*
¼ *cup skim milk*

In a small bowl, mix together the yogurt cheese, salsa and milk. Transfer to a serving bowl and chill until needed.

Preparation time: 5 minutes

Chef's Note: Serve this spicy dip with homemade tortilla chips. They're really easy to make: Cut corn or flour tortillas into wedges. Place in a single layer on a baking sheet and bake at 350° for 10 minutes, or until crisp and beginning to brown at the edges.

Per 2 tablespoons: 18 calories, 0.2 g. fat (10% of calories), 0.3 g. dietary fiber, trace cholesterol, 20 mg. sodium.

MEDITERRANEAN TUNA SPREAD

MAKES ABOUT 1½ CUPS

This rich-tasting spread combines tuna with low-fat cottage cheese and nonfat mayonnaise. The albacore tuna contributes more than interesting flavor—it's a good source of heart-healthy omega-3 fatty acids.

6½	ounces water-packed albacore tuna, drained
½	cup low-fat cottage cheese
¼	cup nonfat mayonnaise
2	tablespoons lemon juice
1	teaspoon dried tarragon
1	teaspoon Dijon mustard

In a food processor or blender, blend the tuna, cottage cheese, mayonnaise, lemon juice, tarragon and mustard until smooth. Stop and scrape down the sides of the container as necessary. Transfer to a serving bowl and chill until needed.

Preparation time: 5 minutes

Per 2 tablespoons: 31 calories, 0.5 g. fat (13% of calories), trace dietary fiber, 6 mg. cholesterol, 163 mg. sodium.

WHITE BEAN AND ROASTED GARLIC SPREAD

*S*erve this flavorful mixture as a spread on toast triangles or crackers. Or use it as a stuffing for celery pieces, hollowed-out cherry tomatoes or Belgian endive leaves.

1   *head (about 12 cloves) garlic, separated but not peeled*
2   *cans (19 ounces each) white beans, rinsed and drained*
¼   *cup lemon juice*
1   *tablespoon olive oil*
2   *tablespoons minced fresh parsley*
¼   *teaspoon ground black pepper*
¼   *cup minced red onions*
¼   *cup minced green peppers*

Place the garlic in a custard cup. Bake at 400° for 15 minutes, or until soft when tested with the tip of a knife. Do not allow the garlic to brown. Let cool slightly, then slip off the skins and trim off the hard stem ends.

Place half of the beans plus the lemon juice, oil and garlic in a food processor. Puree until smooth. Transfer to a medium bowl. Stir in the parsley, black pepper, half of the onions, half of the green peppers and the remaining beans. Roughly mash the whole beans with a fork.

Serve garnished with the remaining onions and green peppers.

Preparation time: 10 minutes
Baking time: 15 minutes

Per 2 tablespoons: 40 calories, 0.7 g. fat (16% of calories), 1 g. dietary fiber, no cholesterol, 1 mg. sodium.

Strawberry Cheese

*T*his slightly sweet cheese is a perfect spread on mini-bagels, toast squares or raw vegetables.

1   *cup nonfat yogurt cheese or low-fat cream cheese*
½   *cup finely chopped strawberries*
1   *tablespoon honey*
1   *teaspoon toasted sesame or poppy seeds*

In a small bowl, stir together the yogurt cheese or cream cheese, strawberries, honey and sesame or poppy seeds.

Preparation time: 5 minutes

Chef's Notes: This basic recipe lends itself to many variations. You may replace the strawberries with minced peaches, chopped apricots, mashed raspberries, chopped blueberries, cooked and chopped cranberries or crushed pineapple.

For a savory spread, replace the fruit and honey with ½ cup peeled, seeded and minced tomatoes plus fresh herbs, such as chives, dill or basil. If desired, stir in a little minced garlic.

Per 2 tablespoons: 21 calories, 0.2 g. fat (9% of calories), 0.3 g. dietary fiber, trace cholesterol, 17 mg. sodium.

FEISTY EGGPLANT SPREAD

MAKES ABOUT 2 CUPS

his spicy spread contains eggplant, which some studies say may help lower cholesterol. Serve the spread on thin rounds of crisp raw vegetables, such as zucchini, yellow squash, jícama, turnips or sweet potatoes.

1	*large eggplant*
⅓	*cup seasoned dry bread crumbs*
⅓	*cup nonfat sour cream*
2	*tablespoons lemon juice*
1	*clove garlic, minced*
¼–½	*teaspoon hot-pepper sauce*
3	*tablespoons minced fresh parsley*

Cut a 5" lengthwise slit in the eggplant and place it on a microwave-safe plate. Microwave on high for 10 minutes, or until the eggplant is very soft and has collapsed. Set aside for 5 minutes, or until cool enough to handle.

Cut open the eggplant and spoon the flesh into a large bowl. Mash it with a fork to break up any long strands. Stir in the bread crumbs, sour cream, lemon juice, garlic and pepper sauce.

Spread on a decorative plate. Sprinkle with the parsley. Serve chilled or at room temperature.

Preparation time: 10 minutes
Cooking time: 10 minutes

Chef's Notes: If you don't have a microwave, broil the eggplant: Pierce it in several places with a fork and place on a baking sheet. Broil about 6" from the heat until blackened on all sides. Set aside until cool enough to handle, then continue with the recipe.

For variety, you may replace the sour cream with nonfat mayonnaise or yogurt cheese. You may also season the spread with herbs, such as oregano, savory, thyme or marjoram. For a real Middle Eastern flavor, add a pinch of cinnamon.

Per 2 tablespoons: 10 calories, trace fat (6% of calories), 0.3 g. dietary fiber, trace cholesterol, 10 mg. sodium.

PIMENTO DIP

MAKES ABOUT 1¹⁄₂ CUPS

Canned pimentos give this dip its rosy color and contribute vitamin A, a nutrient essential for healthy skin and good eyesight.

½ *cup dry-curd cottage cheese*
½ *cup chopped pimentos, well drained*
½ *cup nonfat sour cream*
½ *teaspoon dried basil*

In a food processor, blend the cottage cheese until very smooth. Add the pimentos and blend until smooth. Add the sour cream and basil. Blend just until mixed in. Transfer to a serving bowl and chill until needed.

Preparation time: 5 minutes

Per 2 tablespoons: 14 calories, 0.1 g. fat (5% of calories), trace dietary fiber, trace cholesterol, 9 mg. sodium.

SWEET AND SPICY CURRY DIP

*T*his dip goes especially well with whole-grain crackers or bread sticks.

¼   *cup fruit chutney*
2½   *teaspoons curry powder*
1   *cup nonfat yogurt cheese*
⅛   *teaspoon hot-pepper sauce*

In a small saucepan over medium-low heat, melt the chutney. Stir in the curry powder and cook, stirring frequently, for 1 minute to bring out the flavor of the curry. Cool for 5 minutes.

Place the yogurt cheese in a small bowl. Stir in the chutney and pepper sauce. Transfer to a serving bowl and chill until needed.

Preparation time: 10 minutes

Per 2 tablespoons: 32 calories, 0.2 g. fat (6% of calories), 0.5 g. dietary fiber, trace cholesterol, 35 mg. sodium.

HEALTHY ICE BREAKERS

Always have a selection of nonalcoholic beverages on hand for guests who prefer not to imbibe. For a refreshing change from ordinary soft drinks, try the following pick-me-ups. Made from juice or fresh fruits, they contain vitamins that regular soft drinks lack. If you want to add a little fizz to the drinks, dilute them with sparkling mineral water.

BANANA-BERRY SHAKES

SERVES 8

ou *can* serve luscious low-fat shakes—just take advantage of tropical fruits. They have a creamy texture that would lead you to believe they're high in fat, but they aren't at all. What's more, they're loaded with fiber and brimming with vitamins A and C.

4   *cups sliced strawberries*
2   *large bananas, sliced*
1   *cup orange juice*
1   *cup nonfat vanilla yogurt*
8   *ice cubes*

In a blender, combine 2 cups strawberries, half of the bananas, ½ cup juice, ½ cup yogurt and 4 ice cubes. Puree until thick and smooth.

Repeat with the remaining 2 cups strawberries, bananas, ½ cup juice, ½ cup yogurt and 4 ice cubes.

Preparation time: 5 minutes

Per serving: 85 calories, 0.5 g. fat (5% of calories), 2.6 g. dietary fiber, 1 mg. cholesterol, 19 mg. sodium.

TROPICAL EYE-OPENERS

*H*ere's a refresher for a midsummer lawn party.

2   *large ripe mangoes*
2   *large bananas, sliced*
2   *cups pink grapefruit juice*
1   *cup nonfat frozen vanilla yogurt*
¼   *teaspoon grated nutmeg*
8   *ice cubes*

Peel the mangoes over a bowl to catch the juices. Then use a paring knife to slice away the flesh from the stone. Transfer half to a blender.

Add half of the bananas, 1 cup juice, ½ cup frozen yogurt, ⅛ teaspoon nutmeg and 4 ice cubes. Blend until smooth.

Repeat with the remaining mangoes, bananas, 1 cup juice, ½ cup frozen yogurt, ⅛ teaspoon nutmeg and 4 ice cubes.

Preparation time: 5 minutes

Per serving: 111 calories, 0.4 g. fat (3% of calories), 1.8 g. dietary fiber, no cholesterol, 15 mg. sodium.

KIWI COOLERS

SERVES 8

*K*iwis give this drink an interesting chartreuse color.

9   kiwifruit
4   cups pineapple juice
8   ice cubes
2   cups sparkling water
8   large strawberries

Peel the kiwis and cut into small pieces. Place half in a blender with 2 cups juice and 4 ice cubes. Blend until smooth. Stir in 1 cup sparkling water.

Repeat with the remaining kiwis, 2 cups juice, 4 ice cubes and 1 cup sparkling water.

Pour into tall glasses and garnish each serving with a strawberry.

Preparation time: 5 minutes

Per serving: 138 calories, 0.6 g. fat (4% of calories), 4 g. dietary fiber, no cholesterol, 7 mg. sodium.

HOST AN EASY TREE-TRIMMING PARTY

One way to weather the hectic Christmas season in top form is to get your friends to help with some of the holiday chores—including trimming the tree. They'll be much more inclined to pitch in, of course, if you reward their efforts with tempting snacks. And you can do *that* without overextending yourself. By serving quick, easy, make-ahead goodies such as the ones that follow, you can relax and enjoy your own mini-party.

Menu

FRUIT AND TURKEY PASTRAMI ROLL-UPS

PUMPKIN SOUP

CROSTINI WITH RED-PEPPER PUREE

PEPPERY BISCUITS

HOT MULLED APPLE PUNCH

MAPLE-COATED POPCORN

FRUIT AND TURKEY PASTRAMI ROLL-UPS

SERVES 12

1   cantaloupe or honeydew melon
18   thin slices turkey pastrami (about 9 ounces)
6   lengthwise pineapple slices, 1" wide

Cut the cantaloupe or honeydew in half lengthwise, remove the seeds, and slice into 12 wedges. Remove the rind from the wedges.

Cut the pastrami into pieces that will just wrap around each piece of melon and pineapple. Wrap the fruit and slice into bite-size pieces. Secure the pastrami to the fruit with food picks.

Preparation time: 10 minutes

Per serving: 58 calories, 1.6 g. fat (23% of calories), 0.7 g. dietary fiber, 11 mg. cholesterol, 227 mg. sodium.

PUMPKIN SOUP

SERVES 12

1   *piece (2 pounds) sugar pumpkin, cut into 2" chunks*

2   *cups cubed potatoes*

1   *cup cubed apples*

½   *cup chopped onions*

3   *cups water or defatted chicken stock*

1   *thick (¼") slice fresh ginger, minced*

1   *bay leaf*

1   *clove garlic, chopped*

2–3   *cups low-fat milk*

1   *teaspoon lemon juice*

½   *teaspoon grated nutmeg*

Steam the pumpkin until very tender, about 15 minutes. Set aside until cool enough to handle.

In a 3-quart saucepan, combine the potatoes, apples, onions, water or stock, ginger, bay leaf and garlic. Bring to a boil. Reduce the heat to low and simmer until the vegetables are tender, about 15 minutes. Cool for 5 minutes. Remove and discard the bay leaf.

Remove and discard the skin from the pumpkin pieces. Add the pumpkin to the vegetable mixture. Working in batches, puree the soup in a blender or food processor.

Return the puree to the saucepan. Add enough of the milk to thin the puree to a drinkable consistency. Season with the lemon juice. Warm over low heat. Serve sprinkled with the nutmeg.

Preparation time: 15 minutes
Cooking time: 20 minutes

Chef's Note: If you don't have access to sugar pumpkins, which are a type traditionally used for pumpkin pies, substitute butternut or buttercup squash. Start with a large specimen—about 2½ pounds. Halve it, remove the stem and seeds, then cut into chunks. Steam and peel as above.

Per serving: 60 calories, 0.6 g. fat (8% of calories), 1.4 g. dietary fiber, 2 mg. cholesterol, 25 mg. sodium.

CROSTINI WITH RED-PEPPER PUREE

SERVES 12

Crostini

    12   *thick (½") slices day-old Italian or French bread*

    ½   *clove garlic*

Red-Pepper Puree

    2   *tablespoons minced onions*

    1   *tablespoon olive oil*

    ½   *clove garlic, minced*

    1   *can (14 ounces) Italian tomatoes*

    1   *jar (7 ounces) roasted red peppers, rinsed, drained and diced*

       Pinch of dried oregano or thyme

To make the crostini: Arrange the bread in a single layer on a baking sheet. Bake at 350° for 10 minutes, or until the edges are toasted. Flip the pieces and bake for another 10 minutes, or until evenly toasted. Rub the top of each slice with the garlic.

To make the red-pepper puree: Meanwhile, in a large frying pan over medium heat, sauté the onions in the oil until tender, about 3 minutes. Add the garlic and sauté for 1 minute. Add the tomatoes with their juice, peppers and oregano or thyme. Bring to a boil.

Simmer, stirring and breaking up the tomatoes with the side of a spoon, until the liquid has evaporated and the mixture has thickened, about 15 minutes.

Let cool for 5 minutes, then transfer to a food processor. Chop with on/off turns until slightly chunky. Return to the frying pan. Simmer until very thick. Spread the warm puree on the crostini.

Preparation time: 15 minutes
Cooking time: 20 minutes
Baking time: 20 minutes

Chef's Note: You may prepare the crostini up to three days ahead; cool the pieces and store in plastic bags. You may also prepare the puree ahead. Reheat before using.

Per serving: 119 calories, 2.6 g. fat (20% of calories), 1.1 g. dietary fiber, no cholesterol, 197 mg. sodium.

Spinach and Pimento Omelet (page 73)

53

Grilled Summer Salad (page 217)

Mediterranean Green Beans (page 250)

Turkey Satay (page 160) with rice and steamed carrots

Herbed Angel Hair (page 175)

French Vegetable Soup (page 96)

Broiled Scallops with Grapefruit (page 88)

French Coeur à la Crème (page 285)

PEPPERY BISCUITS

MAKES 25

1	cup unbleached flour
½	cup whole-wheat flour
1	tablespoon baking powder
½	teaspoon ground black pepper
2	tablespoons minced lean ham
½–¾	cup buttermilk
1½	tablespoons olive oil

In a large bowl, mix together the unbleached flour, whole-wheat flour, baking powder and pepper. Stir in the ham.

In a cup, whisk together ½ cup buttermilk and the oil. Pour over the dry ingredients. Toss together with a fork just until the mixture begins to form a mass. If the mixture is too dry, add a little more of the buttermilk.

Turn out the dough onto a lightly floured board and press into a 7" × 7" square. Using a long, thin knife, divide into 25 biscuits (5 across and 5 down).

Coat a baking sheet with no-stick spray. Transfer the biscuits to the sheet with about 1" of space between them. Bake at 400° for 15 minutes, or until golden. Serve warm.

Preparation time: 10 minutes
Baking time: 15 minutes

Chef's Note: Although these biscuits are delicious all by themselves, you may choose to split them in half and serve with a thin layer of spicy chutney, strawberry-flavored yogurt cheese or light cream cheese.

Per biscuit: 35 calories, 1 g. fat (24% of calories), 0.4 g. dietary fiber, trace cholesterol, 51 mg. sodium.

HOT MULLED APPLE PUNCH

SERVES 12

3   quarts apple juice or cider
1   apple, cored and cut into very thin rounds
6   whole cloves
6   allspice berries
1   cinnamon stick
4   Red Zinger tea bags
8   thin lemon slices

Pour the apple juice or cider into a 4-quart saucepan. Stick the apple slices with the cloves and add to the pan. Add the allspice and cinnamon stick. Cover and bring to a simmer over medium heat.

Remove from the heat and add the tea bags. Cover and steep for 15 minutes. Remove the bags before serving.

Ladle into mugs and garnish each with a lemon slice and an apple slice.

Preparation time: 20 minutes
Cooking time: 5 minutes

Per serving: 123 calories, 0.3 g. fat (2% of calories), 0.6 g. dietary fiber, no cholesterol, 7 mg. sodium.

MAPLE-COATED POPCORN

SERVES 12

1   cup maple syrup
9   cups air-popped popcorn
¼   cup broken walnuts

In a deep 2-quart saucepan over medium heat, heat the maple syrup until it reaches 236° on a candy thermometer (or until the mixture forms a soft ball when a small amount is added to a cup of cold water).

Lightly oil a large roasting pan. Add the popcorn and walnuts. Pour the syrup over all. Gently mix with a large oiled spatula (be careful not to touch the very hot mixture). Let cool, stirring occasionally. Break into clumps to serve.

Preparation time: 10 minutes

Per serving: 103 calories, 1.6 g. fat (14% of calories), 0.4 g. dietary fiber, no cholesterol, 4 mg. sodium.

A Lazy Summer Picnic

*I*t's picnic time! The sky's blue, the weather's hot, and you just want to have fun. So find the picnic basket and fill it with an array of healthy foods that taste terrific.

Start your outing on the right foot by leaving behind salads made with heavy binders such as full-fat mayonnaise, sour cream and whipping cream. That doesn't mean you can't enjoy macaroni salad or other old favorites. Just remake them in a lighter mode, either by using reduced-fat ingredients or by substituting a very light vinaigrette.

If you think that deviled eggs are off-limits for the cholesterol conscious, you're in for a treat. Although it's true that you can't take the cholesterol out of an egg yolk, you *can* simply eliminate the yolk entirely. The recipe for Angelic Eggs replaces the standard filling with a creamy potato and mustard mixture.

Here are some foods that travel well and are easy to prepare for spur-of-the-moment picnics. And remember that you don't actually have to *go* anywhere for a delightful repast—your own backyard can be ideal for a relaxing "getaway."

FRESH FRUITADE
ANGELIC EGGS
SKINNY MACARONI SALAD
SUMMER POTATO SALAD
CALIFORNIA BURGERS
ORANGE-SCENTED FIGS AND APRICOTS
GINGERBREAD CAKE

FRESH FRUITADE

SERVES 12

1   *cup brewed orange-spice tea*
⅓   *cup honey or other sweetener*
   Juice of 2 oranges
   Juice of 1 lemon
   Juice of 1 lime
3   *quarts sparkling water*
   Ice cubes

In a 1-quart saucepan, combine the tea and honey or other sweetener. Bring to a boil. Add the orange juice, lemon juice and lime juice. Boil, stirring frequently, for about 7 minutes, or until slightly syrupy. Chill.

For each serving, place 2 tablespoons syrup in a chilled tall glass. Add 1 cup sparkling water. Stir well. Add the ice cubes as desired.

Preparation time: 5 minutes
Cooking time: 10 minutes

Per serving: 35 calories, <0.1 g. fat (1% of calories), 0.1 g. dietary fiber, no cholesterol, 8 mg. sodium.

ANGELIC EGGS

1	large baking potato, peeled, chopped and steamed
3–5	tablespoons nonfat yogurt
1½	tablespoons minced fresh parsley
1½	teaspoons Dijon mustard
¾	teaspoon dried tarragon
¼	teaspoon paprika
6	hard-cooked eggs

Mash the potatoes or press them through a fine strainer into a medium bowl. Stir in 3 tablespoons yogurt. If the mixture is dry, add more of the yogurt. Add the parsley, mustard, tarragon and paprika.

Peel the eggs and cut them in half lengthwise. Use a teaspoon to gently remove the yolks; discard. Set the whites aside.

Use a spoon or a pastry bag fitted with a medium tube to fill the whites with the potato mixture. Wrap well and refrigerate until serving time.

Preparation time: 15 minutes

Per half egg: 26 calories, trace fat (2% of calories), 0.2 g. dietary fiber, no cholesterol, 39 mg. sodium.

Skinny Macaroni Salad

SERVES 12

6   cups cooked penne, elbows or other tube-type
    pasta
3   cups peeled and chopped tomatoes
¾   cup minced red onions
⅓   cup minced fresh basil
2   cloves garlic, minced
2   tablespoons balsamic or apple cider vinegar
2   tablespoons olive oil
½   teaspoon ground black pepper

In a large bowl, combine the pasta, tomatoes, onions, basil, garlic, vinegar, oil and pepper. Cover and let stand at room temperature for at least 30 minutes to allow the flavors to meld.

Preparation time: 15 minutes plus chilling time

Per serving: 90 calories, 2.4 g. fat (23% of calories), 1.4 g. dietary fiber, no cholesterol, 4 mg. sodium.

Summer Potato Salad

SERVES 12

3   pounds boiling potatoes
⅓   cup minced fresh parsley
1   teaspoon dried thyme
6   tablespoons white wine vinegar
3   tablespoons lemon juice
1   tablespoon Dijon mustard
2   cloves garlic, minced
6   tablespoons olive oil
¾   cup thinly sliced onions or celery

Scrub the potatoes and peel them, if desired. Place in a 4-quart saucepan with cold water to cover. Bring to a boil and cook for about 20 minutes, or until easily pierced with a skewer but not mushy. Drain, rinse with cold water, and slice thinly. Place in a large bowl. Toss gently with the parsley and thyme.

In a medium bowl, whisk together the vinegar, lemon juice, mustard and garlic. Slowly whisk in the oil.

Pour the dressing over the warm potatoes. Toss lightly to coat the potatoes with the dressing. Add the onions or celery and toss well. Serve at room temperature or chilled.

Preparation time: 10 minutes
Cooking time: 20 minutes

Per serving: 135 calories, 3.6 g. fat (23% of calories), 1.5 g. dietary fiber, no cholesterol, 25 mg. sodium.

CALIFORNIA BURGERS

SERVES 12

3	*pounds ground turkey breast*
1	*cup minced onions*
1	*cup celery*
1	*cup minced sweet red peppers*
¼	*cup tomato paste*
2	*cloves garlic, minced*
1	*teaspoon ground black pepper*
12	*crusty rolls*
	Shredded lettuce
	Tomato slices

In a large bowl, thoroughly mix the turkey, onions, celery, red peppers, tomato paste, garlic and black pepper.

Form into 12 patties. Grill (or broil or sauté in a no-stick frying pan).

Serve in the rolls with the lettuce and tomatoes.

Preparation time: 10 minutes
Cooking time: 10 minutes

(continued)

Chef's Note: To make the leanest patties possible, purchase boneless, skinless turkey breast. Cut it into chunks and grind it in a food processor using on/off turns. If you're serving fewer than 12, you can freeze the extra turkey mixture for future quick patties. Just form the patties, stack them (separated with pieces of wax paper), wrap well, and freeze.

Per serving: 289 calories, 2.6 g. fat (8% of calories), 3.3 g. dietary fiber, 95 mg. cholesterol, 342 mg. sodium.

ORANGE-SCENTED FIGS AND APRICOTS

SERVES 12

24 *fresh figs, halved*
12 *apricots, halved and pitted*
1 *pint raspberries*
½ *cup orange juice*
2 *tablespoons lime juice*
3 *drops vanilla*
   Pinch of grated nutmeg

In a large bowl, combine the figs, apricots and raspberries.

In a cup, combine the orange juice, lime juice, vanilla and nutmeg. Pour over the fruit and let stand for 20 minutes; stir gently from time to time.

Preparation time: 5 minutes plus marinating time

Per serving: 130 calories, 0.7 g. fat (5% of calories), 5.4 g. dietary fiber, no cholesterol, 2 mg. sodium.

GINGERBREAD CAKE

1¼ cups unbleached flour
1 cup whole-wheat flour
1½ teaspoons powdered ginger
1 teaspoon baking soda
1 teaspoon ground cinnamon
¼ teaspoon allspice
1 cup hot tap water
½ cup molasses
½ cup honey
6 tablespoons oil
¼ cup fat-free egg substitute

In a large bowl, combine the unbleached flour, whole-wheat flour, ginger, baking soda, cinnamon and allspice. Add the water, molasses, honey, oil and egg. Beat with an electric mixer on low speed until all the flour is moistened, about 1 minute. Then beat on medium speed for about 2 minutes, scraping down the sides of the bowl frequently.

Coat an 8" × 8" baking dish with no-stick spray. Pour the batter into the pan. Bake at 325° for 50 minutes, or until a food pick inserted in the center comes out clean. Cool the cake in its pan.

Preparation time: 10 minutes
Baking time: 50 minutes

Per serving: 218 calories, 7.1 g. fat (29% of calories), 1.6 g. dietary fiber, no cholesterol, 82 mg. sodium.

CHAPTER 4

EASY
BREAKFASTS
AND
BRUNCHES

MORNING GLORIES

Spice up your mornings with wonderful low-fat breakfasts—the kind that awaken sleepy appetites and guarantee perfect attendance at the breakfast table. Egg dishes are traditional favorites, but they're loaded with cholesterol. You can avoid that culprit by using egg substitute to create savory omelets and frittatas. Likewise, you can please flapjack lovers with easy low-fat recipes like Apple Pancakes, and you can win over habitual breakfast skippers with delectable muffins (try the honey-glazed ones). When you really feel sociable, throw a healthy brunch featuring Mushroom Puffs, broiled scallops and more. They'll make everyone's day!

HEALTH-LOVERS' EGG DISHES

Do you long for the days when ignorance was bliss and breakfast was a three-egg omelet? That was before you learned that the dietary cholesterol in eggs could send your blood cholesterol (and risk for heart disease) soaring. Well, you can still enjoy your eggs *and* your good health by taking advantage of cholesterol-free egg substitutes. Made largely from egg whites, they are low in calories and high in protein. Many brands contain no fat. And they cook up just fine, making picture-perfect egg dishes for any occasion.

BROCCOLI FRITTATA

SERVES 4

*T*his easy frittata incorporates frozen chopped broccoli, which you don't even need to thaw before using.

1 onion, diced
1 teaspoon olive oil
1 package (10 ounces) frozen chopped broccoli
½ teaspoon dried dill
2 cups fat-free egg substitute
½ cup nonfat cottage cheese
2 teaspoons margarine

In a large no-stick frying pan over medium heat, sauté the onions in the oil for 5 minutes, or until soft. Add the broccoli and dill; sauté for 5 minutes, or until the broccoli is heated through.

In a large bowl, mix the eggs and cottage cheese. Stir in the broccoli mixture.

Wipe out the frying pan, then place it over medium-high heat and let stand for about 2 minutes. Add 1 teaspoon margarine and swirl the pan to distribute it. Add half of the egg mixture. Lift and rotate the pan so that the eggs are evenly distributed. As the eggs set around the edges, lift them to allow uncooked portions to flow underneath.

(continued)

Turn the heat to low, cover the pan, and cook until the top is set. Invert onto a serving plate. Cut into wedges.

Repeat with the remaining 1 teaspoon margarine and egg mixture.

Preparation time: 5 minutes
Cooking time: 20 minutes

Per serving: 134 calories, 3.2 g. fat (21% of calories), 3.4 g. dietary fiber, 3 mg. cholesterol, 278 mg. sodium.

SWEET APPLE FRITTATA

SERVES 4

This spicy-sweet frittata is perfect brunch fare.

1	*tart apple, thinly sliced*
⅓	*cup golden raisins*
1	*tablespoon finely chopped walnuts*
1	*tablespoon honey*
1	*teaspoon ground cinnamon*
½	*teaspoon grated nutmeg*
¼	*teaspoon ground cloves*
1	*teaspoon oil*
2	*cups fat-free egg substitute*
2	*teaspoons margarine*

In a large no-stick frying pan over medium heat, sauté the apples, raisins, walnuts, honey, cinnamon, nutmeg and cloves in the oil for 7 minutes, or until the apples are just tender. Transfer to a large bowl. Add the eggs.

Wipe out the frying pan, then place it over medium-high heat and let stand for about 2 minutes. Add 1 teaspoon margarine and swirl the pan to distribute it. Add half of the egg mixture. Lift and rotate the pan so that the eggs are evenly distributed. As the eggs set around the edges, lift them to allow uncooked portions to flow underneath.

Turn the heat to low, cover the pan, and cook until the top is set. Invert onto a serving plate. Cut into wedges.

Repeat with the remaining 1 teaspoon margarine and egg mixture.

Preparation time: 5 minutes
Cooking time: 15 minutes

Per serving: 166 calories, 4.1 g. fat (21% of calories), 1.5 g. dietary fiber, no cholesterol, 163 mg. sodium.

SPINACH AND PIMENTO OMELET

SERVES 4

*T*his is a type of classic French omelet, which has the filling folded inside a creamy outer layer of eggs.

> 1   *box (10 ounces) frozen spinach, thawed and squeezed dry*
> 1   *cup chopped pimentos*
> 1   *teaspoon dried thyme*
> ¼   *cup chopped scallions*
> 1   *teaspoon olive oil*
> 2   *tablespoons shredded part-skim mozzarella cheese*
> 2   *cups fat-free egg substitute*
> 2   *tablespoons water*
> 2   *teaspoons margarine*
> ½   *cup diced tomatoes*

If necessary, chop the spinach. Place in a medium bowl. Add the pimentos and thyme.

In a large no-stick frying pan over medium heat, sauté the scallions in the oil until soft, about 5 minutes. Add the spinach mixture and warm through. Return to the bowl, add the mozzarella, and set aside.

In another medium bowl, whisk together the eggs and water.

Place the frying pan over medium-high heat and let stand for about 2 minutes. Add 1 teaspoon margarine and swirl the pan to distribute it. Add half of the eggs. Lift and rotate the pan so that the eggs are evenly distributed. As the eggs set around the edges, lift them to allow uncooked portions to flow underneath.

When the eggs are mostly set but not dry (in 2 to 3 minutes), spread half of the spinach mixture over the eggs. Use a spatula to fold the omelet in half. Cut in half and transfer to individual dishes.

Repeat with the remaining 1 teaspoon margarine, eggs and spinach mixture. Sprinkle each serving with about 2 tablespoons tomatoes.

Preparation time: 15 minutes
Cooking time: 10 minutes

Chef's Note: A quick way to thaw frozen spinach is in the microwave. Remove the spinach from its box and place it on a glass pie plate. Microwave on high for 2 minutes. Rotate the dish a half turn. Microwave on high for 2 to 4 minutes, or until defrosted. Squeeze out all the excess moisture.

Per serving: 122 calories, 3.8 g. fat (13% of calories), 1.8 g. dietary fiber, 2 mg. cholesterol, 246 mg. sodium.

SPANISH OMELET

SERVES 4

Spanish omelets really *are* popular in Spain, where they're known as tortillas (no relation to Mexican tortillas). They are close in technique to Italian frittatas, which mix the filling with the eggs before cooking. The potatoes in the filling add a nutritional plus—plenty of dietary fiber.

2   baked potatoes, diced
1   large onion, minced
1   large tomato, seeded and diced
2   tablespoons minced fresh parsley
2   cloves garlic, minced
1   teaspoon olive oil
2   cups fat-free egg substitute
2   teaspoons margarine

In a large no-stick frying pan over medium heat, cook the potatoes, onions, tomatoes, parsley and garlic in the oil until most of the liquid has evaporated from the tomatoes. Transfer to a large bowl and stir in the eggs.

Wipe out the frying pan, then place it over medium-high heat and let stand for about 2 minutes. Add 1 teaspoon margarine and swirl the pan to distribute it. Add half of the egg mixture. Lift and rotate the pan so that the eggs are evenly distributed. As the eggs set around the edges, lift them to allow uncooked portions to flow underneath.

Turn the heat to low, cover the pan, and cook until the top is set. Invert onto a serving plate. Cut into wedges.

Repeat with the remaining 1 teaspoon margarine and egg mixture.

Preparation time: 10 minutes
Cooking time: 15 minutes

Chef's Note: The quickest way to bake potatoes is in the microwave. Scrub them well and prick them all over with a fork. Place side by side on a paper towel directly on the floor of the microwave. Cook on high for 6 to 8 minutes (flip and rearrange the potatoes after 3 minutes), or until easily pierced with a knife. Let stand for 5 minutes to finish cooking. Use immediately or chill for later.

Per serving: 211 calories, 3.3 g. fat (14% of calories), 3.6 g. dietary fiber, no cholesterol, 174 mg. sodium.

Good-for-You 'Cakes

What's breakfast without a short stack of pancakes? Too bad so many flapjack recipes are jam-packed with fat, calories and cholesterol—and practically devoid of fiber. Worse, serving these 'cakes with thick pats of butter and mini-pitchers of syrup further erodes their nutritional profile. Fortunately, you can make really healthy—and delicious—pancakes in no time flat.

BUTTERMILK PANCAKES

SERVES 4

*B*uttermilk is rich and thick like cream, but it has less fat than whole milk.

> 1 cup buttermilk
> 2 egg whites
> ¼ cup nonfat cottage cheese
> 1 tablespoon maple syrup or honey
> ½ teaspoon vanilla
> 1 cup whole-wheat pastry flour
> 1 teaspoon baking powder
> ½ teaspoon baking soda

Place the buttermilk, egg whites, cottage cheese, maple syrup or honey and vanilla in a blender. Process until smooth. Add the flour, baking powder and baking soda. Blend well.

Coat a large no-stick frying pan with no-stick spray. Heat on medium until hot. Ladle about ¼ cup batter into the pan for each pancake. Sizzle until lightly browned and cooked through, about 3½ minutes on each side.

Preparation time: 10 minutes
Cooking time: 15 minutes

Per serving: 161 calories, 1.1 g. fat (6% of calories), 3.8 g. dietary fiber, no cholesterol, 329 mg. sodium.

THREE-WHEAT RICOTTA PANCAKES

SERVES 4

*W*heat flour, wheat germ and bran cereal give these interesting pancakes a rich, nutty flavor and a triple helping of fiber.

½   *cup whole-wheat pastry flour*
½   *cup unbleached flour*
¼   *cup wheat germ*
¼   *cup bran-flakes cereal*
1½   *teaspoons baking powder*
2   *egg whites*
½   *cup part-skim ricotta cheese*
½   *cup skim milk*
1   *tablespoon maple syrup*
1   *teaspoon vanilla*

In a large bowl, combine the pastry flour, unbleached flour, wheat germ, cereal and baking powder.

In a medium bowl, whisk together the egg whites, ricotta, milk, maple syrup and vanilla. Pour the mixture over the dry ingredients and combine well, but don't overmix.

Coat a large no-stick frying pan with no-stick spray. Heat on medium until hot. Spoon in the batter in rounded tablespoons. Sizzle until lightly browned and cooked through, about 3½ minutes on each side.

Preparation time: 10 minutes
Cooking time: 15 minutes

Per serving: 209 calories, 3.4 g. fat (15% of calories), 2.7 g. dietary fiber, 10 mg. cholesterol, 237 mg. sodium.

SPREADING IT ON THICK—OR THIN

Stop! Before you slather that wholesome muffin or those low-fat pancakes with butter, think about all the calories and fat you're adding. Reach instead for no-fat spreads and other toppings that'll keep you—and your breakfast of choice—in perfect form. The following spreads are light, lean and, above all, quick.

- All-fruit preserves contain no fat or added sugar and come in all sorts of tantalizing flavors. Use straight from the jar on muffins and pancakes. Or thin slightly with juice (choose a complementary flavor) for pouring over waffles.

- Make chunky applesauce by cooking cored and sliced apples in a little apple cider until soft. Gravensteins and Crispins are excellent for this application, giving the sauce a silky, buttery texture.

- For a quick jam, combine 2 quarts of pureed unpeeled fruit (such as apricots or plums), ⅓ cup sweetener and 2 tablespoons quick-cooking tapioca. Cook just until the fruit comes to a boil and the tapioca has dissolved. Serve chilled as a spread or warm as a sauce (reheat in the microwave).

- Prepare a beautiful, quick spread by pressing ripe persimmons through a coarse nonaluminum sieve and flavoring the puree with lime or lemon juice.

Here are two easy spreads you can make at home.

MARMALADE

MAKES ABOUT 2 CUPS

This is much easier than traditional marmalade recipes, which can take several hours to cook.

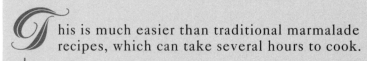

2	*whole navel oranges, coarsely chopped*
½	*cup chopped dates*
½	*cup apple-juice or orange-juice concentrate*

Place the oranges and dates in a food processor and finely chop with on/off turns. Transfer to a 2-quart saucepan. Add the apple-juice or orange-juice concentrate.

Bring to a boil, then reduce the heat to medium-low. Cook, stirring frequently, for about 15 minutes, or until the rind is tender and the marmalade is thick. Let cool.

Preparation time: 5 minutes
Cooking time: 20 minutes

Per tablespoon: 19 calories, trace fat (3% of calories), 0.6 g. dietary fiber, no cholesterol, 1 mg. sodium.

PEACH CHEESE

MAKES ABOUT 1½ CUPS

*Y*ou may use fresh, frozen or canned peaches. If using fresh ones, peel them first by dipping them into boiling water for a few seconds, then removing the peel with a paring knife.

1	*cup nonfat yogurt cheese*
½	*cup chopped peeled peaches*
1	*tablespoon maple syrup*
1	*teaspoon vanilla*
	Pinch of grated nutmeg

In a food processor, combine the yogurt cheese, peaches, maple syrup, vanilla and nutmeg. For a chunky spread, process with on/off turns until the peaches are finely chopped. (For a more creamy spread, process until smooth.)

Preparation time: 10 minutes

Chef's Note: To make yogurt cheese, spoon nonfat yogurt into a yogurt cheese funnel or a sieve lined with cheesecloth. Cover with plastic wrap, set over a bowl, and place in the refrigerator to drain for several hours.

Per tablespoon: 10 calories, trace fat (3% of calories), trace dietary fiber, trace cholesterol, 8 mg. sodium.

GINGERBREAD PANCAKES

SERVES 4

*T*hese pancakes are great topped with fresh fruit and a dollop of vanilla yogurt.

- *1 cup unbleached flour*
- *2 teaspoons baking powder*
- *1 teaspoon cocoa*
- *½ teaspoon powdered ginger*
- *¼ teaspoon ground cinnamon*
- *¼ teaspoon ground cloves*
- *2 tablespoons ground hazelnuts*
- *1 cup skim milk*
- *2 egg whites*
- *2 tablespoons dark molasses*

Sift the flour, baking powder, cocoa, ginger, cinnamon and cloves into a large bowl. Stir in the hazelnuts.

In a medium bowl, whisk together the milk, egg whites and molasses. Make a well in the flour mixture and pour the milk mixture into it. Stir just enough to moisten the dry ingredients. The batter will be lumpy.

Coat a large no-stick frying pan with no-stick spray. Heat on medium until hot. Ladle in the batter, using 2 tablespoons per pancake. Cook for 2 minutes, then flip carefully and cook for 2 minutes more.

Preparation time: 5 minutes
Cooking time: 15 minutes

Per serving: 185 calories, 2.7 g. fat (13% of calories), 1.1 g. dietary fiber, 1 mg. cholesterol, 234 mg. sodium.

APPLE PANCAKES

SERVES 4

*G*inger-spiced pancakes are terrific on frosty winter mornings. And they can be whipped up in about 20 minutes.

⅔ *cup whole-wheat flour*
⅔ *cup unbleached flour*
⅓ *cup cornmeal*
1 *tablespoon baking powder*
1 *teaspoon powdered ginger*
½ *teaspoon baking soda*
2 *cups nonfat yogurt*
¾ *cup fat-free egg substitute*
¼ *cup honey*
2 *tablespoons oil*
1 *large apple, shredded*

In a blender, blend the whole-wheat flour, unbleached flour, cornmeal, baking powder, ginger, baking soda, yogurt, eggs, honey and oil until smooth.

Stir the apples into the batter.

Coat a large no-stick frying pan with no-stick spray. Heat on medium until hot. Ladle in the batter, using 2 to 3 tablespoons for each pancake. Sizzle until lightly browned and cooked through, about 2 minutes on each side.

Preparation time: 5 minutes
Cooking time: 15 minutes

Per serving: 413 calories, 8.1 g. fat (17% of calories), 5.4 g. dietary fiber, 2 mg. cholesterol, 256 mg. sodium.

HOT AND HEARTY CEREALS

oo busy for a hot breakfast? Not with a microwave at your command and a few basic ingredients on hand. With the rest of your day hinging on a good start, you haven't got time *not* to eat right. So rise and shine—and have a great day.

Do the right thing. Your mother probably told you how oatmeal "sticks to your ribs" and keeps you going strong until lunch. You can easily whip up a bowlful in the microwave following package directions. Just be sure to use a large enough bowl and medium (50%) power to prevent the cereal from boiling over and making an extra mess for you to clean up before work. Stir some shredded apples or other fruit into the cooked oatmeal. Top with nonfat vanilla or fruit-flavored yogurt and a sprinkle of cinnamon or ginger.

Have a fruitful morning. Another idea is to cook up a potful of oatmeal on the stove some evening and quickly reheat only what's needed in the morning. For those who love fruit, here's a fiber-packed way to serve the oatmeal: For one serving, slice a banana into a 2-cup glass measure and microwave on high for 1 minute. The banana will become mushy and very sweet. Add ⅔ cup low-fat milk, ½ cup cold cooked oatmeal and 2 sliced dates to the glass; don't bother stirring. Microwave on high for 1 minute, or until the oatmeal is softened. Stir well. Add 1 cup berries or chopped fruit and microwave another minute, or until heated through. If desired, serve with additional milk.

Eat your wheat. Here's a slightly different cereal for those times when you tire of oatmeal. This recipe serves two. In a 9" glass pie plate, combine ½ cup medium cracked wheat and ½ cup apple juice. Cover with vented plastic wrap and microwave on high for 3½ minutes, or until all the juice has been absorbed. Stir in ¼ cup raisins, ¼ cup nonfat yogurt and a pinch of ground cinnamon. Let stand for 2 minutes before serving. Serve with low-fat milk. For an extra treat, top with sliced fruit or fruit compote, such as Lemon-Spice Compote (page 91).

MASTER MUFFINS

Oh, have you seen the muffin man…lately? After indulging in all those high-fat supermarket muffins (especially the jumbo ones), he's put on quite a few pounds. You can avoid that trap yourself by eating lighter muffins such as the ones below.

MAPLE MUFFINS

MAKES 12

*P*repare these muffins ahead and serve at room temperature. They're great with Pear Butter (page 92).

1	*cup whole-wheat flour*
1	*cup unbleached flour*
¼	*cup coarsely chopped pecans*
2	*teaspoons baking powder*
⅔	*cup low-fat milk*
⅔	*cup maple syrup*
½	*cup fat-free egg substitute*
2	*tablespoons oil*

In a large bowl, combine the whole-wheat flour, unbleached flour, pecans and baking powder.

In a medium bowl, whisk together the milk, maple syrup, eggs and oil. Pour over the dry ingredients. Stir with a rubber spatula until the flour is just moistened; do not overmix.

Coat 12 muffin cups with no-stick spray. Divide the batter among the cups. Bake at 375° for 15 to 20 minutes.

Preparation time: 5 minutes
Baking time: 20 minutes

Per muffin: 162 calories, 4.2 g. fat (23% of calories), 1.7 g. dietary fiber, trace cholesterol, 24 mg. sodium.

HONEY-GLAZED MUFFINS

MAKES 12

These unusual muffins are just the thing for a brunch.

Glaze

2	*tablespoons honey*
2	*tablespoons light margarine, softened*
2	*teaspoons grated orange rind (optional)*

Muffins

1	*cup unbleached flour*
¼	*cup wheat germ*
¾	*teaspoon baking soda*
2½	*cups bran-flakes cereal*
¼	*cup currants*
½	*cup fat-free egg substitute*
¼	*cup molasses*
2	*tablespoons honey*
1	*tablespoon oil*
⅔	*cup buttermilk*

To make the glaze: In a cup, mix the honey and margarine. Stir in the orange rind. Coat 12 muffin cups with no-stick spray. Put 1 teaspoon honey mixture in the bottom of each cup.

To make the muffins: In a large bowl, whisk together the flour, wheat germ and baking soda. Stir in the cereal and currants.

In a medium bowl, whisk together the eggs, molasses, honey and oil until smooth. Whisk in the buttermilk. Pour over the dry ingredients. Stir gently until all the flour is moistened.

Divide the batter among the muffin cups. Bake at 375° for 20 minutes. Allow the muffins to cool for 2 minutes, then loosen them from the cups and serve glaze-side up.

Preparation time: 10 minutes
Baking time: 20 minutes

Per muffin: 143 calories, 2.7 g. fat (16% of calories), 1.6 g. dietary fiber, trace cholesterol, 153 mg. sodium.

PEAR MUFFINS

MAKES 12

The high-fiber cereal in these muffins adds crunch to the crust that you usually get from butter and sugar.

1½ cups bran-nuggets cereal
½ cup pear juice
1 pear, coarsely shredded
2 teaspoons finely grated fresh ginger
½ cup nonfat yogurt
¼ cup all-fruit pear butter
¼ cup maple syrup
¼ cup fat-free egg substitute
1 tablespoon oil
1¼ cups unbleached flour
2 teaspoons baking soda
1 teaspoon ground cinnamon

In a medium bowl, combine the cereal, pear juice, pears and ginger. Let soak for 10 minutes. Stir in the yogurt, pear butter, maple syrup, egg and oil.

In a large bowl, combine the flour, baking soda and cinnamon. Pour over the cereal mixture. Stir with a rubber spatula to moisten the flour; do not overmix.

Coat 12 muffin cups with no-stick spray. Divide the batter among the cups. Bake at 400° for 18 to 20 minutes.

Preparation time: 20 minutes
Baking time: 20 minutes

Per muffin: 131 calories, 1.7 g. fat (11% of calories), 3.7 g. dietary fiber, no cholesterol, 218 mg. sodium.

Johnny Appleseed Muffins

MAKES 12

We named these muffins in honor of the legendary tree-planter, who would no doubt approve of the double dose of apples they contain.

1	cup whole-wheat flour
½	cup unbleached flour
1	cup bran-flakes cereal
1	tablespoon baking powder
½	teaspoon baking soda
1	teaspoon ground cinnamon
½	teaspoon grated nutmeg
½	teaspoon ground cloves
1¼	cups applesauce
½	cup fat-free egg substitute
⅓	cup honey
2	tablespoons oil
1	medium apple, shredded

In a large bowl, combine the whole-wheat flour, unbleached flour, cereal, baking powder, baking soda, cinnamon, nutmeg and cloves.

In a medium bowl, whisk together the applesauce, eggs, honey and oil. Stir in the apples. Pour over the dry ingredients. Stir with a rubber spatula until the flour is just moistened; do not overmix.

Coat 12 muffin cups with no-stick spray. Divide the batter among the cups. Bake at 425° for 20 minutes.

Preparation time: 10 minutes
Baking time: 20 minutes

Per muffin: 133 calories, 2.8 g. fat (19% of calories), 2.4 g. dietary fiber, no cholesterol, 173 mg. sodium.

HAVE A HEALTHY BRUNCH

*H*ave you been "cocooning" a little too much lately? Spending time at home with your family certainly has its rewards, but it may leave you feeling exiled from your circle of friends. Get back into circulation with a festive brunch. Informal, relaxing, chummy—it's the ideal way to liven up a weekend. And it's much less trouble than a formal dinner, so you won't feel put out by the effort. The menu that follows will easily feed a dozen of your nearest and dearest. And much of the prep work can be taken care of ahead of time, so you can enjoy your guests' company.

The tantalizing little Mushroom Puffs, for instance, can be assembled ahead and baked when company arrives. You might want to bake them in batches so that latecomers can enjoy them piping hot.

Whip up a batch of muffins ahead of time (choose among the offerings in this chapter). Serve them at room temperature with a low-fat spread such as Pear Butter.

The Lemon-Spice Compote is equally good as a dessert or as a breakfast topping for yogurt. For variety, try other dried fruits, such as prunes, apricots, pears, raisins or blueberries. You may further vary the flavors by using orange or lime rind instead of lemon and by replacing the ginger with vanilla.

Menu

CRANBERRY EYE-OPENERS
BROILED SCALLOPS WITH GRAPEFRUIT
RED AND GREEN SALAD
MUSHROOM PUFFS
LEMON-SPICE COMPOTE
MUFFINS
PEAR BUTTER
BAGELS TO ORDER

CRANBERRY EYE-OPENERS

SERVES 12

8   *cups orange juice*

4   *cups sparkling water*

1   *can (6 ounces) frozen cranberry-juice*
     cocktail, thawed

In a large container, mix the orange juice, water and cranberry juice.

Preparation time: 2 minutes

Chef's Note: To thaw the cranberry juice, either let it stand in the refrigerator overnight or remove the lid and microwave on high for 30 seconds at a time until soft.

Per serving: 108 calories, 0.3 g. fat (3% of calories), 0.2 g. dietary fiber, no cholesterol, 4 mg. sodium.

BROILED SCALLOPS WITH GRAPEFRUIT

SERVES 12

3   *pounds medium sea scallops*

6   *pink grapefruit*

¼   *cup snipped chives*

1   *pound kale*

1   *tablespoon olive oil*

2   *cloves garlic, halved*

Rinse the scallops and pat them dry. Slice each scallop in half horizontally. Place in a large bowl.

Working over the bowl to catch all the juices, peel and section the grapefruit (remove all the inner membranes). Add the sections to the scallops. Squeeze the leftover membranes to extract as much juice as possible. Add the chives and toss gently to combine. Set aside to marinate for 15 minutes.

Meanwhile, wash the kale, trim off tough stems, and break the leaves into small pieces. Drain in a colander, but don't shake off the excess water; it will help to steam-cook the kale later. Set aside.

Transfer the scallops and grapefruit to a large broiler pan. Broil, close to the heat, for 3 minutes. Flip the pieces and broil for 2 minutes.

In a large no-stick frying pan over medium heat, warm the oil. Add the garlic and cook until golden, about 2 minutes. Discard the garlic. Add the kale to the pan and cook, stirring, until its edges start to crisp, about 4 to 6 minutes.

Place the kale on a platter. Top with the scallops and grapefruit.

Preparation time: 10 minutes
Cooking time: 20 minutes

Per serving: 156 calories, 2.2 g. fat (13% of calories), 2.5 g. dietary fiber, 38 mg. cholesterol, 189 mg. sodium.

RED AND GREEN SALAD

SERVES 12

1	*large head romaine lettuce, torn into bite-size pieces*
3	*cups diced tart red apples*
2	*cups diced celery*
¼	*cup chopped walnuts*
1	*ounce blue cheese, crumbled*
1	*cup nonfat mayonnaise*
1	*cup nonfat yogurt*
½	*teaspoon ground black pepper*

In a large bowl, combine the lettuce, apples, celery, walnuts and blue cheese.

In a small bowl, whisk together the mayonnaise, yogurt and pepper. Pour over the salad and toss well.

Preparation time: 10 minutes

Per serving: 77 calories, 2.5 g. fat (27% of calories), 1.7 g. dietary fiber, 2 mg. cholesterol, 321 mg. sodium.

MUSHROOM PUFFS

SERVES 12

1 *pound small mushrooms, halved*
1 *tablespoon oil*
1 *cup thinly sliced scallions*
1 *teaspoon dried thyme*
1 *tablespoon butter-flavored sprinkles*
3 *cups fat-free egg substitute*
3 *cups nonfat ricotta cheese*
1½ *cups nonfat sour cream*
1 *cup dry bread crumbs*
½ *cup grated Parmesan cheese*
Paprika

In a large frying pan over medium-high heat, sauté the mushrooms in the oil for 5 minutes, or until they give up their liquid. Add the scallions and thyme. Continue to sauté for 5 minutes, or until all the liquid has evaporated. Stir in the sprinkles. Remove from the heat and set aside.

In a large bowl, whisk together the eggs, ricotta, sour cream, bread crumbs and Parmesan.

Coat 12 individual (6" diameter) casserole dishes with no-stick spray. Distribute half of the mushroom mixture among the dishes. Divide the egg mixture among the dishes. Sprinkle with the remaining mushroom mixture. Dust lightly with the paprika.

Bake at 375° for 20 minutes, or until puffed and lightly browned.

Preparation time: 10 minutes
Cooking time: 10 minutes
Baking time: 20 minutes

Per serving: 177 calories, 3 g. fat (15% of calories), 1 g. dietary fiber, 3 mg. cholesterol, 333 mg. sodium.

LEMON-SPICE COMPOTE

4   *cups water*

2   *tea bags, preferably Darjeeling*

12   *ounces dried peaches, halved*

8   *ounces dried Black Mission figs, halved*

8   *ounces dried cherries*

2   *slices (about ¼" thick) fresh ginger*

2   *strips (about 2" long) lemon rind*

1   *cinnamon stick*

In a 3-quart saucepan, bring the water to a boil. Remove from the heat. Add the tea bags and let steep for 5 minutes. Remove the bags, pressing to extract the water.

Add the peaches, figs, cherries, ginger, lemon rind and cinnamon stick. Bring to a boil, then reduce the heat to low and simmer, stirring occasionally, until tender, about 15 to 20 minutes.

Remove the ginger, lemon rind and cinnamon stick before serving. Serve warm or chilled.

Preparation time: 10 minutes
Cooking time: 20 minutes

Per serving: 184 calories, 1.3 g. fat (6% of calories), 5.6 g. dietary fiber, no cholesterol, 6 mg. sodium.

PEAR BUTTER

3	*pounds pears*
⅓	*cup pear or apple juice*
1	*tablespoon honey*
1	*tablespoon lemon juice*
¼	*teaspoon ground allspice*
¼	*teaspoon grated nutmeg*

If desired, peel the pears. Core them and cut into 1" chunks. Place in the bowl of a food processor. Using on/off turns, chop finely. Add the pear or apple juice, honey, lemon juice, allspice and nutmeg. Process until smooth.

Transfer to a large frying pan. Cook over medium heat, stirring often to prevent scorching, for 20 minutes, or until thick.

Preparation time: 10 minutes
Cooking time: 20 minutes

Per 2 tablespoons: 57 calories, 0.4 g. fat (5% of calories), 2.2 g. dietary fiber, no cholesterol, 1 mg. sodium.

BAGELS TO ORDER

agels are an ideal addition to the quick and healthy buffet. They're very low in fat and not too high in calories. Most types have no cholesterol whatsoever. It's only egg bagels that contain any, and that amount can vary widely. (Check the label, if there is one.)

Bagels come in such interesting varieties—and sizes—that you can present a wide selection sure to please everybody. Serve them toasted or just as they come from the store; plain or with all sorts of low-fat toppings. Here are some easy ways to dress up a bagel.

- To make a low-fat spread, puree cottage cheese until smooth, then mix in a little cinnamon, chopped fresh fruit or minced raisins. Or turn the cottage cheese into a savory spread by adding minced chives or scallions and some dried thyme, oregano or dill.

- Spread a toasted bagel half with yogurt cheese or reduced-fat cream cheese. Top with a slice of ripe tomato and a sprinkle of basil and Parmesan. Broil for 3 minutes, or until the tomato begins to brown.

- Top a split bagel with a little nonfat mayonnaise, mustard and thinly sliced smoked turkey breast, chicken breast or lean ham. This is particularly good on onion bagels, but raisin, blueberry and other sweet varieties provide an interesting counterpoint to the meat.

- Spread a little crushed pineapple on bagel halves and sprinkle with some shredded reduced-fat cheese. Broil until the cheese has melted.

- Make mini-pizzas by spreading a little tomato sauce on bagel halves and then sprinkling them with Parmesan or reduced-fat Cheddar. Broil until the cheese bubbles.

- Give the pizzas a Mexican flair by using mashed cooked beans, salsa and a sprinkle of low-fat Monterey Jack.

- Toast split bagels and top with tuna salad or salmon salad made using nonfat mayonnaise. Or simply top the bagels with a little mayo, flaked salmon or tuna and a sprinkle of dill or thyme.

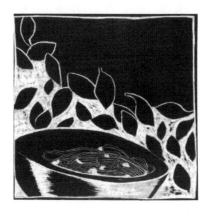

CHAPTER 5

LIGHT
LUNCHEONS

AFTERNOON DELIGHTS

What's your idea of lunch? A greasy burger grabbed on the run? Well, stop running and sit down to tasty low-fat soups, salads and sandwiches that you make from scratch in no time at all. Most can be done ahead and carried along to work or school. You'll love unusual dishes such as Spicy Kale and Sausage Soup and Oriental Chicken Pitas—and you'll marvel at how much flavor they pack, even though they're low in fat. When you have the time for a sit-down lunch at home, enjoy Warm Scallop Salad, Spicy Chicken Taco Salad or other entrées featured here. And don't forget to offer company the gift of good health—the menu on page 118 will show you how.

Simply Delicious Soups

Canned soups let you put a hot lunch on the table fast. But very often, they're too high in sodium and fat to belong in a health-conscious diet. The soups that follow are considerably lower in sodium and fat—especially if made with low-sodium defatted stock.

Velvety Yam Soup

SERVES 4

*W*ith the help of your microwave, you can prepare healthy homemade soup in record time. This rich, thick sweet-potato soup is especially welcome in the middle of winter.

> 2   *medium yams or sweet potatoes (about 8 ounces each)*
> 2   *medium leeks*
> 2   *tablespoons defatted chicken stock*
> ½   *teaspoon dried dill*
> 1½   *cups evaporated skim milk*

Peel the yams or sweet potatoes and slice into ¾" chunks. Place in a 1½-quart casserole. Trim the leeks, slit lengthwise, and wash well to remove all grit. Coarsely chop and add to the dish. Stir in the stock and dill.

Cover the dish with vented plastic wrap and microwave on high for 5 minutes, or until the yams or sweet potatoes are just tender. Let stand for 4 minutes. Transfer the mixture to a blender.

Pour the milk into a 2-cup glass measure and microwave on high for 2 minutes, or until warm. Add to the blender and puree.

Preparation time: 10 minutes
Cooking time: 10 minutes

Per serving: 182 calories, 0.6 g. fat (3% of calories), 3 g. dietary fiber, 4 mg. cholesterol, 133 mg. sodium.

FRENCH VEGETABLE SOUP

*T*his hearty soup contains pistou, which is the French version of pesto sauce.

1   *cup fresh basil leaves*
3   *tablespoons grated Parmesan cheese*
1   *tablespoon chopped walnuts*
1   *clove garlic, minced*
2   *teaspoons olive oil*
6   *cups defatted chicken stock*
1   *can (28 ounces) tomatoes, chopped*
2   *medium carrots, thinly sliced*
1   *cup rinsed and drained canned white beans*
4   *ounces green beans, cut into 1½" pieces*
¼   *cup broken vermicelli*

In a food processor, puree the basil, Parmesan, walnuts, garlic and oil. Set aside.

In a 3-quart saucepan over medium-high heat, bring the stock, tomatoes and carrots to a boil. Reduce the heat to medium and simmer for 15 minutes.

Add the white beans and green beans. Simmer for 4 minutes. Add the vermicelli and simmer for 5 minutes. Stir the basil mixture into the pan.

Preparation time: 10 minutes
Cooking time: 20 minutes

Per serving: 154 calories, 4.6 g. fat (27% of calories), 4.1 g. dietary fiber, 3 mg. cholesterol, 395 mg. sodium.

PEASANT SOUP

*T*his inexpensive soup gets body from an unusual source—stale bread cubes. It's an idea concocted by frugal peasants that's making a comeback.

1	*large onion, diced*
2	*carrots, shredded*
2	*celery stalks, minced*
2	*teaspoons olive oil*
4	*cups defatted chicken stock*
2	*cups stale whole-grain bread cubes*
¼	*teaspoon dried thyme*
¼	*teaspoon ground black pepper*
⅛	*teaspoon crushed fennel seeds*
2	*tablespoons grated sapsago or Parmesan cheese*

In a 3-quart saucepan over medium heat, sauté the onions, carrots and celery in the oil for about 7 minutes, or until fragrant and wilted. Add the stock, bread, thyme, pepper and fennel seeds. Bring to a boil. Reduce the heat and gently simmer for about 20 minutes, stirring frequently to break up the bread.

Serve sprinkled with the sapsago or Parmesan.

Preparation time: 10 minutes
Cooking time: 30 minutes

Chef's Note: If you don't have any stale bread on hand, dry out bread cubes in a 300° oven for about 20 minutes.

Per serving: 95 calories, 2.7 g. fat (24% of calories), 3.6 g. dietary fiber, trace cholesterol, 167 mg. sodium.

SPICY KALE AND SAUSAGE SOUP

SERVES 6

*T*his soup puts nutrient-dense kale to good use.

2 cups defatted chicken stock
1 large baking potato, cut into ½" cubes
1 medium onion, diced
2 ounces frozen reduced-fat turkey sausage links
½ teaspoon dried oregano
¼ teaspoon ground black pepper
⅛ teaspoon ground red pepper
1½ cups skim milk
3 cups shredded kale

In a 3-quart saucepan over medium heat, bring the stock, potatoes, onions, sausage, oregano, black pepper and red pepper to a boil. Cook for 10 minutes, or until the potatoes are softened.

Remove the sausage from the pan. Cut into thin slices and set aside.

Transfer the rest of the mixture to a blender and process for about 10 seconds, or until coarsely pureed. Return the mixture to the saucepan. Stir in the milk and sausage.

While the mixture is cooking, place the kale in a 2-quart casserole. Cover with vented plastic wrap and microwave on high for 4 minutes, or until well wilted. Stir into the pureed mixture.

Preparation time: 10 minutes
Cooking time: 15 minutes

Per serving: 97 calories, 1. 2 g. fat (11% of calories), 2.3 g. dietary fiber, 7 mg. cholesterol, 130 mg. sodium.

Classic Chicken Noodle Soup

SERVES 6

*H*ere's an easy way to have homemade noodle soup.

1	*pound boneless, skinless chicken breasts*
6	*cups defatted chicken stock*
1	*cup thinly sliced carrots*
1	*cup thinly sliced celery*
1	*cup diced onions*
¼	*teaspoon dried oregano*
4	*ounces fine no-yolk noodles*
3	*tablespoons minced fresh parsley*

In a 3-quart saucepan, combine the chicken, stock, carrots, celery, onions and oregano. Bring to a boil over medium-high heat. Lower the heat to medium and simmer for 15 minutes, or until the chicken is tender.

Remove the chicken from the pan and set aside for 5 minutes, or until cool enough to handle. Cut or shred into bite-size pieces.

While the chicken is cooling, stir the noodles into the stock. Cook for 8 minutes, or until just tender. Stir in the parsley and chicken.

Preparation time: 10 minutes
Cooking time: 25 minutes

Per serving: 186 calories, 2.1 g. fat (10% of calories), 0.7 g. dietary fiber, 44 mg. cholesterol, 105 mg. sodium.

CHILLED PEACH SOUP

SERVES 4

*T*his summer-fresh soup takes but a minute to prepare.

12	*ripe peaches*
1½	*cups low-fat milk*
6	*ice cubes, cracked*
½	*cup nonfat sour cream*
2	*teaspoons honey*
1	*teaspoon powdered ginger*
¼	*teaspoon grated nutmeg*

Dip the peaches into boiling water for 20 seconds. Remove the peel. Quarter the peaches and place in a blender with 1 cup milk and the ice cubes. Process on medium-high speed until pureed.

Add the remaining ½ cup milk, sour cream, honey, ginger and nutmeg. Blend well. Serve immediately or chill further.

Preparation time: 10 minutes

Per serving: 181 calories, 1.2 g. fat (6% of calories), 4.2 g. dietary fiber, 4 mg. cholesterol, 66 mg. sodium.

SENSATIONAL LUNCHEON SALADS

Your goal when preparing luncheon salads is to strike a balance between the green leafy ones that provide little or no protein and those that go overboard on protein and fat, such as chef's salads. The following offerings are filling without being heavy.

CANNELLINI BEAN SALAD

SERVES 4

*U*sing canned beans takes all the work out of bean salads. Just be sure to rinse them well with cold water to remove their thick canning liquid and excess sodium.

1   *can (19 ounces) cannellini beans, rinsed and drained*

1   *cup cubed tomatoes*

½   *cup diced green peppers*

½   *cup diced red onions*

½   *cup minced fresh parsley*

2   *ounces part-skim mozzarella cheese, diced*

¼   *cup lemon juice*

3   *tablespoons olive oil*

1   *tablespoon balsamic vinegar*

1   *clove garlic, minced*

2   *teaspoons grated lemon rind*

½   *teaspoon dried thyme*

¼   *teaspoon ground black pepper*

In a large bowl, combine the beans, tomatoes, green peppers, onions, parsley and mozzarella.

In a small bowl, whisk together the lemon juice, oil, vinegar, garlic, lemon rind, thyme and black pepper. Pour over the salad and toss well. Serve chilled or at room temperature.

Preparation time: 10 minutes

Per serving: 203 calories, 6.2 g. fat (26% of calories), 9.5 g. dietary fiber, 8 mg. cholesterol, 520 mg. sodium.

FRESH LIMA SALAD

*T*his is a snap to make when fresh lima beans are in season. Try to choose small, tender ones. Out of season, use frozen baby limas. If you're on a reduced-cholesterol diet, either eliminate the eggs entirely or double the number of eggs and discard the yolks.

2	*cups lima beans*
1½	*cups halved cherry tomatoes*
1	*cup thinly sliced yellow or green peppers*
¼	*cup thinly sliced scallions*
2	*tablespoons chopped fresh basil*
2	*tablespoons snipped chives*
3	*tablespoons lemon juice*
1	*tablespoon water*
1	*tablespoon olive oil*
1	*teaspoon Dijon mustard*
2	*teaspoons minced garlic*
2	*cups torn spinach leaves*
2	*hard-cooked eggs*
1	*cup seasoned whole-grain croutons*

Steam the lima beans until just tender, about 5 minutes. Place in a large bowl. Add the tomatoes, peppers, scallions, basil and chives. Toss to combine.

In a small bowl, whisk together the lemon juice, water, oil, mustard and garlic. Pour over the salad and toss well. Line individual plates with the spinach. Spoon on the salad. Cut the eggs into wedges and add to the plates. Sprinkle with the croutons.

Preparation time: 15 minutes

Per serving: 217 calories, 7 g. fat (28% of calories), 8.6 g. dietary fiber, 107 mg. cholesterol, 144 mg. sodium.

*N*othing is more slimming than greens and fresh vegetables. But don't sabotage your salads with fattening extras. Here's how to keep those light entrée and side-dish salads from gaining weight.

Crisp your own croutons. Commercial varieties can be real fat traps. But if you make your own in the microwave, you can cut the fat entirely. Take 2 slices of bread and spread both sides of each with a super-thin layer of Dijon mustard. Then cut the bread into small cubes. Spread them in a single layer on a sheet of wax paper. Microwave on high for 1½ minutes. Stir well, then microwave on high for another 1½ minutes, or until the bread is dry to the touch. You'll have enough croutons for two entrées or four side dishes.

Perform vegetable magic. Sometimes you just get tired of raw vegetables. But sautéed or oil-marinated ones can sink a lean salad. So when you want a change of pace, turn to the microwave. Quick-cooked zucchini, for instance, is wonderful in spinach salad or with low-fat marinated tomatoes. Carrots, onions, peppers, broccoli and other vegetables can also be microwaved in an instant. Place about 1 cup's worth in a small dish with 1 teaspoon stock or water. Cover with vented plastic wrap and microwave on high for 1 minute, or until just tender. Drain well.

See the lite. You can get familiar tastes with a fraction of the fat if you shop wisely and buy only nonfat or reduced-fat dressings, cheeses and deli meats. Slice cheese and meat into very thin slices, then cut into ¼" slivers. A little will look like a lot scattered throughout the salad.

Spray away. If you crave a real oil-and-vinegar dressing, mix it up in a spray bottle and give your salads a fine misting. Use flavorful ingredients, such as virgin olive oil, walnut oil, sesame oil, balsamic vinegar, herb vinegar or raspberry vinegar. That way, you'll need very little actual dressing to satisfy your taste buds. To keep from clogging the spray bottle, sprinkle herbs and spices directly on the salad. And when using fresh herbs, be generous. Toss in whole leaves of basil, thyme, oregano, sage, parsley, rosemary, coriander and other aromatics.

Turkey Salad with Honey-Cream Dressing

SERVES 4

This delicious salad is good served on a bed of Boston lettuce leaves. Use either leftover poached or roasted turkey or ready-cooked turkey from the supermarket.

1   cup nonfat yogurt
4   ounces rotelle or other shaped pasta
2   cups cooked turkey breast, cut into bite-size pieces
1   cup sliced celery
1   cup orange sections
½   cup sliced water chestnuts, cut into slivers
2   tablespoons minced fresh parsley
2   tablespoons honey
1   tablespoon orange juice
1   teaspoon dry mustard
½   teaspoon ground black pepper
½   teaspoon poppy seeds
2   cups shredded kale

Spoon the yogurt into a yogurt cheese funnel or a strainer lined with cheesecloth. Set over a glass and allow to drain for about 10 minutes.

Cook the pasta in a pot of boiling water for 10 minutes, or until just tender. Drain and rinse with cold water. Place in a large bowl. Add the turkey, celery, oranges, water chestnuts and parsley. Toss well.

Transfer the yogurt to a small bowl. Whisk in the honey, orange juice, mustard, pepper and poppy seeds. Pour over the salad and toss. Line plates with the kale. Top with the salad.

Preparation time: 10 minutes
Cooking time: 10 minutes

AFTERNOON DELIGHTS

Chef's Note: For variety, you could replace the turkey with chicken breast, tuna, small shrimp or crabmeat.

Per serving: 338 calories, 3.5 g. fat (9% of calories), 3.3 g. dietary fiber, 50 mg. cholesterol, 134 mg. sodium.

MOROCCAN RICE SALAD

SERVES 6

*R*ice salads are nice and substantial. You can easily make this salad ahead for a fast lunch. It also travels well, so you can take it along to work.

1	*cup seeded and diced tomatoes*
½	*cup thinly sliced scallions*
½	*cup minced fresh parsley*
¼	*cup minced fresh mint*
¼	*cup minced carrots*
3	*cups cooked aromatic or converted rice*
2	*tablespoons lemon juice*
2	*tablespoons olive oil*
1	*tablespoon water*
1	*clove garlic, minced*
¼	*teaspoon ground black pepper*
¼	*teaspoon ground cumin*
3	*cups torn red leaf or romaine lettuce*

In a large bowl, combine the tomatoes, scallions, parsley, mint and carrots. Add the rice and toss with a fork to combine.

In a small bowl, whisk together the lemon juice, oil, water, garlic, pepper and cumin. Pour over the salad. Toss well.

Line individual plates with the lettuce. Spoon on the salad.

Preparation time: 15 minutes

Per serving: 172 calories, 4.7 g. fat (24% of calories), 2.6 g. dietary fiber, no cholesterol, 14 mg. sodium.

CHICKEN WALDORF SALAD

SERVES 6

*T*his easy variation on the popular Waldorf salad uses quick-cooking brown rice and nonfat mayonnaise. Those changes increase the fiber of the original recipe and reduce the fat considerably.

1¼ *cups defatted chicken stock*

1 *cup quick-cooking brown rice*

1 *red apple, diced*

1 *tablespoon lemon juice*

2 *cups diced cooked chicken breast*

1 *cup seedless red or green grapes*

½ *cup diced celery*

¼ *cup raisins*

½ *cup nonfat mayonnaise*

½ *cup nonfat yogurt*

In a 2-quart saucepan over medium heat, bring the stock to a boil. Add the rice. Cover and cook over medium-low heat for 10 minutes, or until all the stock has been absorbed. Fluff with a fork. Spread in an even layer on a large tray. Place in the freezer or refrigerator for 10 minutes to cool.

In a large bowl, toss the apples with the lemon juice. Add the chicken, grapes, celery and raisins. Toss well. Add the rice and toss again. Stir in the mayonnaise and yogurt.

Preparation time: 20 minutes
Cooking time: 10 minutes

Chef's Note: If you don't have any leftover cooked chicken on hand, you can easily poach boneless, skinless chicken breasts in water or stock for about 15 minutes. Or you can microwave them: Place 2 breasts (about 1 pound total) side by side on a plate with the thicker areas facing outward. Cover with wax paper and microwave on high for 2 minutes. Give the plate a half turn and microwave on high for about 3 minutes, or until the juices run clear when you pierce the chicken with a fork. Cover with foil and allow to stand for 5 minutes. Chop or shred when the chicken is cool enough to handle.

Per serving: 221 calories, 4.1 g. fat (16% of calories), 2.2 g. dietary fiber, 35 mg. cholesterol, 321 mg. sodium.

PITA POCKETS

Pita sandwiches are so easy to make and so convenient for brown bagging that we're featuring four variations here. Three use lean meats, and one is vegetarian, so you can enjoy them in good health. Actually, there's no end to what you can put into a pita. For a really simple lunch, you can try a mixture of shredded vegetables, low-fat cheese and fat-free dressing. Or you can make an instant sandwich from any type of leftover protein-based salad. For a completely different treatment, take advantage of pita's low profile to fashion an open-faced sandwich or even a quick pizza.

If your pita has been refrigerated or is a few days old, it may have hardened enough to make opening the pockets difficult. In that case, wrap a whole pita in a damp paper towel and microwave on high for about 20 seconds to soften it.

ORIENTAL CHICKEN PITAS

SERVES 4

*T*his sandwich pairs cooked chicken breast with snow peas, water chestnuts and Chinese seasonings.

2	*cups shredded cooked chicken breast*
½	*cup chopped snow peas*
½	*cup diced sweet red peppers*
1	*tablespoon toasted sesame seeds*
½	*cup nonfat mayonnaise*
¼	*cup nonfat yogurt*
1	*teaspoon grated fresh ginger*
1	*teaspoon low-sodium soy sauce*
½	*teaspoon sesame oil*
4	*whole-wheat pita breads, halved*
1	*cup mung bean sprouts*

In a medium bowl, combine the chicken, snow peas, peppers and sesame seeds.

In a small bowl, whisk together the mayonnaise, yogurt, ginger, soy sauce and oil. Pour over the salad and mix well.

Spoon into the pita pockets. Top each sandwich half with the sprouts.

Preparation time: 10 minutes

Per serving: 286 calories, 6.5 g. fat (21% of calories), 2 g. dietary fiber, 52 mg. cholesterol, 711 mg. sodium.

SMOKED TURKEY AND ARTICHOKE SANDWICHES

*S*tore-bought smoked turkey, canned artichoke hearts and bottled dressing combine to make an interesting—and very easy—sandwich filling.

4	*ounces smoked turkey breast*
1	*can (14 ounces) artichoke hearts, drained and coarsely chopped*
¼	*cup diced green peppers*
¼	*cup minced onions*
¼	*cup nonfat yogurt*
¼	*cup fat-free Italian dressing*
¼	*teaspoon dried tarragon*
¼	*teaspoon ground black pepper*
4	*pita breads, halved*
	Leaf lettuce
1	*cup alfalfa sprouts*

Thinly slice the turkey, then cut into strips about ½" wide. Place in a medium bowl. Add the artichokes, green peppers and onions.

In a small bowl, whisk together the yogurt, dressing, tarragon and black pepper. Pour over the salad and toss to combine.

Line the pita pockets with the lettuce leaves. Spoon in the filling. Top each sandwich half with the sprouts.

Preparation time: 10 minutes

Per serving: 195 calories, 2.1 g. fat (10% of calories), 4.5 g. dietary fiber, 15 mg. cholesterol, 461 mg. sodium.

EGG POCKETS

SERVES 4

*N*othing could be quicker than scrambling eggs and stuffing them into pita pockets. These easy eggs get a fiber boost from vegetables and whole-wheat pita breads.

1	*cup julienned or shredded carrots*
1	*cup diced mushrooms*
1	*small onion, thinly sliced*
2	*teaspoons margarine*
1½	*cups fat-free egg substitute*
½	*teaspoon dried basil*
¼	*teaspoon dried thyme*
¼	*teaspoon ground black pepper*
¼	*cup shredded reduced-fat Cheddar cheese*
4	*whole-wheat pita breads, halved*
1	*cup alfalfa sprouts or finely shredded spinach*

In a 4-cup glass measure, combine the carrots, mushrooms and onions. Cover with vented plastic wrap and microwave on high for 4 minutes, or until the vegetables are tender.

Coat a large no-stick frying pan with no-stick spray. Place over medium heat for 3 minutes. Add the margarine and vegetables. Sauté for 2 minutes to slightly brown and to evaporate excess liquid from the mushrooms. Add the eggs, basil, thyme and pepper.

Allow the eggs to begin to firm around the edges, then push the set portion to the center. Continue until the eggs are scrambled but not dry. Sprinkle with the Cheddar.

Spoon the eggs into the pita pockets. Top with the sprouts or spinach.

Preparation time: 10 minutes

Cooking time: 10 minutes

Per serving: 225 calories, 5.2 g. fat (21% of calories), 2.1 g. dietary fiber, 7 mg. cholesterol, 402 mg. sodium.

LEAN PORK PITAS

*T*hese hot sandwiches are served with a cooling cucumber sauce, giving them a Middle Eastern flavor.

8   *ounces pork tenderloin*
2   *teaspoons Dijon mustard*
1   *tablespoon olive oil*
1   *tablespoon lemon juice*
1   *clove garlic, minced*
½   *teaspoon dried oregano*
1   *cucumber, peeled and diced*
1   *cup nonfat sour cream*
½   *teaspoon dried dill*
1   *red onion, thinly sliced into rounds*
1   *green pepper, thinly sliced*
4   *pita breads, halved*
1   *cup shredded spinach*
8   *cherry tomatoes, halved*

Cut the pork across the grain into ½" cutlets, then slice each piece into thin strips.

In a large bowl, combine the mustard, oil, lemon juice, garlic and oregano. Add the pork and toss well to coat all the pieces. Let stand about 10 minutes.

In a small bowl, combine the cucumbers, sour cream and dill. Refrigerate until needed.

(continued)

Separate the onions into rings. Place in a 9" glass pie plate. Add the peppers. Cover with vented plastic wrap and microwave on high for 3 minutes, or until soft.

Coat a large no-stick frying pan with no-stick spray and place over medium heat for 3 minutes. Working in batches to avoid overcrowding the pan, add the pork and sauté for about 3 minutes, or until cooked through. Transfer to a plate. Add the onions and peppers to the pan; sauté for 3 minutes, or until lightly browned.

Line the pita pockets with the spinach. Add the pork mixture. Top each sandwich half with a tomato and some cucumber sauce.

Preparation time: 15 minutes
Cooking time: 20 minutes

Chef's Note: The pork will be easier to slice if you freeze it for about 20 minutes first. If you have additional time, you may allow the sliced pieces to marinate in the mustard mixture for up to 8 hours in the refrigerator.

Per serving: 313 calories, 7.1 g. fat (21% of calories), 3.1 g. dietary fiber, 53 mg. cholesterol, 343 mg. sodium.

LIGHT LUNCHEON ENTRÉES

Special-occasion luncheons require hot entrées that are a cut above the usual midday fare. But you don't have to spend extra time in the kitchen to prepare them, as the following elegant dishes prove.

WARM SCALLOP SALAD

SERVES 4

This recipe is an adaptation of one served by the innovative chefs at Chez Eddy, a restaurant located in Houston's Scurlock Tower Medical Center. Although frequented by many hospital patients and their families,

Chez Eddy is also a favorite of both locals and tourists. The menu, inspired by American Heart Association guidelines, proves that you needn't sacrifice taste and eye appeal for the sake of good nutrition. These scallops are a prime example of that philosophy.

2 shallots or scallions, finely chopped
1 tablespoon olive oil
2 tablespoons lime juice
½ teaspoon ground black pepper
2 medium tomatoes, peeled, seeded and chopped
2 tablespoons minced fresh mint
¼ cup defatted chicken stock
1 pound scallops
3 bunches watercress, large stems removed

In a 2-quart saucepan over medium heat, sauté the shallots or scallions in the oil until soft, about 2 minutes. Add the lime juice and pepper. Remove from the heat and stir in the tomatoes and mint. Set aside.

In a large no-stick frying pan over medium-high heat, warm the stock. Add the scallops and simmer for 5 minutes, or until slightly translucent in the middle. Remove from the heat.

Pour half of the tomato mixture over the scallops.

Divide the watercress among individual plates. Spoon on the scallops. Drizzle with the remaining tomato mixture.

Preparation time: 10 minutes
Cooking time: 10 minutes

Per serving: 145 calories, 3.8 g. fat (23% of calories), 1.5 g. dietary fiber, 40 mg. cholesterol, 315 mg. sodium.

BLAZING SHRIMP

SERVES 4

*W*e call this shrimp "blazing" because it gets heat from two types of pepper. If you prefer yours a little milder, adjust the seasonings to taste.

2   *tablespoons lime juice*
1   *tablespoon Worcestershire sauce*
1   *teaspoon hot-pepper sauce*
2   *teaspoons olive oil*
½   *teaspoon dried thyme*
½   *teaspoon dried oregano*
½   *teaspoon ground black pepper*
1   *pound large shrimp, peeled and deveined*
8   *ounces fresh linguini*
1   *cup yellow plum or pear tomatoes, halved*
¼   *cup diced red sweet peppers*
¼   *cup diced yellow peppers*
2   *tablespoons chive pieces (1" lengths)*

In a 9" × 13" baking dish, combine the lime juice, Worcestershire sauce, pepper sauce, oil, thyme, oregano and black pepper. Add the shrimp and toss to coat well.

Spread out the shrimp in an even layer. Bake at 400°, stirring occasionally, for 15 minutes, or until cooked through.

Cook the linguine in a large pot of boiling water for 5 minutes, or until just tender. Drain and toss with the tomatoes, red peppers, yellow peppers and chives. Serve topped with the shrimp.

Preparation time: 10 minutes
Cooking time: 20 minutes
Baking time: 15 minutes

Per serving: 365 calories, 5.2 g. fat (13% of calories), 2.8 g. dietary fiber, 153 mg. cholesterol, 195 mg. sodium.

Turkey Cutlets with Apples

*T*his is a simple way to prepare turkey cutlets that dresses them up a little bit.

4	*large baking potatoes*
1	*teaspoon grated lemon rind*
½	*teaspoon dried tarragon*
1	*clove garlic, minced*
1	*pound turkey cutlets*
2	*teaspoons olive oil*
2	*Granny Smith or other tart baking apples, peeled and cut into ½" wedges*
⅓	*cup apple juice*
½	*cup nonfat sour cream*
2	*tablespoons snipped chives*

Pierce the potatoes all over with a fork. Place a paper towel directly on the floor of the microwave. Arrange the potatoes on the paper towel in a square pattern. Microwave on high for 5 minutes. Flip and rearrange the potatoes. Microwave on high for 5 to 7 minutes, or until easily pierced with a fork. Cover with foil and let stand for at least 5 minutes.

On a plate, combine the lemon rind, tarragon and garlic. Lightly rub the turkey with the mixture.

Warm the oil in a large no-stick frying pan over medium-high heat. Add the turkey and sauté for 3 minutes per side to brown the pieces. Remove to a plate and keep warm.

Add the apples to the pan and sauté for 5 minutes. Stir in the apple juice. Return the turkey to the pan, cover, and cook for 3 minutes to soften the apples.

Using a slotted spoon, divide the turkey and apples among individual dinner plates. Split the potatoes and fluff the flesh with a fork; add to the plates. Whisk the sour cream into the juice remaining in the pan. Spoon over the potatoes. Sprinkle with the chives.

Preparation time: 15 minutes
Cooking time: 20 minutes

Chef's Note: If you don't have a microwave, bake the potatoes at 375° for 1 hour, or until easily pierced with a fork. An alternative for occasions when you're pressed for time is to serve the turkey and apples over rice or pasta.

Per serving: 440 calories, 4.6 g. fat (9% of calories), 6.2 g. dietary fiber, 66 mg. cholesterol, 105 mg. sodium.

SPICY CHICKEN TACO SALAD

SERVES 4

*T*he microwave speeds up the time required for this main-course Mexican salad. Forming the tortillas into little salad bowls takes just a few minutes but makes an impressive presentation. Serve this salad on a bed of shredded lettuce. Have on hand chopped tomatoes, minced fresh coriander, nonfat yogurt or sour cream and bottled salsa so that diners can top their individual taco salads as they please.

1	*pound boneless, skinless chicken breasts*
2	*tablespoons orange juice*
4	*flour tortillas*
½	*cup nonfat yogurt*
1	*teaspoon lemon juice*
1	*teaspoon chili powder*
¼	*teaspoon ground cumin*
⅛	*teaspoon ground cloves*
3	*tablespoons minced fresh parsley*
1	*celery stalk, minced*
1	*scallion, minced*
1	*shallot, minced*

If the chicken pieces aren't of equal thickness, place them between sheets of wax paper and pound with a meat mallet. Arrange around the edge of a 9" glass pie plate. Sprinkle with the orange juice and cover with vented plastic wrap. Microwave on high for 2 minutes.

Turn over the pieces and rotate the dish a half turn. Cover again and microwave on high for another 3 minutes. Let stand for 5 minutes, or until cool enough to handle. Shred into bite-size pieces.

Meanwhile, place 4 custard cups (1 cup or larger) upside down on a baking sheet or in a broiler pan. Lightly coat the tortillas on both sides with no-stick spray. Drape them over the cups, and very lightly mold them around the cups (be careful not to tear or break the tortillas if they're not pliable). Bake at 400° for 10 minutes, or until lightly browned. Carefully remove from the cups and set aside on a wire rack.

In a large bowl, combine the yogurt, lemon juice, chili powder, cumin and cloves. Stir in the parsley, celery, scallions, shallots and chicken. Mix well. If desired, chill before serving.

Spoon the salad into the tortilla cups.

Preparation time: 15 minutes
Cooking time: 10 minutes
Baking time: 10 minutes

Chef's Note: If you don't have a microwave, poach the chicken in water or stock for about 15 minutes, or until cooked through.

Per serving: 236 calories, 3.6 g. fat (14% of calories), 0.9 g. dietary fiber, 67 mg. cholesterol, 143 mg. sodium.

LET'S DO LUNCH

*A*re you hosting a noontime get-together? Maybe you're surprising a co-worker with a bridal or baby shower. Maybe it's your turn to have the bridge club over. Or maybe you've offered to feed the gang after a morning of shopping or museum hopping. You'll want a menu that is impressive but that is not an imposition on your time and culinary talents. You'll certainly want dishes that can be prepared ahead and either reheated or served cold. The following meal would do nicely.

Menu

CORN CHOWDER
GARDEN SALAD WITH GREEN GODDESS DRESSING
SANDWICH SMORGASBORD
CRANBERRY POACHED PEARS

CORN CHOWDER

SERVES 8

3	cups defatted chicken stock
3	cups water
2	baking potatoes, peeled and diced
1	large onion, diced
1	clove garlic, minced
1	teaspoon dried basil
½	teaspoon ground black pepper
¼	teaspoon dried thyme
3	cups corn
2	small zucchini, diced
1	cup evaporated skim milk

In a 4-quart pot over medium-high heat, bring the stock, water, potatoes, onions, garlic, basil, pepper and thyme to a boil. Cook for

10 minutes, or until the potatoes are tender.

Let cool for a few minutes, then ladle half of the vegetables and about 2 cups liquid into a blender. Add 1 cup corn. Process for 30 seconds, or until coarsely pureed. Return to the saucepan.

Stir in the zucchini and remaining 2 cups corn. Cook over medium heat for 8 minutes, or until the zucchini is tender. Stir in the milk and heat briefly.

Preparation time: 15 minutes
Cooking time: 20 minutes

Per serving: 122 calories, 0.5 g. fat (3% of calories), 2.3 g. dietary fiber, 1 mg. cholesterol, 54 mg. sodium.

GARDEN SALAD WITH GREEN GODDESS DRESSING

SERVES 8

2   cups low-fat cottage cheese
½   cup nonfat mayonnaise
2   tablespoons lemon juice
2   tablespoons grated Parmesan cheese
1   tablespoon minced shallots or scallions
1   tablespoon minced fresh parsley
1   teaspoon Dijon mustard
½   teaspoon dried tarragon
½   teaspoon ground black pepper
1   clove garlic, minced
6   cups mixed greens, torn into bite-size pieces
2   cups very thinly sliced carrots
2   cups bite-size broccoli florets
1   pint cherry tomatoes, halved
1   cup sliced mushrooms

In a food processor, puree the cottage cheese for 3 minutes, or until very smooth. Transfer to a large bowl. Whisk in the mayonnaise, lemon juice, Parmesan, shallots or scallions, parsley, mustard, tarragon, pepper and garlic. Cover and refrigerate until needed.

(continued)

In a large salad bowl, toss together the greens, carrots, broccoli, tomatoes and mushrooms. Divide among individual plates. Drizzle with the dressing.

Preparation time: 15 minutes

Per serving: 107 calories, 2 g. fat (16% of calories), 2.8 g. dietary fiber, 6 mg. cholesterol, 480 mg. sodium.

SANDWICH SMORGASBORD

*C*reate a simply elegant buffet for your luncheon with a smorgasbord of open-faced sandwiches. In general, the sandwiches will consist of several layers: bread, a spread, greens, protein and garnishes.

- Choose a firm-grained, hearty bread that won't sag when it's picked up. Try thinly sliced rye, pumpernickel, black bread or French baguettes. Cut the larger slices into halves or even quarters.

- Add moisture to the sandwiches with a lean spread, such as nonfat mayonnaise, low-fat cream cheese or yogurt cheese. For added interest, flavor them with herbs, spices, horseradish, pureed pimentos or chopped olives.

- Give the sandwiches color and crunch with a greens layer. Good choices include red or green garden lettuce (oak leaf is unusual and appealing), green or ornamental kale, spinach, arugula, radicchio and chard. Use only a leaf or two to keep the sandwich from becoming bulky.

- For your protein, use thinly sliced chicken breast, turkey breast, lean roast beef or well-trimmed ham from the deli department. Or use a little smoked salmon, a few small shrimp or a slice of hard-cooked egg. Or prepare your own chicken salad, turkey salad, tuna salad or shrimp salad using nonfat mayonnaise.

- Top off your creations with more crunch and color. Thinly slice some red radishes, carrots, cucumbers or other raw vegetables, and arrange a few pieces over the protein layer. For the final embellishment, add a fresh herb leaf. Basil, sage and dill are pretty and delicious.

CRANBERRY POACHED PEARS

SERVES 8

4	*cups water*
2	*tablespoons lime juice*
1	*cinnamon stick*
12	*whole cloves*
1	*teaspoon star anise pieces*
3	*lemon tea bags*
8	*Bosc pears, peeled, halved and cored*
2	*cups cranberries*
¼	*cup honey*
½	*teaspoon vanilla*
1	*quart nonfat frozen vanilla yogurt*
	Mint leaves

In a 4-quart pot, combine the water, lime juice, cinnamon stick, cloves, star anise and tea bags. Add the pears and submerge as much as possible.

Over high heat, bring almost to a boil—you'll see steam rising. Then reduce the heat to medium and simmer for 15 to 20 minutes, or until the pears are just tender when pierced with a sharp knife.

Remove the pears with a slotted spoon and place on individual dessert dishes.

Strain the liquid into a bowl. Measure out 1½ cups and return to the pot. Add the cranberries, honey and vanilla. Cook over medium heat for 10 to 15 minutes, or until the cranberries pop. If desired, chill.

Place a small scoop of frozen yogurt in the hollowed-out part of each pear. Using a slotted spoon, spoon the cranberries over the pears and frozen yogurt. Garnish with the mint leaves.

Preparation time: 10 minutes
Cooking time: 35 minutes

Per serving: 225 calories, 0.6 g. fat (2% of calories), 5.1 g. dietary fiber, no cholesterol, 72 mg. sodium.

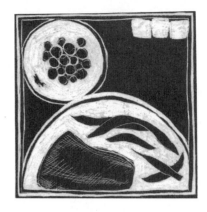

CHAPTER 6

THE MAIN EVENT

Define a satisfying main course. Is it something like breaded fish, stuffed peppers, ravioli or chili? If so, take heart—you *can* enjoy such succulent fare and still watch your intake of fat, calories and cholesterol. The recipes in this chapter prove it! And many of them can be prepared in the microwave, so they're on the table fast. Even cassoulet, a French bean and meat casserole that's generally an all-day production, can be ready for the oven in about 10 minutes and baked in another 30. In the same vein, you can serve stir-fries, tacos and interesting pasta dishes in the time it takes to heat a TV dinner. Really, it's so easy to make the healthy choice.

THE BOUNTY OF THE SEA

Seafood is a natural choice for meals in a hurry. Fish fillets and steaks cook super fast—the general rule of thumb being 10 minutes per inch of thickness. Similarly, scallops, oysters, shrimp and other shellfish take just minutes to prepare. Healthwise, seafood is a good catch. All types contain heart-healthy omega-3 fatty acids, which can help lower harmful blood cholesterol.

HONEY-MUSTARD COD

SERVES 4

This dish is a favorite among patrons of The Heartland spa in Gilman, Illinois. Serve the fish with herbed rice, steamed spinach and lemon wedges.

4   *cod fillets (4 ounces each)*
1   *tablespoon Dijon mustard*
1   *tablespoon coarse mustard*
1   *tablespoon nonfat yogurt*
1   *tablespoon nonfat mayonnaise*
1   *tablespoon honey*

Coat a baking sheet with no-stick spray. Place the cod on the sheet.

In a small bowl, combine the Dijon mustard, coarse mustard, yogurt, mayonnaise and honey. Divide the mixture among the fillets, covering the top surface of each.

Bake at 400° for 20 minutes. Lay a sheet of foil over the fish, turn off the oven, and let the fish stand for 5 minutes.

Preparation time: 5 minutes
Baking time: 25 minutes

Per serving: 122 calories, 1.1 g. fat (8% of calories), trace dietary fiber, 49 mg. cholesterol, 164 mg. sodium.

ORANGE-POACHED FLOUNDER

SERVES 4

*P*oaching is one of the simplest ways to cook fish. This recipe would also work nicely for scallops or shrimp. Serve the fish with quick-cooking brown rice and a mixture of carrots and parsnips.

>   1   *cup water*
>   ½   *cup orange juice*
>   2   *teaspoons lemon juice*
>   ¼   *teaspoon powdered ginger*
>   4   *flounder fillets (4 ounces each)*
>   1   *teaspoon cornstarch*
>   2   *tablespoons water*

In a large frying pan, combine the 1 cup water, orange juice, lemon juice and ginger. Bring to a boil, then reduce the heat to a simmer. Add the fish and simmer for 5 minutes, or until the fish flakes easily with a fork.

Use a slotted spoon or spatula to remove the fish to a serving plate. Keep warm.

In a cup, dissolve the cornstarch in the 2 tablespoons water. Add to the liquid in the pan. Bring to a boil and stir until slightly thickened. Serve over the fish.

Preparation time: 5 minutes
Cooking time: 10 minutes

Per serving: 121 calories, 1.4 g. fat (11% of calories), 0.3 g. dietary fiber, 55 mg. cholesterol, 94 mg. sodium.

Chocolate-Ginger Sorbet (page 262)

Cannellini Bean Salad (page 101) and Fresh Lima Salad (page 102)

126

Santa Fe Corn (page 247) and Southwestern Cornbread (page 259)

Grilled Turkey Steaks (page 141) with Herb-Flavored Corn on the Cob (page 218)

Ginger Bass in Foil (page 216)

129

Apple Crumb Pie (page 227)

Pumpkin Soup (page 51) with Peppery Biscuits (page 61)

131

Turkey and Broccoli Stir-Fry (page 158)

CAPE COD SCALLOPS WITH TOMATOES

*T*his dish has the consistency of a chunky stew. Serve it over rice or pasta.

   1¼   *pounds sea scallops*
   3   *tablespoons minced fresh parsley*
   2   *tablespoons lemon juice*
   ½   *teaspoon dried basil*
   ¼   *teaspoon dried rosemary*
   1   *clove garlic, minced*
   1   *teaspoon olive oil*
   2   *cups sliced mushrooms*
   1   *cup sliced onions*
   1½   *cups diced tomatoes*
   1   *cup defatted chicken stock*

In a medium bowl, combine the scallops, parsley, lemon juice, basil, rosemary and garlic. Set aside.

In a large no-stick frying pan over medium-high heat, warm the oil for 30 seconds. Add the mushrooms and onions; sauté for 5 minutes. Add the tomatoes and stock. Bring to a simmer.

Add the scallop mixture to the pan. Simmer for 5 minutes, or until the scallops are cooked through. Using a slotted spoon, remove the scallops and vegetables to a serving bowl, and keep warm.

Raise the heat to high and boil the stock until reduced by half, about 5 minutes. Pour over the scallops.

Preparation time: 10 minutes
Cooking time: 20 minutes

Per serving: 182 calories, 3 g. fat (15% of calories), 2 g. dietary fiber, 47 mg. cholesterol, 256 mg. sodium.

FISH BAKED IN AN HERB CRUST

*H*ere's a fat-lowering technique you can use with all types of fish fillets. Instead of frying the fish in a classic batter coating, which would absorb lots of fat, encase the fish in a thin herb crust, very lightly sauté it, and then finish cooking it in the oven. This recipe comes from Emile Mooser, chef/owner of Emile's in San Jose, California.

4 catfish fillets (6 ounces each)
2 teaspoons olive oil
1 sweet red pepper, chopped
1½ cups defatted chicken stock
1 cup chopped plum tomatoes
2 cups loosely packed fresh basil
1 cup dry bread crumbs

Rub the fish all over with 1 teaspoon oil. Set aside for 5 minutes to marinate.

Meanwhile, place the peppers and the remaining 1 teaspoon oil in a large no-stick frying pan. Over medium-high heat, sauté for 5 minutes. Add the stock and tomatoes. Cover and simmer for 10 minutes, or until the vegetables are softened. Transfer to a blender or food processor and puree. The mixture should lightly coat the back of a spoon. If it is too thin, return it to the pan and cook until properly thickened. Keep warm.

While the vegetables are cooking, coarsely chop the basil. Place in a food processor. Add the bread crumbs. With on/off turns, process until finely chopped and well mixed. Do not process into a paste. Transfer to a large plate or a sheet of wax paper. Dredge the fish in the crumb mixture to coat both sides; press firmly so that the mixture adheres.

Coat a large no-stick frying pan with no-stick spray. Over medium-high heat, sear the fish for 3 minutes per side. Transfer to a baking sheet. Bake at 400° for 4 minutes per side, or until crispy and firm to the touch. Serve the fish with the tomato mixture.

Preparation time: 10 minutes
Cooking time: 15 minutes
Baking time: 10 minutes

Per serving: 304 calories, 6.2 g. fat (18% of calories), 2.4 g. dietary fiber, 82 mg. cholesterol, 342 mg. sodium.

HADDOCK WITH A PECAN COATING

SERVES 4

*T*his is a very simple way to bread fish. The small amount of nuts gives an interesting flavor to the haddock but doesn't add too much fat to this lean fish. Serve the haddock with reduced-fat cole slaw, applesauce and rotelle or other pasta.

¼   *cup seasoned dry bread crumbs*
2   *tablespoons ground pecans*
4   *haddock fillets (4 ounces each)*
1   *teaspoon olive oil*

In a shallow dish, combine the bread crumbs and pecans. Dredge the fish in the mixture to coat all sides well.

In a large no-stick frying pan over medium heat, sauté the fish in the oil for about 4 minutes per side, or until cooked through.

Preparation time: 5 minutes
Cooking time: 10 minutes

Per serving: 156 calories, 4.5 g. fat (27% of calories), 0.4 g. dietary fiber, 65 mg. cholesterol, 124 mg. sodium.

MAGNIFICENT MARINADES

*F*at-free marinades impart wonderful flavor to lean, quick-cooking delicacies such as seafood and boneless cuts of poultry. And they can be as simple or as complex as you like. Because most marinades contain at least one acidic ingredient, you should prepare them in a glass or other nonreactive container. Add the fish or poultry, and turn the pieces to coat all sides. Seafood really doesn't need to be marinated for more than an hour, and an even lesser amount of time will benefit its flavor. Poultry can stand a longer marinating—but if you do it for more than an hour, cover the dish with plastic wrap and refrigerate it.

The best ways to cook marinated food are on the grill, under the broiler and in the oven. Although seafood and boneless poultry take very little time to prepare, you may baste them with marinade a few times as they cook to add an extra layer of flavor and to keep them from drying out.

Discard any leftover marinade—it has been in contact with raw fish or poultry and could contain undesirable bacteria.

MARINADES FOR SEAFOOD

- Balsamic vinegar, mustard and ginger
- Lemon juice, crushed fennel seed and garlic
- Lime juice, Worcestershire sauce and hot-pepper sauce
- Orange juice, garlic, soy sauce and five-spice powder
- Chicken stock, soy sauce, ginger and honey
- White wine vinegar, rosemary, lemon rind and onions
- Red wine vinegar, tarragon, oregano and garlic

MARINADES FOR POULTRY

- Yogurt, mint, garlic and hot-pepper sauce
- Raspberry or sherry vinegar, thyme and black pepper
- Orange juice, tomato puree, honey and orange rind
- Lime juice, yogurt and curry powder
- Chicken stock, lemon juice and smooth cranberry sauce
- Apple cider vinegar, Worcestershire sauce, cumin, ginger and garlic

FABULOUS FOWL

Poultry is as quick and easy to prepare as fish, especially if you purchase boneless, skinless cutlets. And it's much lower in calories and fat than red meat. The following recipes put lean chicken and turkey to tasty use.

TUSCANY CHICKEN

SERVES 4

*T*his recipe uses ingredients favored by Italian cooks, including tomatoes, olive oil, basil and garlic. Serve over fettuccine or angel hair pasta.

> 1 teaspoon olive oil
> 4 boneless, skinless chicken breast halves
>   (4 ounces each)
> 2 tomatoes, diced
> 1 clove garlic, minced
> 2 tablespoons red wine vinegar
> 2 tablespoons water
> 2 tablespoons minced fresh basil

In a large no-stick frying pan over medium heat, warm the oil for 1 minute. Add the chicken and sauté for 5 minutes per side. Remove to a plate.

Add the tomatoes, garlic, vinegar and water to the pan. Cover and cook for 5 minutes, or until the tomatoes are softened and have given up some of their juice. Add the chicken, cover, and cook for 5 minutes, or until the chicken is cooked through. Sprinkle with the basil.

Preparation time: 5 minutes
Cooking time: 20 minutes

Per serving: 149 calories, 2.7 g. fat (17% of calories), 0.8 g. dietary fiber, 66 mg. cholesterol, 80 mg. sodium.

GINGER CHICKEN

SERVES 4

*T*his recipe works equally well with turkey breast and boneless chicken thighs. If using the thighs, take a few extra minutes to remove as much visible fat as possible with a sharp knife. Since this recipe has a creamy sauce, serve it over rice, couscous, bulgur or pasta. If desired, you may prepare the chicken ahead and gently reheat just before serving.

1   *large onion, finely diced*
1   *teaspoon olive oil*
2   *cups defatted chicken stock*
1   *tablespoon minced fresh ginger*
1   *tablespoon cornstarch*
2   *tablespoons water*
4   *boneless, skinless chicken breast halves*
    (4 ounces each)
2   *tablespoons minced fresh parsley*
2   *tablespoons snipped chives*

In a large no-stick frying pan over medium heat, sauté the onions in the oil for 5 minutes. Add the stock and ginger. Bring to a boil.

In a cup, dissolve the cornstarch in the water. Add to the pan and stir until the mixture starts to thicken. Add the chicken to the pan. Cover and simmer for 10 minutes, or until cooked through. Sprinkle with the parsley and chives.

Preparation time: 10 minutes
Cooking time: 15 minutes

Per serving: 178 calories, 3.3 g. fat (17% of calories), 0.8 g. dietary fiber, 66 mg. cholesterol, 117 mg. sodium.

Turkey Roll-Ups

*T*hese little stuffed cutlets are good with mashed potatoes and steamed peas. If desired, you may prepare the turkey ahead and reheat individual portions in the microwave. For variety, you may also chill the cooked turkey and cut it into ½" sections for hors d'oeuvres.

4	boneless, skinless turkey cutlets (4 ounces each)
12	ounces mushrooms, minced
1	small onion, minced
1	teaspoon olive oil
¼	cup seasoned dry bread crumbs
3	tablespoons nonfat ricotta cheese
2	tablespoons fat-free egg substitute
1	tablespoon grated Parmesan cheese

If the cutlets are thicker than ¼", place them between sheets of wax paper and pound with a mallet until evenly thick. Be careful not to tear the flesh.

In a large no-stick frying pan over medium-high heat, sauté the mushrooms and onions in the oil until all the moisture has evaporated, about 5 minutes. Transfer to a medium bowl. Stir in the bread crumbs, ricotta, egg and Parmesan. Mix well.

Divide the mushroom mixture into 4 portions and shape each into a log. Place each log in the middle of a turkey piece and roll to enclose the filling. Coat a steamer basket with no-stick spray. Place the turkey rolls in the basket and steam for 15 minutes, or until the turkey is cooked through.

Preparation time: 15 minutes
Cooking time: 20 minutes

Per serving: 218 calories, 4.2 g. fat (18% of calories), 1.8 g. dietary fiber, 67 mg. cholesterol, 171 mg. sodium.

Turkey Stir-Fry

*Y*ou may vary the vegetables to accommodate what's on hand. Serve the stir-fry over rice.

1   *pound boneless, skinless turkey breast*
1   *tablespoon minced fresh ginger*
1   *clove garlic, minced*
1   *tablespoon all-fruit apricot preserves*
1   *tablespoon low-sodium soy sauce*
1   *tablespoon white vinegar*
1   *large onion, thinly sliced*
4   *ounces snow peas*
1   *sweet red pepper, thinly sliced*
2   *teaspoons oil*
1   *tablespoon cornstarch*
¾   *cup defatted chicken stock*

Cut the turkey into thin strips. Place in a large bowl. Add the ginger, garlic, preserves, soy sauce and vinegar. Stir well to combine. Set aside.

In a wok or large frying pan over medium-high heat, stir-fry the onions, snow peas and peppers in the oil until just tender, about 5 minutes. Remove with a slotted spoon and set aside.

Add the turkey, with the marinade, to the pan. Stir-fry until the turkey is cooked through, about 5 minutes. Add the vegetables.

In a cup, dissolve the cornstarch in the stock. Add to the pan. Stir until thick.

Preparation time: 15 minutes
Cooking time: 15 minutes

Per serving: 250 calories, 5.5 g. fat (20% of calories), 2.1 g. dietary fiber, 79 mg. cholesterol, 288 mg. sodium.

GRILLED TURKEY STEAKS

SERVES 4

*H*ere's a very easy way to prepare turkey. Buy cutlets that are about ½" thick, or get a whole boneless breast and cut the pieces yourself.

1	*pound turkey steaks*
1	*tablespoon Dijon mustard*
1	*teaspoon dried tarragon*
¼	*teaspoon ground black pepper*

Blanch the steaks in boiling water for about 2 minutes. (This step sets the protein and allows the steaks to grill without overcooking on the surface.) Remove from the water and pat dry.

Rub the steaks on all sides with the mustard. Sprinkle on the tarragon and pepper. Grill 5" from the heat for 5 minutes per side, or until cooked through.

Preparation time: 5 minutes
Cooking time: 10 minutes

Per serving: 135 calories, 1.9 g. fat (13% of calories), no dietary fiber, 68 mg. cholesterol, 120 mg. sodium.

EASY STUFFED PEPPERS

*T*his is a good way to use up leftover cooked rice. You may also replace the rice with an equal amount of bulgur, couscous or millet. For a festive dinner, use a combination of peppers in different colors, such as red, green, yellow and orange. This is a good make-ahead dish. Reheat individual portions in the microwave.

4	*large peppers*
12	*ounces ground turkey*
1	*cup finely chopped onions*
1	*teaspoon dried oregano*
1½	*cups cooked rice*
¼	*cup grated Parmesan cheese*
¼	*cup fat-free egg substitute*
1	*cup tomato sauce*

Cut the peppers in half lengthwise. Remove and discard the stems and seeds. Blanch the peppers in boiling water for 3 minutes. Drain and set aside.

Crumble the turkey into a 2-quart casserole. Sprinkle with the onions and oregano. Cover with vented plastic wrap and microwave on high for 4 minutes. Break up the turkey with a spoon and mix well. Cover and microwave on high for 3 minutes, or until the turkey is cooked through and the onions are translucent. Carefully drain off any accumulated fat.

Stir in the rice, Parmesan, egg and ½ cup tomato sauce. Divide the mixture among the pepper halves.

Arrange the peppers in a 9" × 13" baking dish. Top with the remaining ½ cup tomato sauce. Cover loosely with wax paper. Microwave on high for 6 minutes. Rearrange the peppers and give the dish a half turn. Cover and microwave on high for 6 minutes.

Preparation time: 10 minutes

Cooking time: 25 minutes

Chef's Notes: If your microwave can't accommodate a 9" × 13" baking dish, divide the peppers between two smaller pans. Microwave each pan for a total of 6 minutes.

If you don't have a microwave, brown the turkey and onions in a no-stick frying pan. Mix with the remaining stuffing ingredients and fill the peppers. Arrange in a baking dish, top with the tomato sauce, and cover with foil. Bake at 350° for about 30 minutes.

Per serving: 271 calories, 4.4 g. fat (15% of calories), 3.9 g. dietary fiber, 54 mg. cholesterol, 211 mg. sodium.

QUICK CASSOULET

SERVES 4

Cassoulet is a classic French bean and meat casserole that generally takes a long time to prepare. You can make it much faster by using canned beans. What's more, you can turn out a considerably leaner version by replacing the traditional pork, lamb, duck and regular sausage with smoked turkey breast and turkey sausage.

6	*ounces mild or spicy turkey sausage links*
1	*large onion, diced*
1	*tart apple, diced*
1	*cup defatted chicken stock*
2	*tablespoons tomato paste*
2	*cans (19 ounces each) navy beans, rinsed and drained*
3	*ounces smoked turkey breast, diced*
½	*teaspoon dried thyme*
½	*teaspoon ground black pepper*
1	*cup fresh bread crumbs*
½	*cup minced fresh parsley*
2	*teaspoons olive oil*

In a large no-stick frying pan over medium heat, brown the sausage. Remove to a cutting board and slice into ½" pieces. Return to the pan and add the onions, apples and 2 tablespoons stock. Sauté for 5 minutes, or until the onions and apples are softened. Stir in the tomato paste and the remaining stock. Transfer to a large bowl.

Stir in the beans, turkey, thyme and pepper.

Coat a 3-quart casserole with no-stick spray. Add the bean mixture.

In a small bowl, mix the bread crumbs, parsley and oil until the oil is well distributed. Sprinkle over the bean mixture. Bake at 350° for 30 minutes.

Preparation time: 10 minutes
Cooking time: 10 minutes
Baking time: 30 minutes

Chef's Note: To make fresh bread crumbs, tear bread slices into large chunks. Place in a food processor and crumble with on/off turns. You may use any type of bread, including whole-wheat, oat, multigrain or white.

Per serving: 356 calories, 6.5 g. fat (16% of calories), 9.9 g. dietary fiber, 26 mg. cholesterol, 810 mg. sodium.

HEARTY MEATLESS MEALS

You can serve satisfying vegetarian entrées by making good use of quick-cooking, low-fat ingredients such as pasta, lentils and canned beans. And don't overlook tofu as a protein-rich replacement for meat in casseroles, stir-fries, chili and other main dishes.

CURRIED RAVIOLI

SERVES 4

*R*eady-made cheese ravioli is available in most markets and cooks in minutes. For an unusual flavor, top it with a curried white sauce. Serve with Italian bread and cooked carrots or snap peas.

2	*tablespoons unbleached flour*
1½	*cups skim milk*
1	*tablespoon butter-flavored sprinkles*
½	*teaspoon curry powder*
¼	*teaspoon ground black pepper*
9	*ounces cheese ravioli*

Place the flour in a 2-quart saucepan. Whisk in about ¼ cup milk to form a smooth paste. Whisk in the remaining 1¼ cups milk, sprinkles, curry powder and pepper. Whisk over medium heat until the mixture comes to a boil and thickens, about 5 minutes.

Cook the ravioli in a large pot of boiling water until just tender, about 4 minutes. Drain and divide among 4 serving plates. Top with the sauce.

Preparation time: 5 minutes
Cooking time: 10 minutes

Per serving: 256 calories, 8.5 g. fat (30% of calories), 0.2 g. dietary fiber, 58 mg. cholesterol, 367 mg. sodium.

ROTELLE WITH BEANS AND PECANS

SERVES 4

This dish is very easy to prepare—just whip up the sauce in a blender or food processor and toss it with warm pasta and green beans. For extra flavor, toast the pecans first.

1   cup nonfat ricotta cheese
⅓   cup skim milk
¼   cup chopped pecans
1   clove garlic, minced
½   teaspoon ground black pepper
¼   teaspoon dried basil
8   ounces rotelle
8   ounces tender young green beans
2   tablespoons grated Parmesan cheese

In a blender or food processor, process the ricotta, milk, pecans, garlic, pepper and basil until smooth, about 2 minutes. Set the sauce aside.

Cook the rotelle in a large pot of boiling water until just tender, about 10 minutes. Drain and place in a large serving bowl.

Meanwhile, steam the beans until just tender, about 5 minutes. Add to the rotelle and toss lightly. Top with the sauce and toss well. Sprinkle with the Parmesan.

Preparation time: 5 minutes
Cooking time: 10 minutes

Per serving: 346 calories, 6.5 g. fat (17% of calories), 2.7 g. dietary fiber, 3 mg. cholesterol, 147 mg. sodium.

ELBOWS AND CHEESE

This version of macaroni and cheese is much lower in fat than traditional recipes.

1½   cups elbow macaroni
⅔   cup shredded reduced-fat Cheddar cheese
½   cup dry-curd cottage cheese
½   cup skim milk
½   cup fat-free egg substitute
¼   teaspoon hot-pepper sauce
2   teaspoons Dijon mustard
½   cup seasoned dry bread crumbs

Cook the macaroni in a large pot of boiling water until just tender, about 10 minutes. Drain.

Coat a 1-quart casserole dish with no-stick spray. Add the Cheddar and macaroni. Toss to combine.

In a blender, puree the cottage cheese, milk, eggs, pepper sauce and 1 teaspoon mustard. Pour over the macaroni and stir lightly to distribute.

In a cup, mix the bread crumbs with the remaining 1 teaspoon mustard. Sprinkle over the casserole. Bake at 375° for 25 minutes.

Preparation time: 10 minutes
Cooking time: 10 minutes
Baking time: 25 minutes

Per serving: 264 calories, 5.1 g. fat (18% of calories), 2 g. dietary fiber, 15 mg. cholesterol, 229 mg. sodium.

LENTIL TACOS

SERVES 4

*L*entils give these vegetarian tacos a meaty texture—but none of the cholesterol or fat you'd find in meat. You can easily make the lentil mixture ahead and reheat it for tacos in an instant.

1   cup minced onions
½   cup minced celery
1   clove garlic, minced
1   teaspoon olive oil
1   cup red lentils
1   tablespoon chili powder
2   teaspoons ground cumin
1   teaspoon dried oregano
2   cups defatted chicken stock
2   tablespoons raisins
1   cup mild or spicy salsa
8   corn tortillas
    Shredded lettuce
    Chopped tomatoes

In a large frying pan over medium heat, sauté the onions, celery and garlic in the oil for 5 minutes. Stir in the lentils, chili powder, cumin and oregano. Cook for 1 minute. Add the stock and raisins. Cover and cook for 20 minutes, or until the lentils are tender.

Remove the lid and cook, stirring often, until the lentils are thickened, about 10 minutes. Stir in the salsa.

Wrap the tortillas in a damp paper towel and microwave on high for 1 minute, or until soft. Divide the lentil mixture among the tortillas. Top with the lettuce and tomatoes.

Preparation time: 10 minutes

Cooking time: 40 minutes

Chef's Note: If you don't have a microwave, wrap the tortillas in foil and heat at 350° for about 10 minutes.

Per serving: 409 calories, 7 g. fat (14% of calories), 10.4 g. dietary fiber, no cholesterol, 421 mg. sodium.

LEMON-BASIL CAPELLINI

SERVES 4

utter-flavored sprinkles give this dish a buttery flavor without adding a lot of fat and calories.

8 *ounces capellini*
½ *cup defatted chicken stock*
1 *clove garlic, minced*
2 *tablespoons butter-flavored sprinkles*
2 *tablespoons lemon juice*
¼ *cup minced fresh parsley*
¼ *cup minced fresh basil*

Cook the capellini in a large pot of boiling water until just tender, about 5 minutes. Drain and place in a large serving bowl.

Meanwhile, bring the stock and garlic to a boil in a 1-quart saucepan. Remove from the heat and stir in the sprinkles, lemon juice, parsley and basil. Pour over the pasta and toss well.

Preparation time: 5 minutes
Cooking time: 7 minutes

Per serving: 232 calories, 1.1 g. fat (4% of calories), 1 g. dietary fiber, no cholesterol, 116 mg. sodium.

VEGETARIAN CHILI

SERVES 4

*T*ofu adds protein to chili without contributing the cholesterol and high amount of fat that regular ground beef would.

2   *cups tomato juice*
½   *cup bulgur*
½   *cup chopped onions*
½   *cup chopped carrots*
½   *cup chopped green peppers*
1   *teaspoon olive oil*
2   *tablespoons chili powder*
1½   *teaspoons ground cumin*
¼   *teaspoon ground red pepper*
1   *can (about 14 ounces) chopped tomatoes*
1   *can (19 ounces) kidney beans, rinsed and drained*
8   *ounces firm tofu, cubed*

In a 1-quart saucepan over medium heat, bring the tomato juice to a boil. Stir in the bulgur. Fluff with a fork. Cover, remove from the heat, and set aside for 15 minutes.

Meanwhile, in a 3-quart saucepan over medium heat, sauté the onions, carrots and green peppers in the oil for about 5 minutes. Stir in the chili powder, cumin and red pepper; cook for 1 minute. Stir in the tomatoes with their juice, beans and tofu. Simmer for 10 minutes. Add the bulgur to the pot. Simmer for 10 minutes.

Preparation time: 15 minutes
Cooking time: 30 minutes

Per serving: 295 calories, 7.9 g. fat (22% of calories), 12.1 g. dietary fiber, no cholesterol, 337 mg. sodium.

THE MAIN EVENT

PASTA WITH ZUCCHINI AND FRESH TOMATOES

SERVES 6

*M*ake this dish when summer-ripe tomatoes abound. Serve it with a simple green salad tossed with fat-free vinaigrette or Italian dressing.

4	*small zucchini (about 1 pound total)*
2	*tablespoons lemon juice*
3	*cloves garlic, minced*
2	*onions, thinly sliced crosswise and separated into rings*
1	*tablespoon white wine vinegar*
3	*large tomatoes, thinly sliced*
¼	*cup minced fresh basil*
1	*tablespoon minced fresh parsley*
½	*teaspoon red-pepper flakes*
1	*pound ziti*

Halve the zucchini lengthwise and slice into ½" cross sections. Place in a large bowl. Add the lemon juice and toss well. Set aside.

In a large no-stick frying pan over medium-high heat, cook the garlic for 30 seconds, stirring constantly; don't let it burn. Add the onions, vinegar and zucchini. Cook for 3 to 4 minutes.

Add the tomatoes, basil, parsley and pepper flakes. Cover the pan, reduce the heat, and simmer until the zucchini is tender, about 5 to 7 minutes.

Meanwhile, cook the ziti in a large pot of boiling water until just tender, about 8 minutes. Drain and place in a large shallow bowl. Add the zucchini mixture and toss well.

Preparation time: 10 minutes
Cooking time: 15 minutes

Per serving: 323 calories, 1.7 g. fat (5% of calories), 4.3 g. dietary fiber, no cholesterol, 9 mg. sodium.

TOFU: INSTANT PROTEIN

An Oriental favorite, tofu is a cheeselike product derived from soybean milk. But unlike regular cheese, this protein-rich food is low in calories and saturated fat—with no cholesterol. It's also ready to eat right from the package, so you can toss it into salads, stir-fries and other quick dishes. Thanks to its basic blandness, it marries well with all sorts of other foods and seasonings, taking on their individual flavors.

Tofu comes in two basic textures: firm, and soft. The general rule is to use firm tofu in dishes where it must retain its shape and soft tofu in recipes where it will be blended, creamed or mashed.

You can achieve a third texture at home by freezing tofu. Once frozen, thawed and drained, tofu has a chewy, meatlike texture. You can slice or crumble it as a substitute for meat or poultry in chili, soups, spaghetti sauce or stir-fry dishes.

Here are some additional ways to use this versatile bean curd.

- Crumble or dice it into vegetarian curry dishes.
- Mash and mix with egg substitute before scrambling; add minced fresh herbs.
- Make a luncheon salad by combining tofu with mixed greens, raw vegetables and perhaps canned beans. Toss with fat-free vinaigrette and serve with garlic bread.

CHAPTER 7

QUICK
ENTRÉES
FOR 1 OR 2

ℋOME ALONE

𝒜re you on your own tonight? That's no reason to give
dinner short shrift. The pages that follow feature main
courses so easy that you'll want to enjoy them often. From
Juicy Burgers (they contain a secret ingredient that makes them
moist without extra fat) and Shells with Meaty Marinara Sauce
to individual Tuna Tarts and Herbed Angel Hair—these
entrées are special enough to remind you that you *deserve* to eat
well, whether or not you're dining solo. (And if you do have
company, we've provided quantities for two servings in all
recipes.) A tip: When you prepare full-size recipes, freeze the
extras in single-serving packets for really quick future meals.

MUSHROOM-STUFFED COD

─────

*W*rapping fish in lettuce leaves before baking keeps it moist and succulent. Be sure to buy cod fillets that are at least 1″ thick so that you can cut a pocket in them for the savory mushroom stuffing. If you don't have celery root, substitute regular celery, jícama or parsnips. Serve the fish over rice or pasta.

Ingredients	For 1	For 2
Diced mushrooms	⅓ cup	⅔ cup
Minced onions	1 tablespoon	2 tablespoons
Minced fresh parsley	2 tablespoons	¼ cup
Lemon juice	1 teaspoon	2 teaspoons
Dried tarragon	⅛ teaspoon	¼ teaspoon
Ground black pepper	pinch	⅛ teaspoon
Cod fillet (6 ounces, 1″ thick)	1	2
Large iceberg lettuce leaf	1	2
Julienned carrots	½ cup	1 cup
Julienned celery root	½ cup	1 cup
Defatted chicken stock, heated to boiling	¼ cup	½ cup

In a 1-cup (2-cup) glass measure, combine the mushrooms and onions. Cover with vented plastic wrap. Microwave on high for 2 (3) minutes, or until soft. Drain off any liquid. Stir in the parsley, lemon juice, tarragon and pepper.

With a sharp knife, cut a horizontal pocket in the fish. Fill with the mushroom mixture.

Dip the lettuce into boiling water for 10 seconds. Rinse with cold water to cool, then pat dry with paper towels. Place a fillet on each leaf and fold to enclose.

Place the carrots, celery root and stock in the bottom of a 1-quart (1½-quart) casserole. Add the fish. Cover tightly with foil and bake at 400° for 10 minutes.

Preparation time: 15 minutes
Cooking time: 5 minutes
Baking time: 10 minutes

Chef's Note: If you don't have a microwave, cook the mushrooms and onions in a small frying pan for about 6 minutes, or until the vegetables are softened and the liquid has evaporated.

Per serving: 220 calories, 2 g. fat (8% of calories), 2.8 g. dietary fiber, 74 mg. cholesterol, 215 mg. sodium.

TUNA TARTS

These individual tarts are super easy to prepare because they don't require a piecrust. Serve with a tossed salad for a complete meal.

Ingredients	For 1	For 2
Water-packed canned tuna, drained and flaked	*3½ ounces*	*7 ounces*
Fat-free egg substitute	*½ cup*	*1 cup*
Nonfat sour cream	*¼ cup*	*½ cup*
Dijon mustard	*¼ teaspoon*	*½ teaspoon*
Dried oregano	*¼ teaspoon*	*½ teaspoon*
Seasoned dry bread crumbs	*1 tablespoon*	*2 tablespoons*

In a medium bowl, mix the tuna, eggs, sour cream, mustard and oregano.

Coat 1 (2) 2-cup casserole dish(es) with no-stick spray. Add the bread crumbs and swirl to coat evenly. Add the tuna mixture. Bake at 400° for 25 minutes, or until the filling is set.

Preparation time: 10 minutes
Baking time: 25 minutes

Per serving: 215 calories, 2.8 g. fat (12% of calories), 0.2 g. dietary fiber, 42 mg. cholesterol, 614 mg. sodium.

CURRIED SOLE

*P*reparing food *en papillote* (in paper packets) cuts down on cleanup time, since you don't get a baking dish dirty. You can even eat the food straight from the packet to minimize plate washing. Parchment is the material traditionally used, but you may substitute aluminum foil.

Ingredients	For 1	For 2
Water	*2 tablespoons*	*¼ cup*
Peanut butter	*1 tablespoon*	*2 tablespoons*
Honey	*1 tablespoon*	*2 tablespoons*
Curry powder	*¾ teaspoon*	*1½ teaspoons*
Banana	*1 medium*	*2 medium*
Sole fillet (6 ounces)	*1*	*2*
Raisins	*2 tablespoons*	*¼ cup*
Grated coconut	*1 teaspoon*	*2 teaspoons*
Nonfat sour cream	*2 tablespoons*	*¼ cup*

Cut 1 large square of parchment or foil for each serving. Fold in half and cut into a large heart shape. Open and coat one side with no-stick spray.

In a small bowl, mix the water, peanut butter, honey and curry powder until smooth.

Cut each banana in half lengthwise and place the pieces parallel on one half of the paper (near the fold). Cover with a fillet and spoon on the peanut butter mixture. Sprinkle with the raisins and coconut. Top with the sour cream.

Fold the paper over the fish and align the edges. Seal each packet well (use overlapping folds, starting at the top of the heart shape). Place on a baking sheet. Bake at 400° for 20 minutes.

Preparation time: 10 minutes
Baking time: 20 minutes

Per serving: 506 calories, 11.3 g. fat (20% of calories), 4.4 g. dietary fiber, 82 mg. cholesterol, 241 mg. sodium.

FLOUNDER IN A MINT MARINADE

*F*ish fillets are always a smart choice when cooking for one or two because they come already divided into individual portions. This quick mint and garlic marinade also works well on any other white fish as well as on scallops and shrimp. Serve the fish with microwave-baked potatoes and steamed carrots, broccoli or green beans.

Ingredients	For 1	For 2
Lemon juice	*2 teaspoons*	*4 teaspoons*
Minced fresh mint	*1 teaspoon*	*2 teaspoons*
Minced fresh parsley	*1 teaspoon*	*2 teaspoons*
Olive oil	*½ teaspoon*	*1 teaspoon*
Garlic, minced	*½ clove*	*1 clove*
Flounder fillet (6 ounces)	*1*	*2*

In a shallow dish, combine the lemon juice, mint, parsley, oil and garlic. Add the fish and turn to coat both sides. Let stand for 10 minutes.

Coat a baking sheet with no-stick spray. Add the fish and broil about 6" from the heat for about 5 minutes, or until cooked through (do not flip). Carefully remove with a metal spatula to avoid breaking the fish.

Preparation time: 15 minutes
Cooking time: 5 minutes

Per serving: 181 calories, 4.3 g. fat (22% of calories), 0.1 g. dietary fiber, 82 mg. cholesterol, 139 mg. sodium.

TURKEY AND BROCCOLI STIR-FRY

*S*tir-fries are an excellent choice when you're home alone. You can use whatever ingredients you're hungry for at the moment, and you can adjust the quantities to match your appetite. For a really fast meal, serve quick-cooking brown rice. Start it cooking before you cut up the ingredients for the stir-fry.

Ingredients	For 1	For 2
Boneless, skinless turkey breast	*4 ounces*	*8 ounces*
Low-sodium soy sauce	*1½ teaspoons*	*1 tablespoon*
Honey	*1½ teaspoons*	*1 tablespoon*
Garlic, minced	*1 clove*	*2 cloves*
Oil	*1 teaspoon*	*2 teaspoons*
Broccoli florets	*½ cup*	*1 cup*
Sliced sweet red peppers	*½ cup*	*1 cup*
Defatted chicken stock	*2 tablespoons*	*¼ cup*
Hot cooked brown rice	*¾ cup*	*1½ cups*

Cut the turkey into ½" × 1½" strips. In a medium bowl, stir together the soy sauce, honey and garlic. Add the turkey and toss to coat.

In a wok or large frying pan over medium-high heat, heat the oil for 1 minute. Add the turkey and stir-fry for 3 minutes, or until opaque. Remove with a slotted spoon and keep warm.

Add the broccoli and peppers to the pan. Stir-fry for 2 minutes. Add the stock and continue to stir-fry for 2 minutes, or until the vegetables are crisp-tender. Return the turkey to the pan and toss briefly. Serve over the rice.

Preparation time: 10 minutes
Cooking time: 10 minutes

Per serving: 403 calories, 8.2 g. fat (18% of calories), 4.6 g. dietary fiber, 68 mg. cholesterol, 404 mg. sodium.

PINEAPPLE TURKEY BREAST

*P*ineapple, lime juice and spices give this easy dish an exotic air. Serve it with rice and your choice of frozen vegetables.

Ingredients	For 1	For 2
Boneless, skinless turkey breast, cut into 1" cubes	*4 ounces*	*8 ounces*
Finely chopped onions	*¼ cup*	*½ cup*
Oil	*½ teaspoon*	*1 teaspoon*
Ground cinnamon	*⅛ teaspoon*	*¼ teaspoon*
Ground cumin	*⅛ teaspoon*	*¼ teaspoon*
Paprika	*⅛ teaspoon*	*¼ teaspoon*
Pineapple cubes	*½ cup*	*1 cup*
Raisins	*1 tablespoon*	*2 tablespoons*
Lime juice	*1 tablespoon*	*2 tablespoons*
Minced fresh coriander or parsley	*1 tablespoon*	*2 tablespoons*

In a large no-stick frying pan over medium heat, sauté the turkey and onions in the oil for 5 minutes, or until the turkey is cooked through. Stir in the cinnamon, cumin and paprika.

Add the pineapple, raisins and lime juice to the pan. Cook for 2 minutes. Serve sprinkled with the coriander or parsley.

Preparation time: 10 minutes
Cooking time: 10 minutes

Per serving: 237 calories, 4.6 g. fat (17% of calories), 2.1 g. dietary fiber, 66 mg. cholesterol, 72 mg. sodium.

Turkey Satay

---

*y*ou may also prepare this Indonesian type of kabob with chicken breast, shrimp or scallops.

Ingredients	For 1	For 2
Water	6 tablespoons	¾ cup
Quick-cooking brown rice	6 tablespoons	¾ cup
Sliced carrots	½ cup	1 cup
Boneless, skinless turkey breast, cut into thin strips or 1" cubes	4 ounces	8 ounces
Low-sodium soy sauce	1 teaspoon	2 teaspoons
Honey	1 teaspoon	2 teaspoons
Powdered ginger	¼ teaspoon	½ teaspoon
Minced garlic	¼ teaspoon	½ teaspoon
Defatted chicken stock	3 tablespoons	6 tablespoons
Peanut butter	1 tablespoon	2 tablespoons
Lemon juice	1 teaspoon	2 teaspoons
Ground cumin	¼ teaspoon	½ teaspoon

In a 1-quart saucepan over medium-high heat, bring the water to a boil. Stir in the rice. Cover, reduce the heat, and simmer for 5 minutes. Remove from the heat, stir, and let stand for 5 minutes.

Meanwhile, steam the carrots for 5 minutes, or until tender. Set aside and keep warm.

In a medium bowl, mix the turkey, soy sauce, honey, ginger and garlic. Thread the turkey onto metal skewers. Broil about 4" from the heat for 4 minutes per side, or until cooked through.

In a 1-quart saucepan, mix the stock, peanut butter, lemon juice and cumin. Whisking constantly, bring to a boil over medium heat. Remove from the heat.

Serve the turkey with the rice and carrots. Drizzle with the sauce.

Preparation time: 10 minutes

Cooking time: 10 minutes

Per serving: 428 calories, 11.3 g. fat (24% of calories), 5.6 g. dietary fiber, 66 mg. cholesterol, 419 mg. sodium

New Mexican Chicken

This Southwest-inspired dish is a snap to prepare. Serve with rice, mashed canned black beans and nonfat yogurt.

Ingredients	For 1	For 2
Unbleached flour	*1 teaspoon*	*2 teaspoons*
Ground cumin	*¼ teaspoon*	*½ teaspoon*
Boneless, skinless chicken breast (4 ounces)	*1*	*2*
Oil	*½ teaspoon*	*1 teaspoon*
Chunky salsa	*¼ cup*	*½ cup*
Lime juice	*1 tablespoon*	*2 tablespoons*
Chopped fresh coriander	*1 tablespoon*	*2 tablespoons*

On a sheet of wax paper, combine the flour and cumin. Dredge the chicken in the mixture to coat well.

In a small (large) frying pan over medium heat, heat the oil for 2 minutes. Add the chicken and sauté for 2 minutes per side. Add the salsa and lime juice. Flip the chicken to coat well.

Cover and cook for about 7 minutes, or until the chicken is cooked through. Stir in the coriander.

Preparation time: 10 minutes
Cooking time: 15 minutes

Per serving: 180 calories, 5.2 g. fat (25% of calories), 0.1 g. dietary fiber, 66 mg. cholesterol, 297 mg. sodium.

Warm Chicken Salad

*H*ere's an interesting way to use leftover cooked chicken (or turkey) breast.

Ingredients	For 1	For 2
Shredded cooked chicken breast	½ cup	1 cup
Diced sweet red peppers	½ cup	1 cup
Nonfat mayonnaise	2 tablespoons	¼ cup
Lemon juice	1 tablespoon	2 tablespoons
Minced scallions	1 tablespoon	2 tablespoons
No-salt herb blend	½ teaspoon	1 teaspoon
Shredded nonfat mozzarella cheese	¼ cup	½ cup
Shredded lettuce	1 cup	2 cups

In a large bowl, mix the chicken, peppers, mayonnaise, lemon juice, scallions and herb blend.

Coat a small baking sheet with no-stick spray. Form the chicken mixture into 1 (2) flat mound(s). Place on the sheet. Sprinkle the chicken mixture with the mozzarella. Broil about 4" from the heat for 5 minutes, or until the cheese has melted and the chicken is warmed through.

Place the lettuce on 1 (2) dinner plate(s). Use a metal spatula to transfer the chicken mixture to the plate(s).

Preparation time: 10 minutes
Cooking time: 5 minutes

Per serving: 181 calories, 5.5 g. fat (20% of calories), 1.5 g. dietary fiber, 72 mg. cholesterol, 926 mg. sodium.

Dinner from the Pantry

What *do* you eat when you're home alone and there's "nothing in the house"? You can save yourself a trip to the nearest fast-food place by keeping your pantry stocked for just such occasions. For starters, make sure you have a variety of condiments on hand, such as hot-pepper sauce, chutney, Worcestershire sauce, herb vinegar, tomato paste, mustard and hoisin sauce. These flavor enhancers can enliven leftover poultry, fish or grains in innumerable ways. They can also convert a few frozen vegetables and egg substitute into a gourmet omelet or scrambled eggs. Here are other ways to ensure yourself quick and healthy meals.

Know beans. Keep canned beans in the pantry for instant full-meal salads or other dishes. One salad idea—perfect any time of the year: Toss rinsed and drained chick-peas or white beans with canned tuna, chopped peppers and fresh or dried herbs. Dress with vinegar and a bare splash of oil. For extra zip, sprinkle on some capers, hearts of palm or olives.

Cultivate grains. Quick-cooking grains such as bulgur, couscous and almost-instant rice keep well and are ready in no time flat. For a quick side dish, sauté some chopped onions and minced garlic or garlic powder in a little oil. Stir in couscous, bulgur or quick-cooking rice. Add boiling canned stock and curry powder or other seasonings. Throw in some drained canned protein, such as shrimp, crab, mussels, chicken or turkey. Cover, remove from the heat, and let stand for 10 minutes. Fluff with a fork and serve.

Think Italian. You can throw together an instant antipasto if you remember to keep pimentos, artichokes, tuna, beans, baby corn, hot cherry peppers, pickled red beets and such in the pantry. When buying these items, look for ones that are light on oil and sodium. Arrange a selection on a large platter lined with torn greens and sprinkle with lemon juice.

Veg out. Defrost a bag of mixed vegetables in the microwave, drain well, and toss with chopped tomatoes and cubes of stale bread for a Tuscan bread salad. Add some store-bought fat-free Italian dressing and let the salad marinate while you unwind from a hard day.

FETTUCCINE WITH OLIVES AND BROCCOLI

*Y*ou save time when preparing this dish by cooking the broccoli right in with the pasta.

Ingredients	For 1	For 2
Fettuccine	*3 ounces*	*6 ounces*
Broccoli florets	*1 cup*	*2 cups*
Julienned sweet yellow peppers	*½ cup*	*1 cup*
Sliced onions	*¼ cup*	*½ cup*
Olive oil	*1 teaspoon*	*2 teaspoons*
Sliced black olives	*¼ cup*	*½ cup*
Dried oregano	*¼ teaspoon*	*½ teaspoon*
Ground black pepper	*¼ teaspoon*	*½ teaspoon*
Grated Parmesan cheese	*1 tablespoon*	*2 tablespoons*

Bring a large pot of water to a boil. Add the fettuccine and cook for 5 minutes. Add the broccoli and cook for 5 minutes, or until the fettuccine is just tender. Drain and keep warm.

Meanwhile, in a large frying pan over medium heat, sauté the yellow peppers and onions in the oil for 5 minutes, or until limp. Add the olives, oregano and black pepper. Cook for 2 minutes.

Toss together the pasta and vegetables. Sprinkle with the Parmesan.

Preparation time: 10 minutes
Cooking time: 15 minutes

Per serving: 457 calories, 11 g. fat (21% of calories), 5.6 g. dietary fiber, 5 mg. cholesterol, 227 mg. sodium.

Lentil Tacos (page 148) with Salsa Cruda (page 193)

Chicken Cacciatore with Spaghetti (page 220)

Chicken Waldorf Salad (page 106)

Fresh Fruit Tart (page 264)

Seared Pineapple and Peaches (page 218)

Crostini with Red-Pepper Puree (page 52)

Elbows and Cheese (page 147)

Fettuccine with Olives and Broccoli (page 164)

172

BASIL AND MUSHROOM OMELET

*O*melets aren't just for breakfast. This one makes a satisfying, quick dinner. Serve it with toast and quick-cooking grits.

Ingredients	For 1	For 2
Sliced mushrooms	*1 cup*	*2 cups*
Fat-free egg substitute	*¾ cup*	*1½ cups*
Water	*1 tablespoon*	*2 tablespoons*
Dried basil	*½ teaspoon*	*1 teaspoon*
Ground black pepper	*¼ teaspoon*	*½ teaspoon*
Margarine	*1 teaspoon*	*2 teaspoons*
Grated Parmesan cheese	*1 tablespoon*	*2 tablespoons*

Place the mushrooms in a 2-cup (4-cup) glass measure and cover with vented plastic wrap. Microwave on high for 2 (3) minutes, or until the mushrooms are wilted. Drain off any liquid.

In a medium bowl, whisk together the eggs, water, basil and pepper.

In a medium (large) no-stick frying pan over medium heat, melt the margarine. Swirl the pan to coat the bottom. Add the egg mixture. As the eggs begin to set, pull the outer edges toward the center with a fork or spatula; allow uncooked portions to run underneath. Continue until the eggs are just barely set.

Sprinkle with the mushrooms and Parmesan. Fold the omelet in half. Transfer to 1 (2) serving plate(s).

Preparation time: 10 minutes
Cooking time: 10 minutes

Chef's Note: If you don't have a microwave, cook the mushrooms in a little bit of stock until they soften and give up their natural juices. Then cook a few minutes longer to evaporate the liquid.

Per serving: 158 calories, 6 g. fat (34% of calories), 1 g. dietary fiber, 5 mg. cholesterol, 404 mg. sodium.

Mexican Bean Casseroles

These easy little pies take advantage of canned pinto beans. Just rinse the beans well to remove excess sodium, then mash and mix with a few other ingredients. While the casseroles are baking, you can toss together a salad of shredded lettuce, diced tomatoes, a few sliced black olives and nonfat vinaigrette. For an even lower sodium level, use freshly cooked dried beans that you've prepared without added salt.

Ingredients	For 1	For 2
Diced green peppers	¼ cup	½ cup
Scallion, minced	1	2
Oil	½ teaspoon	1 teaspoon
Canned pinto beans, rinsed and drained	¾ cup	1½ cups
Diced tomatoes	⅓ cup	⅔ cup
Chili powder	½ teaspoon	1 teaspoon
Dried oregano	¼ teaspoon	½ teaspoon
Ground coriander	¼ teaspoon	½ teaspoon
Fat-free egg substitute	¼ cup	½ cup
Shredded reduced-fat Monterey Jack cheese	2 tablespoons	¼ cup

In a 1-quart (2-quart) saucepan over medium heat, sauté the peppers and scallions in the oil for 5 minutes, or until soft. Stir in the beans, tomatoes, chili powder, oregano and coriander. Cook, stirring constantly, for 2 minutes. Remove from the heat and stir in the egg(s).

Coat 1 (2) 2-cup casserole dish(es) with no-stick spray. Add the bean mixture and spread evenly. Sprinkle with the Monterey Jack. Bake at 375° for 20 minutes, or until the filling is set.

Preparation time: 5 minutes
Cooking time: 5 minutes

Baking time: 20 minutes

Per serving: 260 calories, 6.1 g. fat (20% of calories), 1.2 g. dietary fiber, 9 mg. cholesterol, 621 mg. sodium.

HERBED ANGEL HAIR

*A*ngel hair pasta cooks very quickly, so keep your eye on it to avoid having it turn mushy. This sauce is so simple, you can toss it together in a minute. Feel free to vary the herbs according to what's in season.

Ingredients	For 1	For 2
Angel hair pasta	3 ounces	6 ounces
Nonfat sour cream	½ cup	1 cup
Minced fresh basil	1½ tablespoons	3 tablespoons
Minced fresh parsley	1 tablespoon	2 tablespoons
Diced black olives	1 tablespoon	2 tablespoons
Snipped chives	1 teaspoon	2 teaspoons

Cook the pasta in a pot of boiling water until just tender. Drain and return to the pot.

In a small (medium) bowl, stir together the sour cream, basil, parsley, olives and chives. Pour over the pasta and toss to coat well. Warm over low heat for 1 minute.

Preparation time: 5 minutes
Cooking time: 5 minutes

Per serving: 403 calories, 2.1 g. fat (5% of calories), 1.5 g. dietary fiber, no cholesterol, 108 mg. sodium.

SHELLS WITH MEATY MARINARA SAUCE

This made-from-scratch marinara sauce takes only about 30 minutes but tastes like it has simmered all day. It's ideal served over medium shells, but you may certainly substitute other types of pasta.

Ingredients	For 1	For 2
Olive oil	1½ teaspoons	1 tablespoon
Ground turkey	3 ounces	6 ounces
Minced onions	½ cup	1 cup
Garlic, minced	1 clove	2 cloves
Canned plum tomatoes, drained and chopped	1½ cups	3 cups
Dried oregano	¼ teaspoon	½ teaspoon
Dried basil	¼ teaspoon	½ teaspoon
Dried savory	¼ teaspoon	½ teaspoon
Medium shells	3 ounces	6 ounces
Grated Parmesan cheese	1 tablespoon	2 tablespoons

In a 2-quart saucepan (large frying pan) over medium-high heat, heat the oil for 1 minute. Crumble the turkey into the pan, and stir to brown and break up the pieces. Add the onions and garlic; stir for 2 minutes.

Stir in the tomatoes, oregano, basil and savory. Reduce the heat to medium and cook, stirring frequently, for 20 minutes, or until thick.

Meanwhile, cook the shells in boiling water for 10 minutes, or until tender. Drain and keep warm. Serve topped with the sauce and Parmesan.

Preparation time: 5 minutes
Cooking time: 25 minutes

Per serving: 609 calories, 12.4 g. fat (18% of calories), 5 g. dietary fiber, 56 mg. cholesterol, 227 mg. sodium.

JUICY BURGERS

*T*here are a few ways to decrease the fat—especially the saturated variety—in hamburgers. One is to use the very leanest ground beef you can buy. Look for meat labeled at least 92 percent fat-free. Or buy a very lean cut of beef, such as top round or eye of round, trim away all visible fat, and grind it yourself in your food processor. Another way to cut fat is to replace part of the beef with tofu, which also adds moisture to the burgers so that they turn out juicy. Serve your burgers with lettuce, tomato slices, thin pickle chips and ketchup.

Ingredients	For 1	For 2
Extra-lean ground beef	*4 ounces*	*8 ounces*
Mashed soft tofu, well drained	*¼ cup*	*½ cup*
Minced onions	*¼ cup*	*½ cup*
Dry bread crumbs	*3 tablespoons*	*6 tablespoons*
Ketchup	*1 tablespoon*	*2 tablespoons*
Fat-free egg substitute	*1 tablespoon*	*2 tablespoons*
Dried oregano	*¼ teaspoon*	*½ teaspoon*
Kaiser roll	*1*	*2*

In a large bowl, mix the beef, tofu, onions, bread crumbs, ketchup, egg and oregano. Form into 1 patty (2 patties). Cook in a no-stick frying pan over medium heat until browned on both sides and cooked through, about 10 minutes. Serve in the roll(s).

Preparation time: 10 minutes
Cooking time: 10 minutes

Per serving: 460 calories, 10.8 g. fat (21% of calories), 2.8 g. dietary fiber, 65 mg. cholesterol, 650 mg. sodium.

CHAPTER 8

NO-FUSS
FAMILY
SUPPERS

$\mathscr{I}$T'S BEEN A LONG DAY

$\mathscr{D}$o you enjoy sitting down with the whole family on weeknights for a relaxing dinner? It's a time for everyone to catch up on the day's happenings and just generally relish each other's company. *You'll* be able to enjoy yourself that much more if you aren't harried from a long bout of dinner preparations. And you'll feel good about what you're serving if you know that your meals are helping your loved ones stay fit, trim and healthy. In the pages that follow, we offer a variety of low-fat dinner menus that cater to your cravings for all sorts of meals, from Chinese to all-American. And they can be ready in a cool 45 minutes or less.

A YANKEE SUPPER

*T*his hearty New England–inspired dinner should hit the spot on really cold evenings. The clam chowder gets body from nourishing potatoes rather than cream. And the low-fat dessert is a snap to prepare.

Menu

HOT AND HEARTY CHOWDER
QUICK CORNMEAL MUFFINS
APPLES STUFFED WITH PRUNES

HOT AND HEARTY CHOWDER

SERVES 4

12	*shucked chowder clams*
5	*cups defatted chicken stock*
2	*large baking potatoes, peeled and diced*
1	*large onion, diced*
1	*carrot, diced*
1	*stalk celery, diced*
1	*tablespoon minced fresh parsley*
1	*bay leaf*
½	*teaspoon dried oregano*
¼	*teaspoon dried tarragon*
¼	*teaspoon ground black pepper*
8	*ounces cod, cut into 1" pieces*
1	*cup low-fat or evaporated skim milk*

In a 3-quart saucepan, combine the clams and 2 cups stock. Bring to a boil over high heat, then reduce the heat to medium and simmer for 3 minutes. Remove the clams with a slotted spoon and set aside.

Add the potatoes, onions, carrots, celery, parsley, bay leaf, oregano, tarragon, pepper and remaining 3 cups stock to the saucepan. Bring to a boil, then cook over medium heat for 15 minutes, or until the vegetables are softened. Remove and discard the bay leaf.

Ladle about half of the vegetables and about 1 cup liquid into a blender. Blend until smooth. Return to the pan. Add the cod and simmer for 5 minutes, or until the cod is cooked through.

Chop the clams finely and add to the pan. Stir in the milk and heat briefly.

Preparation time: 10 minutes
Cooking time: 25 minutes

Per serving: 252 calories, 4.1 g. fat (15% of calories), 2.5 g. dietary fiber, 50 mg. cholesterol, 215 mg. sodium.

QUICK CORNMEAL MUFFINS

MAKES 12

1 cup cornmeal
½ cup whole-wheat flour
½ cup unbleached flour
1 tablespoon baking powder
1 teaspoon dried sage
1 cup skim milk
¼ cup fat-free egg substitute
2 tablespoons honey
2 tablespoons oil

In a large bowl, whisk together the cornmeal, whole-wheat flour, unbleached flour, baking powder and sage.

In a medium bowl, whisk together the milk, egg, honey and oil. Pour over the dry ingredients and mix until well combined.

Coat 12 muffin cups with no-stick spray. Divide the batter among the cups, filling them about halfway. Bake at 450° for 15 minutes, or until golden.

Preparation time: 10 minutes
Baking time: 15 minutes

Chef's Note: You can give these muffins a Mexican accent by replacing the sage with 1½ teaspoons chili powder, ½ teaspoon ground cumin and ¼ teaspoon ground black pepper. Add 2 to 4 tablespoons drained and finely chopped canned chili peppers to the milk mixture. (You can control the hotness of these muffins by your choice of mild or jalapeño peppers and how much of them you use. Three tablespoons of jalapeños produces downright hot muffins.)

Per muffin: 112 calories, 2.8 g. fat (22% of calories), 2.3 g. dietary fiber, trace cholesterol, 94 mg. sodium.

APPLES STUFFED WITH PRUNES

SERVES 4

4	*large McIntosh apples*
1	*teaspoon lemon juice*
¼	*cup finely chopped prunes*
1	*tablespoon ground walnuts*
1	*teaspoon honey*
¼	*teaspoon ground cinnamon*
¼	*cup orange or apple juice*

Core the apples and remove about 1" of the peel from around the tops. Rub the exposed surfaces with the lemon juice. Prick the skins in several places with a fork to keep the apples from bursting.

In a small bowl, combine the prunes, walnuts, honey and cinnamon. Divide the mixture among the apples, stuffing it into the cored areas.

Arrange the apples in a 3-quart casserole dish. Add the orange or apple juice to the casserole. Cover with vented plastic wrap. Microwave on high for 4 minutes. Give the dish a half turn and microwave on high for 3 minutes, or until the apples are tender and easily pierced with a sharp knife.

Preparation time: 5 minutes
Cooking time: 10 minutes

Chef's Note: If you don't have a microwave, core the apples, then slice them in half through the cored areas for quicker cooking. Stuff with the prune mixture (you might want to double it) and place, cut side up, in a 7" × 11" baking dish. Add ½ cup orange or apple juice, cover tightly with foil, and bake at 375° for 30 minutes, or until tender but not collapsed.

Per serving: 153 calories, 3.4 g. fat (18% of calories), 4.1 g. dietary fiber, no cholesterol, 2 mg. sodium.

NEW BASICS

*C*hicken with noodles and a green vegetable is a dinnertime
classic. But traditional recipes—especially those that fry the
chicken—can be very high in fat. Here's how to update that family
favorite. The simple banana dessert can be in the oven while you
eat the rest of your dinner. Serve it as is or spoon the softened fruit
over frozen yogurt.

Menu

LEMON CHICKEN WITH NOODLES
BROCCOLI PARMESAN
BAKED BANANAS

LEMON CHICKEN WITH NOODLES

SERVES 4

8   *ounces medium no-yolk egg noodles*
4   *boneless, skinless chicken breast halves*
    (about 1 pound total)
1   *tablespoon olive oil*
1   *tablespoon lemon juice*
1   *teaspoon paprika*
¼   *teaspoon ground black pepper*

Cook the noodles in a large pot of boiling water for 8 minutes, or
until just tender. Drain and keep warm.

Meanwhile, place the chicken between sheets of wax paper and
pound lightly with a mallet to an even thickness.

In a small shallow container, mix the oil, lemon juice, paprika
and pepper. Dredge the chicken in the mixture to coat both sides.

Heat a large no-stick frying pan over medium-high heat for 1
minute. Add the chicken. Cover and cook for 8 to 10 minutes, or

until the chicken is opaque; do not overcook. Serve over the noodles.

Preparation time: 5 minutes
Cooking time: 15 minutes

Per serving: 360 calories, 5.9 g. fat (15% of calories), 4.5 g. dietary fiber, 66 mg. cholesterol, 99 mg. sodium.

BROCCOLI PARMESAN

SERVES 4

1	pound broccoli
2	tablespoons water
¼	teaspoon dried thyme
2	tablespoons grated Parmesan cheese

Trim and peel tough stalks. Cut the broccoli into thin spears. Arrange on a large plate in a circular pattern, with the florets in the center and the stems at the rim. Sprinkle with the water and thyme. Cover with vented plastic wrap.

Microwave on high for 4 minutes. Rotate the dish a half turn. Microwave on high for 3 minutes, or until the stems are easily pierced with a sharp knife. Do not overcook. Allow to stand for 5 minutes.

Drain. Then sprinkle with the Parmesan.

Preparation time: 5 minutes
Cooking time: 10 minutes

Per serving: 46 calories, 1.3 g. fat (22% of calories), 3.2 g. dietary fiber, 2 mg. cholesterol, 90 mg. sodium.

BAKED BANANAS

4   *large bananas*
¼   *cup pineapple juice*
1   *teaspoon honey*
⅛   *teaspoon grated nutmeg*

With a sharp knife, remove the stem end from each banana. Remove a 1" wide strip of peel down the length of each.

In a small bowl, combine the pineapple juice, honey and nutmeg. Brush the exposed banana flesh with the juice mixture. Arrange the bananas in a shallow baking dish. Bake at 300°, basting occasionally with the juice, for 25 minutes, or until the bananas are softened.

Preparation time: 5 minutes
Baking time: 25 minutes

Per serving: 119 calories, 0.6 g. fat (4% of calories), 1.8 g. dietary fiber, no cholesterol, 1 mg. sodium.

THE '90s MALT SHOP

*H*ere's a new, lower-fat twist on the burgers and ever-popular sundaes that are a malt-shop staple. These low-fat burgers have tuna as their base. Top them with ketchup or a lean tartar sauce made from nonfat mayonnaise, minced pickles, lemon juice and minced parsley or dill. Serve the burgers with a simple green salad and nonfat blue cheese dressing.

TUNA BURGERS
GREEN SALAD WITH
NONFAT BLUE CHEESE DRESSING
ZUCCHINI FRIES
STRAWBERRY SUNDAES

TUNA BURGERS

SERVES 4

1   *can (12½ ounces) low-sodium water-packed*
    albacore tuna, drained and flaked
½   *cup wheat germ*
2   *scallions, minced*
1   *tablespoon minced fresh parsley*
½   *teaspoon dried oregano*
¼   *cup nonfat mayonnaise*
¼   *cup fat-free egg substitute*
1   *tablespoon ketchup*
2   *teaspoons oil*
4   *Kaiser or crusty hamburger rolls*

In a medium bowl, combine the tuna, wheat germ, scallions, parsley and oregano.

In a cup, combine the mayonnaise, egg and ketchup. Pour over the tuna and mix well. Form into 4 patties.

In a large no-stick frying pan over medium heat, sauté the patties in the oil until browned and heated through, about 3 minutes per side. Serve on the rolls.

Preparation time: 10 minutes
Cooking time: 10 minutes

Per serving: 360 calories, 7.4 g. fat (20% of calories), 3 g. dietary fiber, 36 mg. cholesterol, 599 mg. sodium.

ZUCCHINI FRIES

SERVES 4

2 thin (1" diameter) zucchini
2 thin (1" diameter) yellow squash
½ teaspoon oil
1 teaspoon minced fresh basil

Cut the zucchini and squash into fries about 2" long and ½" thick.

In a large no-stick frying pan over medium-high heat, sauté the vegetables in the oil for 5 minutes, or until lightly browned. Sprinkle with the basil.

Preparation time: 10 minutes
Cooking time: 5 minutes

Per serving: 36 calories, 0.9 g. fat (21% of calories), 2.6 g. dietary fiber, no cholesterol, 5 mg. sodium.

STRAWBERRY SUNDAES

SERVES 4

¼ cup apple juice
1 tablespoon unflavored gelatin
3 cups sliced strawberries
2 cups nonfat plain or vanilla yogurt
¼ cup orange juice

Place the apple juice in a custard cup. Sprinkle with the gelatin. Let stand for a few minutes to soften. Stir well, then microwave on high for 30 seconds, or until the gelatin has dissolved.

Puree 2 cups strawberries in a food processor. With the motor running, pour in the gelatin. Mix well.

Transfer to a bowl and fold in the yogurt. Process in an ice-cream maker according to the manufacturer's instructions.

While the yogurt is freezing, puree the orange juice and remaining 1 cup strawberries in a food processor. Transfer to a 9" glass pie plate. Microwave on high for 2 minutes, or until the color is bright and the sauce is bubbly. Serve warm or at room temperature over the frozen yogurt.

Preparation time: 10 minutes plus freezing time

Per serving: 110 calories, 0.6 g. fat (5% of calories), 2 g. dietary fiber, 2 mg. cholesterol, 91 mg. sodium.

PRESTO PESTO

*L*et pasta be the main course when you want dinner on the table in a hurry. Keep in mind that thin varieties cook faster than thick ones and that fresh pasta takes but a minute.

Menu

ANGEL HAIR WITH ROSEMARY PESTO
CRUSTY ITALIAN BREAD
TOMATOES AU GRATIN
PINEAPPLE POUND CAKE

ANGEL HAIR WITH ROSEMARY PESTO

SERVES 4

1   *clove garlic*
½   *cup fresh oregano leaves*
2   *tablespoons fresh rosemary leaves*
1   *tablespoon grated orange rind*
1   *cup chopped scallions*
¼   *teaspoon red-pepper flakes*
¼   *cup olive oil*
1   *tablespoon red wine vinegar*
12   *ounces angel hair pasta*

With a food processor running, drop the garlic, oregano, rosemary and orange rind through the feed tube.

(continued)

Stop and scrap down the sides of the container.

With the machine running again, add the scallions and pepper flakes, then the oil and vinegar. Scrape down the sides of the container. Continue processing with on/off turns until the rosemary is well minced and the mixture has formed a paste.

Cook the pasta in a large pot of boiling water for 4 minutes, or until just tender. Do not overcook. Drain and place in a large bowl. Add the pesto and toss to combine well.

Preparation time: 10 minutes
Cooking time: 5 minutes

Per serving: 429 calories, 12.1 g. fat (25% of calories), 1.7 g. dietary fiber, no cholesterol, 10 mg. sodium.

TOMATOES AU GRATIN

SERVES 4

4   *large tomatoes*
⅓   *cup seasoned dry bread crumbs*
2   *tablespoons grated Parmesan cheese*
2   *tablespoons minced fresh parsley*
1   *tablespoon lemon juice*
¼   *teaspoon olive oil*
¼   *teaspoon garlic powder*

Cut the tomatoes in half crosswise. Gently squeeze the pieces to remove the seeds and excess juice. Place, cut side up, in a small casserole dish. Bake at 350° for 10 minutes.

In a small bowl, mix the bread crumbs, Parmesan, parsley, lemon juice, oil and garlic powder. Carefully spoon the mixture over the tomatoes and into the cavities left by the seeds. Bake for 15 minutes, or until the tomatoes are softened and the crumbs are lightly browned.

Preparation time: 5 minutes
Baking time: 25 minutes

Per serving: 80 calories, 2.3 g. fat (25% of calories), 2 g. dietary fiber, 2 mg. cholesterol, 131 mg. sodium.

PINEAPPLE POUND CAKE

SERVES 8

1   *package (0.9 ounce) sugar-free vanilla instant pudding mix*

1½   *cups skim milk*

½   *teaspoon almond extract*

1   *can (20 ounces) crushed pineapple in juice*

¼   *cup chopped toasted almonds*

1   *fat-free pound cake (12 ounces)*
    Mandarin orange slices or sliced strawberries

Place the pudding mix in a large bowl; add the milk and almond extract. Whisk for 2 minutes. Let stand for 5 minutes to thicken.

Place the pineapple in a strainer and press with the back of a spoon to remove as much of the juice as possible; reserve the juice for another use. Fold the pineapple and almonds into the pudding.

Cut the cake into 8 slices. Spoon the pudding mixture over the slices. Top with the oranges or strawberries.

Preparation time: 20 minutes

Chef's Note: For a more elegant presentation, cut the cake horizontally into 3 layers. Place 1 layer, cut side up, on a serving platter. Spread with a third of the pudding mixture. Top with the second layer and more pudding mixture; repeat with the third layer, ending with the pudding mixture on top. Decorate with the oranges or strawberries. If the layers slide while the pudding mixture is still soft, hold them in place by spearing the cake with skewers at the corners. Chill before serving.

Per serving: 187 calories, 2.3 g. fat (11% of calories), 0.9 g. dietary fiber, 1 mg. cholesterol, 194 mg. sodium.

MANDARIN MONDAY

*J*ust another manic Monday? Unwind by preparing an easy Chinese dinner. Thinly sliced turkey cutlets make the main dish really easy. And the dessert can be made ahead.

Menu

SWEET-AND-SOUR TURKEY BREAST
GREEN BEANS WITH OYSTER SAUCE
APRICOT PARFAITS

SWEET-AND-SOUR TURKEY BREAST

SERVES 4

2 cups water
1 cup long-grain white rice
1 pound turkey breast cutlets (about ¼" thick)
1 tablespoon unbleached flour
1 teaspoon oil
¼ cup white vinegar
¼ cup orange juice
2 tablespoons honey
2 tablespoons tomato paste
¼ teaspoon garlic powder
¼ teaspoon ground black pepper

In a 2-quart saucepan over high heat, bring the water to a boil. Stir in the rice. Reduce the heat to medium-low, cover the pan, and simmer for about 20 minutes, or until the rice is tender and all the liquid has been absorbed. Let stand for 5 minutes, then fluff with a fork.

Meanwhile, dredge the turkey in the flour to coat lightly. Heat the oil in a large no-stick frying pan over medium-high heat for 2 minutes. Add the turkey, working in batches if necessary. Cook for about 3 minutes per side, or until lightly browned.

Reduce the heat to medium. In a bowl, whisk together the vinegar, orange juice, honey, tomato paste, garlic powder and pepper. Pour over the turkey. Cover and cook for about 10 minutes, or until the sauce is slightly thickened. (If it becomes too thick, thin with a little water.)

Serve the turkey over the rice.

Preparation time: 15 minutes
Cooking time: 20 minutes

Per serving: 363 calories, 3.3 g. fat (8% of calories), 1.1 g. dietary fiber, 68 mg. cholesterol, 143 mg. sodium.

GREEN BEANS WITH OYSTER SAUCE

SERVES 4

2 tablespoons oyster sauce
1 tablespoon vinegar
1 teaspoon cornstarch
1 teaspoon oil
2 cloves garlic, halved
1 pound green beans
1 tablespoon sesame seeds

In a cup, combine the oyster sauce, vinegar and cornstarch; stir until smooth and set aside.

In a wok or large frying pan over medium-high heat, combine the oil and garlic. Stir for about 30 seconds, then discard the garlic. Quickly add the beans and stir-fry for 2 minutes.

Make a space in the bottom of the wok and add the sauce. Quickly stir until thick. (This won't take long, so be careful not to burn the sauce.) Toss the beans to coat with the sauce. Sprinkle with the sesame seeds.

Preparation time: 10 minutes
Cooking time: 5 minutes

Per serving: 66 calories, 2 g. fat (24% of calories), 3.1 g. dietary fiber, no cholesterol, 305 mg. sodium.

APRICOT PARFAITS

SERVES 4

1 *pound soft tofu, well drained*
¼ *cup pineapple juice concentrate*
1 *tablespoon honey*
½ *teaspoon almond extract*
1 *can (1 pound) apricot halves, packed in juice*
2 *tablespoons toasted shredded coconut*

In a blender, process the tofu, juice concentrate, honey and almond extract until very smooth.

Drain the apricots and reserve the juice for another use. Cut each apricot half into 2 or 3 pieces.

Spoon a few tablespoons of the tofu mixture into the bottoms of 4 parfait glasses. Top with a few apricot pieces. Continue to layer until the tofu and apricots are used. Sprinkle with the coconut. Serve immediately or chill.

Preparation time: 10 minutes

Per serving: 197 calories, 6.7 g. fat (29% of calories), 1.7 g. dietary fiber, no cholesterol, 21 mg. sodium.

AN EVENING SOUTH OF THE BORDER

*M*exican food can also be very quick to prepare. Just keep it simple, as in this dinner of bean enchiladas, homemade salsa, steamed rice and a no-fuss dessert.

Menu

BEAN ENCHILADAS
SALSA CRUDA
STEAMED RICE
MELON BALLS WITH LEMON-LIME SAUCE

Bean Enchiladas

SERVES 4

2   cans (15 ounces each) pinto beans, rinsed
    and well drained
1   tablespoon chili powder
8   flour tortillas
½   cup shredded reduced-fat Monterey Jack
    cheese

Place the beans in a large bowl and mash coarsely with a potato masher. Stir in the chili powder.

Wrap the tortillas in a damp paper towel and microwave on high for 45 seconds, or until pliable. Divide the bean mixture among the tortillas. Sprinkle the mixture with the Monterey Jack. Roll the tortillas to enclose the mixture.

Coat a 9" × 13" baking dish with no-stick spray. Place the enchiladas, seam side down, in the dish. Cover with foil and bake at 350° for 20 minutes, or until heated through.

Preparation time: 10 minutes
Baking time: 20 minutes

Per serving: 363 calories, 6 g. fat (15% of calories), 2.2 g. dietary fiber, 5 mg. cholesterol, 752 mg. sodium.

Salsa Cruda

SERVES 4

2   cups seeded and diced tomatoes
½   cup minced fresh coriander
¼   cup lime juice
2   cloves garlic, minced
½   teaspoon hot-pepper sauce

In a medium bowl, combine the tomatoes, coriander, lime juice, garlic and pepper sauce.

Preparation time: 5 minutes

Per serving: 20 calories, 0.2 g. fat (11% of calories), 0.8 g. dietary fiber, no cholesterol, 2 mg. sodium.

MELON CHUNKS WITH LEMON-LIME SAUCE

⅓ cup all-fruit apricot preserves
Grated rind of 1 lemon
Grated rind of 1 lime
1 tablespoon lemon juice
1 tablespoon lime juice
6 cups melon chunks
1 cup halved strawberries

In a 1-quart saucepan over medium heat, bring the preserves, lemon rind, lime rind, lemon juice and lime juice to a boil. Reduce the heat to low and simmer for 5 minutes. Transfer to a large bowl and place in the refrigerator for 5 minutes to cool but not thicken the sauce.

Add the melons and strawberries. Toss well. Serve in pretty dessert bowls.

Preparation time: 10 minutes
Cooking time: 5 minutes

Per serving: 133 calories, 0.6 g. fat (4% of calories), 3.4 g. dietary fiber, no cholesterol, 47 mg. sodium.

FRIDAY IN FLORENCE

*I*t doesn't have to be Friday. Maybe Wednesday is traditionally pasta day at your house. But no matter when you're hungry for an Italian dinner, this meal will satisfy your craving nicely.

Menu

SPAGHETTI AND MEATBALLS
GARLIC BREAD
CUCUMBER AND DILL SALAD
CREAMY RICE PUDDING

SPAGHETTI AND MEATBALLS

SERVES 4

8	ounces ground turkey breast
1½	slices whole-wheat bread, crumbled
1	egg white
2	teaspoons minced garlic
½	cup defatted chicken stock
1	small onion, finely chopped
2	sweet red peppers, finely chopped
2	cups chopped mushrooms
4	large tomatoes, seeded and coarsely chopped
¼	cup tomato paste
1	teaspoon dried basil
½	teaspoon dried oregano
1	teaspoon honey
8	ounces spaghetti

In a medium bowl, combine the turkey, bread, egg white and garlic. Shape into 1" balls.

Coat a Dutch oven or large frying pan with no-stick spray. Heat over medium heat, add the meatballs, and brown on all sides. Remove to a platter and set aside.

Add the stock to the pan and scrape up the cooked-on bits with a spatula. Add the onions and sauté, stirring frequently, until soft but not browned. Add the peppers and mushrooms; cook for 5 minutes.

Add the tomatoes, tomato paste, basil, oregano and honey. Cover and cook for 15 minutes, stirring frequently to prevent scorching.

Working in batches, transfer the mixture to a blender or food processor and puree. Return the sauce to the pan. Add the meatballs and heat through.

Cook the spaghetti in a large pot of boiling water until just tender, about 10 minutes. Drain and serve with the meatballs and sauce.

Preparation time: 15 minutes
Cooking time: 30 minutes

Per serving: 390 calories, 3.4 g. fat (8% of calories), 5.2 g. dietary fiber, 33 mg. cholesterol, 149 mg. sodium.

GARLIC BREAD

2 *tablespoons butter-flavored sprinkles*
2 *tablespoons hot tap water*
1 *tablespoon grated Parmesan cheese*
1 *teaspoon dried oregano*
1 *clove garlic, minced*
1 *loaf French bread, cut into 8 slices*

In a cup, stir the sprinkles into the water until dissolved. Stir in the Parmesan, oregano and garlic.

With a pastry brush, lightly coat both sides of each bread slice with the mixture. Form the bread back into a loaf and place on a sheet of aluminum foil. Wrap well. Bake at 350° for 15 minutes.

Preparation time: 5 minutes
Baking time: 15 minutes

Per slice: 109 calories, 1.6 g. fat (14% of calories), 0.8 g. dietary fiber, 1 mg. cholesterol, 257 mg. sodium.

CUCUMBER AND DILL SALAD

SERVES 4

1 *cup nonfat yogurt*
1 *teaspoon lemon juice*
1 *tablespoon minced fresh dill*
1 *tablespoon honey*
3 *medium cucumbers*
Mixed greens

In a large mixing bowl, combine the yogurt, lemon juice, dill and honey. Chill for at least 15 minutes.

Just before serving, peel and seed the cucumbers. Slice very thinly, then gently combine with the yogurt mixture. Divide the greens among salad plates. Top with the cucumber mixture.

Preparation time: 20 minutes

Per serving: 90 calories, 0.6 g. fat (5% of calories), 3.2 g. dietary fiber, 1 mg. cholesterol, 56 mg. sodium.

CREAMY RICE PUDDING

SERVES 6

3	cups skim milk
⅓	cup honey
1	teaspoon vanilla
¼	teaspoon grated nutmeg
¼	teaspoon ground cinnamon
1½	cups cooked rice
½	cup fat-free egg substitute

In a 2-quart casserole, whisk together the milk, honey, vanilla, nutmeg and cinnamon. Stir in the rice. Microwave on high for 10 minutes. Stir well, then microwave on high for 10 minutes.

Whisk in the eggs. Microwave on high for 2 minutes. Stir and let stand for at least 10 minutes to thicken further. Serve warm or cold.

Preparation time: 15 minutes
Cooking time: 15 minutes

Chef's Note: For variety, stir ⅓ to ½ cup dried fruit into the mixture before cooking. Try raisins, currants, cherries, blueberries or chopped apricots or prunes. You may also serve the pudding over fresh fruit. Sliced strawberries are especially good. If you don't have a microwave, combine all the ingredients except the eggs and bake at 350° for 1 hour, stirring occasionally. Whisk in the eggs and bake for 10 minutes.

Per serving: 178 calories, 0.4 g. fat (2% of calories), 0.6 g. dietary fiber, 2 mg. cholesterol, 92 mg. sodium.

LET'S CELEBRATE

 id something special happen this week? Have a family celebration with this elegant but easy dinner.

Menu

PEPPERED LAMB LOIN
SQUASH SOUFFLÉ
HONEY-GLAZED CARROTS
CHEESE BLINTZES

PEPPERED LAMB LOIN

SERVES 4

1   *pound boneless lamb loin, trimmed of all visible fat*
2   *tablespoons freshly cracked peppercorns*
¼   *cup sherry vinegar or white wine vinegar*
1   *tablespoon minced shallots*
1   *cup defatted beef stock*
2   *tablespoons minced fresh mint*
1   *tablespoon margarine*
8   *ounces medium no-yolk egg noodles*

Cut the lamb into 4 fillets. Firmly press the peppercorns into both sides of each piece.

Coat a no-stick frying pan with no-stick spray. Over medium-high heat, heat the pan until hot. Sear each fillet on both sides.

Transfer the meat to an ovenproof pan and finish cooking at 400° for 10 to 15 minutes.

In the same frying pan, combine the sherry vinegar or white wine vinegar and shallots. Cook for a few minutes, scraping any browned bits from the bottom of the pan. Add the stock. Stir in the mint and margarine. Keep warm.

Meanwhile, cook the noodles in a large pot of boiling water until just tender. Drain and keep warm.

Cut the lamb into very thin slices and place on a plate with the noodles. Drizzle with the sauce.

Preparation time: 10 minutes
Cooking time: 5 minutes
Baking time: 15 minutes

Per serving: 412 calories, 11 g. fat (24% of calories), 1.8 g. dietary fiber, 80 mg. cholesterol, 150 mg. sodium.

SQUASH SOUFFLÉ

SERVES 4

1	*pound butternut squash, peeled, seeded and cubed*
¼	*cup fat-free egg substitute*
¼	*teaspoon ground cinnamon*
⅛	*teaspoon grated nutmeg*
2	*egg whites*
½	*tart apple, such as Winesap*
1	*tablespoon margarine, melted*
1	*tablespoon maple syrup*

Steam the squash until very tender, about 10 minutes. Transfer to a food processor. Add the egg, cinnamon and nutmeg. Puree, then transfer to a large bowl.

In a separate bowl, beat the egg whites with clean beaters until stiff. Fold into the squash.

Coat a 1-quart baking dish with no-stick spray. Spread the squash in the dish, smoothing the top with a rubber spatula.

Peel and core the apple. Cut into paper-thin slices. Arrange the slices in a circle atop the squash.

In a cup, mix the margarine and maple syrup. Pour over the apples. Bake at 350° for 30 minutes, or until golden and slightly puffed.

Preparation time: 15 minutes
Baking time: 30 minutes

Per serving: 106 calories, 3 g. fat (24% of calories), 1.7 g. dietary fiber, no cholesterol, 85 mg. sodium.

FAST FOOD

*S*ome members of your family—such as the kids—might get home a lot earlier than others. And they probably want something to eat the minute they walk in the door. Keep them out of the cookie jar until dinnertime by having the fixings for these healthy snacks on hand.

Turkey time. Keep sliced roasted turkey breast in the fridge for sandwiches. Simply line a pita with lettuce and tuck in the turkey. For an even quicker snack, just munch the turkey as finger food.

Cheese and crudités. Have small chunks of low-fat cheese and strips of colorful sweet peppers or carrots in little plastic bags in the refrigerator for very portable snacks. For sweeter treats, use peeled and sectioned citrus fruits. For interesting colors and flavors, mix pink grapefruit with oranges and tangerines.

Tops in pops. Popped corn is a great high-fiber snack that most everybody likes. It's satisfying but not heavy enough to spoil anyone's appetite for dinner. Investing in a hot-air popper will keep the fat content of the popcorn down. And one of those appliances is safer for kids to use than poppers that heat oil. For a change of pace, toss the popped corn with raisins and a few cracked peanuts.

Quick 'cakes. You can freeze extra pancakes for quick and tasty snacks. To reheat them quickly, wrap individually in dampened paper towels and microwave on high for about 30 seconds, or until heated through. Top with maple yogurt, which you make by mixing maple syrup and yogurt.

Sundaes will never be the same. Make healthful sundaes by layering nonfat frozen yogurt with chopped fruit and nuts. Try vanilla yogurt with chopped bananas and a few pecans. Or have strawberry yogurt with fresh strawberries and some pistachios. You can even make the sundaes ahead and store them in the freezer.

Shake it. For quick shakes, pour 1 cup skim milk into a blender, then add a small peeled banana, 2 tablespoons peanut butter and sweetener to taste. Whiz until thick and smooth.

HONEY-GLAZED CARROTS

SERVES 4

1 *pound carrots, thickly sliced on the diagonal*
1 *cup defatted chicken stock*
2 *tablespoons honey*
1 *tablespoon Dijon mustard*

In a large frying pan, combine the carrots, stock, honey and mustard. Cover and cook over medium heat for 10 minutes, or until the carrots are tender.

Remove the cover and cook over medium-high heat, stirring often, for 5 minutes, or until the stock has been reduced to a glaze.

Preparation time: 10 minutes
Cooking time: 15 minutes

Per serving: 94 calories, 0.6 g. fat (6% of calories), 3.7 g. dietary fiber, no cholesterol, 109 mg. sodium.

CHEESE BLINTZES

MAKES 8

⅔ *cup skim milk*
⅓ *cup whole-wheat flour*
¼ *cup fat-free egg substitute*
½ *teaspoon baking powder*
2 *tablespoons honey*
1 *tablespoon grated orange rind*
¼ *teaspoon ground cinnamon*
1½ *cups nonfat sour cream*
1 *teaspoon oil*
2 *cups blueberries*
1 *cup applesauce*

In a blender, process the milk, flour, egg and baking powder until smooth, scraping down the sides of the container as needed.

Coat a small no-stick frying pan with no-stick spray. Place the pan over medium-high heat. Pour in about 3 tablespoons batter and swirl it around to coat the bottom of the pan.

(continued)

Cook the blintz for about 1 minute, or until the top is dry and the bottom is lightly browned. Flip the blintz out onto a rack or tea towel by turning the pan upside down. Continue making blintzes with the remaining batter.

In a small bowl, mix the honey, orange rind, cinnamon and 1 cup sour cream.

To fill, lay each blintz on a counter. Spoon 1 rounded tablespoon of the filling onto the middle. Fold the bottom of the blintz over the filling. Then fold in the sides. Finish by rolling the whole thing up into a little pouch.

Coat a large no-stick frying pan with no-stick spray. Heat over medium heat. Add the oil and sauté the blintzes for a few minutes on each side to lightly brown.

Serve topped with the blueberries, applesauce and remaining ½ cup sour cream.

Preparation time: 10 minutes
Cooking time: 20 minutes

Per blintz: 112 calories, 0.9 g. fat (7% of calories), 1.9 g. dietary fiber, trace cholesterol, 74 mg. sodium.

FISHING FOR COMPLIMENTS

*Y*ou'll get plenty of raves when you serve this low-fat fish dinner. To save time, finish off the meal with store-bought gingersnaps, which are much lower in fat than many other types of cookies, and a scoop of nonfat frozen vanilla yogurt.

Menu

LEMON HALIBUT
POTATO CRISPS
COLORFUL PEPPER SALAD
GINGERSNAPS WITH FROZEN VANILLA YOGURT

LEMON HALIBUT

  1 onion, thinly sliced
  1 tablespoon olive oil
  2 cups defatted chicken stock
  1 head romaine lettuce, cut into 1" squares
    Juice of 2 lemons
    Pinch of ground black pepper
  4 halibut fillets (6 ounces each)
  2 tablespoons water
  1 tablespoon cornstarch
  ¼ cup snipped chives
  1 tablespoon rinsed capers

In a large no-stick frying pan over medium heat, sauté the onions in the oil until transparent, about 5 minutes. Add the stock and bring to a boil. Add the lettuce and cook for 2 to 3 minutes, or until the lettuce just starts to wilt.

Stir in the lemon juice and pepper. Add the fish and cook for 5 minutes, or until just firm to the touch.

Carefully drain the excess liquid from the frying pan into a 2-quart saucepan. Over high heat, cook until reduced by half, about 5 to 7 minutes.

In a cup, mix the water and cornstarch until smooth. Add to the saucepan and cook for a few minutes to thicken the sauce. Stir in the chives and capers.

To serve, transfer portions of lettuce and fish to dinner plates. Spoon on the sauce.

Preparation time: 10 minutes
Cooking time: 20 minutes

Per serving: 277 calories, 8.2 g. fat (27% of calories), 2.1 g. dietary fiber, 54 mg. cholesterol, 185 mg. sodium.

POTATO CRISPS

SERVES 4

12 ounces small potatoes
1 tablespoon water
2 teaspoons olive oil
½ teaspoon dried oregano

Slice the potatoes into ¼" disks. Arrange on a 9" glass pie plate. Sprinkle with the water. Cover with vented plastic wrap and microwave on high for 3 minutes, or until just tender.

Drain well and pat dry with paper towels. Toss with the oil and oregano.

Heat a large, well-seasoned cast-iron frying pan over high heat for 2 minutes. Reduce the heat to medium-high and add the potatoes. Sizzle, flipping the pieces often, for about 15 minutes, or until lightly browned and slightly puffed.

Preparation time: 5 minutes
Cooking time: 20 minutes

Chef's Note: If you don't have a microwave, steam the potatoes for about 5 minutes, or until just tender but not breaking apart.

Per serving: 83 calories, 2.4 g. fat (25% of calories), 2.4 g. dietary fiber, no cholesterol, 6 mg. sodium.

COLORFUL PEPPER SALAD

SERVES 4

1 red onion, halved and thinly sliced
2 teaspoons olive oil
3 peppers, cut into 1" chunks
1 clove garlic, minced
1 cucumber, thinly sliced
2 tablespoons lemon juice
¼ teaspoon ground cumin
¼ teaspoon ground black pepper
⅛ teaspoon paprika
⅛ teaspoon ground red pepper

In a large no-stick frying pan over medium heat, sauté the onions in the oil for 7 minutes. Add the peppers. Sauté for 5 minutes, or until crisp-tender. Stir in the garlic and sauté for 1 minute. Transfer to a large bowl and stir in the cucumbers.

In a cup, whisk together the lemon juice, cumin, black pepper, paprika and red pepper. Pour over the salad. Toss well. Serve warm or at room temperature.

Preparation time: 10 minutes
Cooking time: 15 minutes

Per serving: 54 calories, 1.4 g. fat (22% of calories), 2.3 g. dietary fiber, no cholesterol, 4 mg. sodium.

Southern Hospitality

*T*his Dixie-inspired dinner would work just as nicely for breakfast or Sunday brunch.

Menu

CHEESE GRITS
SCRAMBLED EGGS WITH TOAST
SPICY TURKEY LINKS
HOT APPLES WITH OAT TOPPING

CHEESE GRITS

SERVES 4

4 *cups defatted chicken stock*
1 *cup quick-cooking grits*
¾ *cup frozen corn*
¼ *cup grated Parmesan cheese*
½ *teaspoon dried thyme*
½ *teaspoon ground black pepper*

In a 2-quart saucepan over medium-high heat, bring the stock to a boil. Whisk in the grits. Reduce the heat to medium-low, cover the pan, and cook, stirring occasionally, for 7 minutes, or until thick.

Stir in the corn, Parmesan, thyme and pepper. Remove from the heat and let stand for 5 minutes to warm the corn.

Preparation time: 10 minutes
Cooking time: 10 minutes

Per serving: 236 calories, 3.8 g. fat (14% of calories), 5.4 g. dietary fiber, 5 mg. cholesterol, 199 mg. sodium.

SCRAMBLED EGGS WITH TOAST

SERVES 4

½	cup minced sweet red peppers
½	cup minced mushrooms
¼	cup minced celery
2	teaspoons olive oil
2	cups fat-free egg substitute
¼	cup nonfat sour cream
2	tablespoons snipped chives
¼	teaspoon dried marjoram
¼	teaspoon dried sage
8	slices whole-wheat bread

In a large no-stick frying pan over medium heat, sauté the peppers, mushrooms and celery in the oil for 5 minutes, or until tender.

In a small bowl, whisk together the eggs, sour cream, chives, marjoram and sage. Pour into the pan and scramble, stirring occasionally, until set.

Just before serving, toast the bread.

Preparation time: 10 minutes
Cooking time: 10 minutes

Per serving: 224 calories, 4.8 g. fat (19% of calories), 6.8 g. dietary fiber, no cholesterol, 533 mg. sodium.

SPICY TURKEY LINKS

1   *pound boneless, skinless turkey breast, cut into 1" cubes*
½   *small onion, minced*
1   *egg white*
1   *tablespoon tomato paste*
1   *teaspoon dried thyme*
½   *teaspoon dried sage*
½   *teaspoon crushed fennel seeds*
¼   *teaspoon poultry seasoning*
⅛   *teaspoon ground allspice*
⅛   *teaspoon ground red pepper*
2   *tablespoons unbleached flour*
2   *teaspoons olive oil*

In a food processor, combine the turkey, onions, egg white, tomato paste, thyme, sage, fennel seeds, poultry seasoning, allspice and red pepper. Process with on/off turns until the turkey is evenly ground.

Wet your hands and form the mixture into 8 links, using about ¼ cup mixture for each.

Place the flour on a piece of wax paper. Lightly roll each link in it.

In a large no-stick frying pan over medium-high heat, heat the oil. Add the links and sizzle for 8 minutes, or until burnished on all sides and cooked through.

Preparation time: 15 minutes
Cooking time: 10 minutes

Per serving: 185 calories, 4.4 g. fat (22% of calories), 1.1 g. dietary fiber, 66 mg. cholesterol, 86 mg. sodium.

Hot Apples with Oat Topping

SERVES 4

Apples

    4   *tart apples, such as Granny Smith*

    2   *tablespoons cornstarch*

    ¼   *cup maple syrup*

    2   *teaspoons lemon juice*

    1   *teaspoon ground cinnamon*

Oat Topping

    1   *cup quick-cooking rolled oats*

    2   *tablespoons maple syrup*

    2   *teaspoons oil*

    1   *teaspoon vanilla*

To make the apples: Peel and core the apples, then cut into small chunks. Place in a 9" glass pie plate and toss with the cornstarch. Drizzle with the maple syrup, lemon juice and cinnamon. Stir well. Cover with vented plastic wrap and microwave on high for 6 minutes. Stir well, cover, and microwave on high for 6 minutes, or until the apples are tender. Let stand for 5 minutes.

To make the oat topping: Place the oats in another 9" glass pie plate. Drizzle with the maple syrup, oil and vanilla. Mix well. Microwave on high for 1 minute. Stir well. Repeat 3 or 4 times, or until the oats are crisp and very lightly browned but not burned. Sprinkle over the apples.

Preparation time: 10 minutes
Cooking time: 20 minutes

Chef's Note: If you don't have a microwave, combine the apple mixture in an 8" × 8" baking dish and cover with foil. Bake at 350° for 30 minutes. Uncover and sprinkle with the oat mixture. Bake, uncovered, for 20 minutes, or until the apples are just tender and the oats are lightly browned. If the oats brown too quickly, cover loosely with foil.

Per serving: 275 calories, 4.1 g. fat (13% of calories), 4.2 g. dietary fiber, no cholesterol, 7 mg. sodium.

CHAPTER 9

FESTIVE
MEALS
READY IN
AN HOUR
OR LESS

COMPANY'S COMING

D o you have a fondness for informal dinner parties—
simple get-togethers planned just a few days ahead?
They're a cozy way to unwind after work or to while away a lazy
weekend. One way to make these occasions easier on yourself is
to have guests pitch in and bring some of the food. But when all
you want them to bring is their charming selves, you'll need no-
fuss menus that won't be a drain on your time and energy. The
menus that follow are a little more elaborate than simple family
suppers, but they're not really more work. Many dishes can be
prepared ahead. And even without that forethought, you can
have a nice little—healthy—feast on the table in about an hour.

Fish 'n' Chips

*I*nvite the gang for a good old-fashioned fish fry—complete with slimmed-down versions of tartar sauce, fries and cole slaw. Make things easy on yourself by preparing the appetizer, dill sauce and slaw ahead. Further lighten your load by serving a simple steamed green vegetable, such as snow peas, and a no-bother dessert of angel food cake topped with black raspberries and pureed strawberries.

Menu

STUFFED CHERRY TOMATOES
LIGHT AND LUSCIOUS FISH FRY
DILL SAUCE
OVEN FRIES
TWO-CABBAGE COLE SLAW
STEAMED SNOW PEAS
FESTIVE ANGEL FOOD CAKE WITH BERRIES

STUFFED CHERRY TOMATOES

SERVES 8

24   *red or yellow cherry tomatoes*
½   *cup dry-curd cottage cheese*
¼   *cup minced spinach*
1   *tablespoon minced fresh basil*
2   *teaspoons snipped chives*

Slice off the very tops of the tomatoes. Use a small spoon to remove the insides; discard. Turn the tomatoes upside down to drain while you prepare the filling.

In a small bowl, mix the cottage cheese, spinach, basil and chives. Spoon into the tomatoes (or place in a pastry bag fitted with a large decorative tip; pipe the filling into the tomatoes).

Preparation time: 15 minutes

Chef's Notes: For variety, you may replace the cottage cheese filling with pureed chicken, tuna or salmon salad. For brunch, use scrambled eggs; garnish with tiny herb sprigs. For a Mexican flavor, try guacamole.

You may also turn these cold hors d'oeuvres into warm ones. For best results, use firm-walled tomatoes that won't collapse when heated. Prepare the filling as above, but replace the cottage cheese with 3 tablespoons dry bread crumbs plus 2 ounces softened Neufchâtel cheese. Blend well, then pipe the filling into the tomatoes. Arrange the tomatoes in a baking dish and bake at 350° for about 15 minutes, or until the tomatoes just begin to soften. Do not overbake, or the tomatoes will split. Let stand for about 10 minutes, or until just barely warm, before serving.

Per serving: 21 calories, 0.2 g. fat (10% of calories), 0.9 g. dietary fiber, 1 mg. cholesterol, 8 mg. sodium.

LIGHT AND LUSCIOUS FISH FRY

SERVES 8

2   *pounds haddock fillet*
2   *tablespoons Dijon mustard*
2   *tablespoons nonfat yogurt*
2   *tablespoons snipped chives*
2   *tablespoons minced fresh parsley*
    Pinch of ground red pepper
2   *cups dry bread crumbs*

Rinse the fish and pat dry. Cut into 16 equal pieces.

In a cup, combine the mustard, yogurt, chives, parsley and pepper. Rub this mixture onto all sides of the fish. Refrigerate for about 20 minutes.

Thoroughly coat the fish pieces with the bread crumbs.

Coat a baking sheet with no-stick spray. Add the fish in a single layer, with space between the pieces. Bake at 375° for 10 to 12 minutes, or until the fish flakes easily when tested with a fork.

Preparation time: 5 minutes plus chilling time
Baking time: 15 minutes

Per serving: 201 calories, 2.2 g. fat (10% of calories), 1 g. dietary fiber, 65 mg. cholesterol, 313 mg. sodium.

DILL SAUCE

MAKES ABOUT 1 CUP

¾ cup nonfat mayonnaise
3 tablespoons minced gherkin pickles
1 tablespoon minced fresh dill
1 tablespoon minced fresh parsley
2 teaspoons snipped chives
2 teaspoons lemon juice
1 teaspoon Dijon mustard

In a small bowl, mix the mayonnaise, pickles, dill, parsley, chives, lemon juice and mustard. Chill until serving time.

Preparation time: 5 minutes

Per 2 tablespoons: 27 calories, trace fat (1% of calories), 0.1 g. dietary fiber, no cholesterol, 342 mg. sodium.

OVEN FRIES

SERVES 8

6 large baking potatoes
½ teaspoon oil

Cut each potato lengthwise into 8 spears. Pat dry with paper towels to remove surface moisture. Place the potatoes in a large jelly-roll pan. Drizzle with the oil and mix well with your hands to coat the pieces evenly.

Arrange the pieces, cut sides up, in a single layer. (If necessary, use 2 pans.) Bake at 375° for 30 to 40 minutes, or until the pieces are golden and slightly puffed.

Preparation time: 5 minutes
Baking time: 40 minutes

Per serving: 85 calories, 0.4 g. fat (4% of calories), 2.3 g. dietary fiber, no cholesterol, 8 mg. sodium.

Two-Cabbage Cole Slaw

3   cups thinly sliced green cabbage
3   cups thinly sliced red cabbage
2   carrots, shredded
1   green pepper, julienned
2   scallions, minced
⅓   cup nonfat mayonnaise
⅓   cup nonfat yogurt
3   tablespoons white vinegar
½   teaspoon ground black pepper
⅛   teaspoon celery seeds

In a large bowl, mix the green cabbage, red cabbage, carrots, green peppers and scallions.

In a small bowl, whisk together the mayonnaise, yogurt, vinegar, black pepper and celery seeds. Pour over the salad and toss well to combine. Chill.

Preparation time: 15 minutes plus chilling time

Per serving: 38 calories, 0.2 g. fat (4% of calories), 2 g. dietary fiber, trace cholesterol, 148 mg. sodium.

GRILLED TO PERFECTION

ookouts are a great American tradition, especially when company's coming. As long as you've got the grill hot, you might as well use it for as many dishes as possible. For this meal, the fish, salad, corn and dessert all are prepared over coals. You can make the gazpacho beverage ahead and have it chilling in the fridge. Before your guests arrive, get the pita chips ready for the oven.

Menu

GAZPACHO ON THE ROCKS
PITA CHIPS
GINGER BASS IN FOIL
GRILLED SUMMER SALAD
HERB-FLAVORED CORN ON THE COB
SEARED PINEAPPLE AND PEACHES

GAZPACHO ON THE ROCKS

SERVES 8

2   cans (24 ounces each) reduced-sodium vegetable-cocktail juice
2   tablespoons chopped celery
2   tablespoons chopped onions
2   tablespoons lemon juice
2   cloves garlic, chopped
¼   teaspoon hot-pepper sauce

Pour about 3 cups juice into a blender. Add the celery, onions, lemon juice, garlic and pepper sauce. Process on high speed until smooth. Pour into a large pitcher and add the remaining juice. Serve over ice or chill.

Preparation time: 5 minutes

Per serving: 33 calories, 0.1 g. fat (3% of calories), 2 g. dietary fiber, no cholesterol, 20 mg. sodium.

PITA CHIPS

SERVES 8

6   *large pita breads*
1   *tablespoon olive oil*
1   *tablespoon butter-flavored sprinkles*
½   *teaspoon dried oregano*
¼   *teaspoon ground black pepper*
¼   *teaspoon chili powder*

Cut each pita in half to form 2 pockets. Then carefully separate each pocket into 2 semicircles by cutting open the closed edge.

In a cup, combine the oil, sprinkles, oregano, pepper and chili powder. Lightly brush the interior side of each pita with the mixture. Cut each piece into 4 wedges.

Arrange the chips in a single layer on large baking sheets. Bake at 375° for 5 to 10 minutes, or until crisped. Serve warm.

Preparation time: 10 minutes
Baking time: 10 minutes

Chef's Note: If preparing just a portion of the chips, you may microwave them. Line a large microwave-safe plate with a paper towel. Arrange 16 wedges at a time around the outer edge of the plate with the points facing in. Microwave on high for 2 minutes. Rotate the plate a half turn. Microwave for 1 to 2 minutes, or until the wedges begin to curl and brown.

Per serving: 97 calories, 2.1 g. fat (20% of calories), 0.5 g. dietary fiber, no cholesterol, 187 mg. sodium.

HOT TIPS

A prime key to grilling success is knowing when the coals are ready and just how far away to position the food. Always use enough charcoal to form a closely packed layer a little larger than the food will cover. Allow about 30 minutes for the coals to become hot enough for cooking. Then use long tongs to knock off their coat of white ash.

Use an impeccably clean grilling rack. Coat with no-stick spray, then set it 5" to 6" above the coals. Cook thin or quick-cooking foods right in the middle of the grill, over the highest heat. Put very delicate foods, such as thin fish fillets or soft vegetables, on perforated foil or in a wire grilling basket. Place longer-cooking items, such as whole potatoes, off to the side so that they won't char before they're cooked through.

GINGER BASS IN FOIL

SERVES 8

2 *thin zucchini, julienned*
2 *thin yellow squash, julienned*
1 *large carrot, julienned*
2 *tablespoons minced fresh ginger*
8 *bass fillets (6 ounces each)*
1 *lemon, quartered lengthwise*
2 *cloves garlic, minced*
½ *teaspoon ground black pepper*

Cut 8 large pieces of foil (16" × 16"). Fold each in half to make a double thickness.

In a large bowl, mix the zucchini, squash, carrots and ginger. Divide into 8 portions and place 1 portion on each piece of foil. Top each portion with a fillet.

Squeeze the lemon over the fish. Sprinkle with the garlic and pepper.

Fold the foil over the fish and crimp the edges to tightly seal the packets.

Grill over medium-high heat for 15 to 20 minutes. If desired, serve right in the foil.

Preparation time: 10 minutes
Cooking time: 20 minutes

Chef's Note: You may also bake the fish. Place the packets on baking sheets. Bake at 425° for 15 to 20 minutes.

Per serving: 211 calories, 8.5 g. fat (34% of calories), 1.3 g. dietary fiber, 116 mg. cholesterol, 123 mg. sodium.

GRILLED SUMMER SALAD

SERVES 8

4	heads Belgian endive, halved lengthwise
2	heads radicchio or romaine lettuce, quartered lengthwise
2	medium zucchini, thickly sliced on the diagonal
2	teaspoons olive oil
2	teaspoons minced fresh basil
2	large firm tomatoes
¼	cup balsamic vinegar

Place the endive, lettuce and zucchini in a large baking dish. Drizzle with the oil. Sprinkle with the basil. Toss lightly to combine and to coat the vegetables with the oil.

Cut the tomatoes in half through their cores. Trim the cores. Cut each half lengthwise into 1" wide wedges.

Prepare a grill and arrange the zucchini slices over the hottest coals. Surround with the endive and lettuce. Add the tomatoes, positioning them near the outer edges of the rack. Grill for about 3 minutes. Carefully flip the pieces and grill for 3 to 5 minutes, or until browned and soft.

Remove the pieces with a metal spatula and divide among 8 plates. Sprinkle with the vinegar.

Preparation time: 10 minutes
Cooking time: 10 minutes

Per serving: 40 calories, 1.3 g. fat (30% of calories), 1.3 g. dietary fiber, no cholesterol, 7 mg. sodium.

HERB-FLAVORED CORN ON THE COB

SERVES 8

8   *ears corn with husks*
¼   *teaspoon olive oil*
1   *teaspoon dried dill*
    Butter-flavored sprinkles

Pull down the husks of each ear of corn, but don't remove them. Remove and discard the silk.

Very lightly rub each ear with the oil, then lightly dust with the dill and sprinkles. Replace the husks, making sure that all the corn kernels are covered. If necessary, secure the husks with damp kitchen string.

Place the ears around the edge of the grill (medium-low heat), about 5" from the hottest coals. Grill for about 20 minutes, flipping the ears occasionally, until cooked through.

Preparation time: 5 minutes
Cooking time: 20 minutes

Chef's Note: You may also microwave the corn. Prepare the ears as above, then arrange 4 in a square pattern on a large, flat plate. Microwave on high for 2 minutes. Turn and rotate the ears. Repeat 3 times for a total of 8 minutes. Microwave the remaining 4 ears the same way.

Per serving: 87 calories, 1.2 g. fat (10% of calories), 6.6 g. dietary fiber, no cholesterol, 30 mg. sodium.

SEARED PINEAPPLE AND PEACHES

SERVES 8

2   *cups nonfat yogurt*
½   *cup skim milk*
4   *cups raspberries*
2   *ripe pineapples*
4   *peaches*
2   *cups blueberries*

Combine the yogurt, milk and 2 cups raspberries in a blender container. Puree on medium speed. Transfer to a bowl and chill.

Slice the tops and bottoms off the pineapples. With a sharp knife, remove the outer peel and the inner core of each. Slice the flesh crosswise into 1" thick pieces. Halve the peaches and remove the pits.

Prepare a grill and place the pineapples and peaches directly on the rack. Grill over medium-high heat for about 4 minutes per side, or until golden brown.

Use a metal spatula to transfer the fruit to dessert plates. Sprinkle with the blueberries and remaining 2 cups raspberries. Top with the sauce.

Preparation time: 5 minutes
Cooking time: 10 minutes

Per serving: 190 calories, 1.4 g. fat (6% of calories), 6.3 g. dietary fiber, 1 mg. cholesterol, 55 mg. sodium.

THAT'S ITALIAN!

Turn your house into an Italian trattoria for a few selected friends. Set the scene with traditional red-checkered tablecloths and candles stuck in decorative bottles. Have store-bought bread sticks and nonalcoholic wine or carbonated fruit drinks on hand for guests to nosh on while you prepare the dinner.

Menu

CHILLED HONEYDEW SOUP
CHICKEN CACCIATORE WITH SPAGHETTI
BROILED VEGETABLES DIABLO
GREEN AND ORANGE SALAD
PEACH CRISP

CHILLED HONEYDEW SOUP

SERVES 8

2 honeydew melons
Juice of 1 lime
1 teaspoon fennel seeds, crushed

Halve the melons and scoop out the seeds. Peel, then cut the flesh into chunks. Transfer about a third of the chunks to a blender. Add the lime juice and fennel seeds. Puree on high speed. Transfer to a large bowl. Working in batches, puree the remaining melon chunks. Add to the bowl and stir well.

Preparation time: 5 minutes

Per serving: 28 calories, 0.1 g. fat (3% of calories), 0.7 g. dietary fiber, no cholesterol, 8 mg. sodium.

CHICKEN CACCIATORE WITH SPAGHETTI

SERVES 8

1 tablespoon olive oil
8 boneless, skinless chicken breast halves (about 4 ounces each)
1 cup diced onions
1 clove garlic, minced
2 cups tomato sauce
½ cup defatted chicken stock
1 pound spaghetti
¼ cup grated Parmesan cheese

In a large no-stick frying pan or Dutch oven over medium heat, heat 1½ teaspoons oil. Add 4 chicken breast halves and brown on both sides. Remove to a plate. Repeat with the remaining 1½ teaspoons oil and 4 chicken breast halves.

Add the onions and garlic. Sauté for 5 minutes, or until soft. Add the tomato sauce and stock. Stir well. Add the chicken breast halves and spoon sauce over them. Cover and cook for 15 minutes, or until the chicken is cooked through.

Meanwhile, cook the spaghetti in a large pot of boiling water for

10 minutes, or until just tender. Drain and place on a large platter. Top with the chicken and sauce. Sprinkle with the Parmesan.

Preparation time: 10 minutes
Cooking time: 25 minutes

Per serving: 397 calories, 5 g. fat (12% of calories), 2 g. dietary fiber, 68 mg. cholesterol, 158 mg. sodium.

BROILED VEGETABLES DIABLO

SERVES 8

3	tablespoons red wine vinegar
3	tablespoons defatted chicken stock
1	tablespoon low-sodium soy sauce
1	tablespoon Dijon mustard
1	tablespoon minced fresh parsley
2	teaspoons olive oil
2	cloves garlic, minced
½	teaspoon ground black pepper
3	sweet red or green peppers, cut into flat wedges
1	pound small mushrooms, stems cut flush with the caps
3	large red onions, cut crosswise into ½" rounds
4	thin zucchini, halved crosswise and lengthwise

In a small bowl, whisk together the vinegar, stock, soy sauce, mustard, parsley, oil, garlic and black pepper.

In a large bowl or glass baking dish, combine the red or green peppers, mushrooms, onions and zucchini. Pour on the marinade and toss lightly to coat, being careful not to separate the rings of the onions. Set aside for 15 to 30 minutes.

Lightly coat a large jelly-roll pan with no-stick spray. Using a slotted spoon, remove the vegetables from the marinade and place in a single layer in the pan. Reserve any leftover marinade.

Broil 4" to 6" from the heat, turning the vegetables as needed, until all sides are nicely browned but not burned. Brush occasionally with the reserved marinade. Cooking time will be at least 10 minutes.

Transfer the vegetables to a platter and brush lightly with any leftover marinade.

Preparation time: 15 minutes plus marinating time
Cooking time: 10 minutes

Per serving: 68 calories, 1.7 g. fat (21% of calories), 3.1 g. dietary fiber, no cholesterol, 108 mg. sodium.

GREEN AND ORANGE SALAD

SERVES 8

8   navel oranges
¼   cup minced parsley
2   tablespoons snipped chives
3   tablespoons orange juice
1½   tablespoons olive oil
1   tablespoon Dijon mustard
1   clove garlic, minced
     Boston or Bibb lettuce

Peel and section the oranges, removing all the membranes. Place in a large bowl. Sprinkle with the parsley and chives.

In a small bowl, whisk together the orange juice, oil, mustard and garlic. Pour over the oranges and toss well. Serve on a bed of lettuce leaves.

Preparation time: 15 minutes

Per serving: 91 calories, 2.8 g. fat (26% of calories), 3.5 g. dietary fiber, no cholesterol, 26 mg. sodium.

PEACH CRISP

SERVES 8

⅔ *cup rolled oats*

½ *cup oat bran*

¼ *cup maple syrup*

1 *teaspoon vanilla*

¼ *cup all-fruit peach preserves*

2 *tablespoons cornstarch*

1 *tablespoon lemon juice*

¼ *teaspoon almond extract*

8 *cups sliced peeled peaches*

In a 9" glass pie plate, combine the oats, oat bran, maple syrup and vanilla. Mix well to distribute the liquid ingredients and to break up the clumps of oats. Spread the mixture evenly in the pan. Microwave on high, stirring every 45 seconds, until the mixture is almost dry to the touch, a total of 5 to 6 minutes. Set aside.

Place the preserves in a large bowl and microwave on high for 25 seconds to soften. Stir in the cornstarch, lemon juice and almond extract. Add the peaches and mix well.

Place the peaches in a 9" × 9" or 7" × 11" baking dish. Microwave on high for 3 minutes. Stir well, then microwave on high for 3 minutes. Stir. Continue microwaving at 1-minute intervals until the mixture is thick and bubbling. (The exact time will depend on the size and shape of the pan, the ripeness and initial temperature of the peaches and the thickness of the slices).

Sprinkle with the oat mixture. Serve warm or chilled.

Preparation time: 10 minutes
Cooking time: 15 minutes

Chef's Note: If you don't have a microwave, soften the preserves in a saucepan and then mix with the rest of the peach-filling ingredients. Spread in a baking dish. Mix the oat-topping ingredients and sprinkle over the peaches. Bake at 350° for about 30 minutes, or until the filling is bubbly and the topping is lightly browned.

Per serving: 153 calories, 1 g. fat (5% of calories), 3.9 g. dietary fiber, no cholesterol, 11 mg. sodium.

FOR MEAT-LOVERS

*I*f you count some avowed meat-eaters among your friends, you can serve them this delicious dinner, which pairs well-trimmed top round with low-fat gravy and fancy stuffed potatoes.

Menu

ASPARAGUS SOUP
LONDON BROIL
LEAN GRAVY
CHEESE-STUFFED POTATOES
ORANGE-GLAZED CARROTS
APPLE CRUMB PIE

ASPARAGUS SOUP

SERVES 8

7	*cups defatted chicken stock*
½	*cup white wine vinegar*
2	*teaspoons honey*
7	*ounces asparagus, trimmed and cut into 1" pieces*
7	*ounces canned baby corn, drained*
¼	*cup snipped chives*

In a 3-quart saucepan, combine the stock, vinegar and honey. Bring to a boil. Reduce the heat to a gentle simmer.

Add the asparagus and corn. Simmer until the asparagus is tender but still vibrant green, about 3 minutes for thin stalks. Serve sprinkled with the chives.

Preparation time: 5 minutes
Cooking time: 8 minutes

Per serving: 49 calories, 0.2 g. fat (3% of calories), 1 g. dietary fiber, no cholesterol, 354 mg. sodium.

LONDON BROIL

1   tablespoon Worcestershire sauce
3   cloves garlic, minced
¾   teaspoon ground allspice
¾   teaspoon dried thyme
½   teaspoon dry mustard
2   pounds top round, about 2" thick

In a large glass baking dish, combine the Worcestershire sauce, garlic, allspice, thyme and mustard. Add the meat to the dish and rub the marinade over the surface.

Allow to marinate for 30 minutes. Broil or grill the meat for about 8 minutes per side for rare. Carve into thin slices.

Preparation time: 5 minutes plus marinating time
Cooking time: 10 minutes

Per serving: 239 calories, 6.6 g. fat (26% of calories), no dietary fiber, 101 mg. cholesterol, 70 mg. sodium.

LEAN GRAVY

MAKES 2 CUPS

2   tablespoons cornstarch
2   cups defatted beef stock

In a 1-quart saucepan, dissolve the cornstarch in about ¼ cup stock. Whisk in the remaining 1¾ cups stock. Cook over medium heat until the stock comes to a boil and thickens.

Preparation time: 1 minute
Cooking time: 5 minutes

Per ¼ cup: 23 calories, 0.3 g. fat (12% of calories), trace dietary fiber, trace cholesterol, 5 mg. sodium.

CHEESE-STUFFED POTATOES

SERVES 8

4   *large potatoes, baked*
⅔   *cup dry-curd cottage cheese*
⅓   *cup buttermilk*
1   *large carrot, finely shredded*
2   *tablespoons minced fresh parsley*
1   *teaspoon dried thyme*
    Pinch of paprika
2   *tablespoons grated Parmesan cheese*

Slice the potatoes in half lengthwise. Scoop out the centers with a spoon, leaving ¼" thick shells.

Mash the centers roughly with a fork and place in a medium bowl. Add the cottage cheese, buttermilk, carrots, parsley, thyme and paprika. Mix well. Spoon the filling into the potato shells. Sprinkle with the Parmesan.

Bake at 350° for 15 minutes, or until heated through. (If the potatoes are still warm from being baked, you may simply broil the stuffed halves until the tops are lightly browned and the filling is warmed through.)

Preparation time: 10 minutes
Cooking time: 5 minutes

Per serving: 86 calories, 0.8 g. fat (8% of calories), 2.1 g. dietary fiber, 2 mg. cholesterol, 55 mg. sodium.

ORANGE-GLAZED CARROTS

SERVES 8

2   *pounds carrots, thickly sliced*
2   *tablespoons orange marmalade*
2   *tablespoons orange juice*
2   *tablespoons prepared horseradish*

Place the carrots in a large no-stick frying pan. Add cold water to cover.

Cover and cook over medium heat for 10 minutes, or until just tender. Drain.

Add the marmalade, orange juice and horseradish to the pan. Cook, stirring frequently, until all the liquid has evaporated and the carrots are glazed.

Preparation time: 5 minutes
Cooking time: 15 minutes

Per serving: 66 calories, 0.2 g. fat (3% of calories), 3.7 g. dietary fiber, no cholesterol, 81 mg. sodium.

APPLE CRUMB PIE

SERVES 8

8	large baking apples, peeled and thinly sliced
1	tablespoon lemon juice
½	cup maple syrup
1	cup unbleached flour
2	tablespoons butter-flavored sprinkles
2	tablespoons oil
1	tablespoon corn syrup
½	teaspoon ground cinnamon
¼	teaspoon ground allspice

In a large bowl, combine the apples, lemon juice and ¼ cup maple syrup. Set aside.

In a food processor, combine the flour, sprinkles, oil, corn syrup, cinnamon, allspice and remaining ¼ cup maple syrup. Process with on/off turns until well mixed and crumbly. Sprinkle about two-thirds of the mixture over the apples and toss to mix well.

Divide the apples between 2 (9") pie plates or place in a 9" × 13" baking dish. Sprinkle with the remaining crumbs.

Bake at 375° for 20 minutes. Cover loosely with foil and bake another 20 minutes, or until the apples are tender but not mushy.

Preparation time: 15 minutes
Baking time: 40 minutes

Per serving: 227 calories, 3.9 g. fat (15% of calories), 3.1 g. dietary fiber, no cholesterol, 54 mg. sodium.

A Pizza Party

*E*verybody loves pizza. Making your own is easier than you might think. And preparing pizza at home lets you control the amount of fat in an otherwise high-calorie item. What's more, you can top your pies with interesting foods generally not available at the pizzeria. To add to the festive air of your party, give guests two different pizzas to choose from and colorful sundaes for dessert.

Menu

RASPBERRY JULEPS
SMOKED CHICKEN APPETIZERS
BROCCOLI PIZZA
TURKEY AND MUSHROOM PIZZA
EASY PEA SALAD
SUMMER SUNDAES

RASPBERRY JULEPS

SERVES 8

¼   *cup fresh mint leaves*
¼   *cup lemon juice*
2   *tablespoons honey*
6   *cups orange juice*
1⅓   *cups raspberry puree*

In a blender, combine the mint, lemon juice and honey. Puree until the mint is very finely chopped. Pour into a large pitcher. Stir in the orange juice and raspberry puree. Serve over ice.

Preparation time: 2 minutes
Chef's Note: When preparing these juleps, don't be tempted to blend the orange juice and raspberry puree in the blender, or the mixture will separate.

Per serving: 112 calories, 0.5 g. fat (4% of calories), 2.4 g. dietary fiber, no cholesterol, 2 mg. sodium.

SMOKED CHICKEN APPETIZERS

3   tablespoons all-fruit preserves

6   ounces lightly smoked chicken breast, sliced
    paper-thin

2   tart apples, cut into 8 wedges

1   papaya, cut into lengthwise slices ½" wide

24 strawberries

1   tablespoon curry powder

1   cup nonfat yogurt

Place the preserves in a small bowl and microwave on high for 1 minute, or until melted. (Or melt in a small saucepan over medium-low heat.) Lightly brush the top surface of each chicken slice with the preserves.

Wrap the chicken around each piece of fruit, cutting the meat to fit. Cut the apple slices in half and the papaya slices into bite-size pieces; leave the strawberries whole. Fasten the chicken in place with food picks.

Heat the curry powder in a small no-stick frying pan over medium heat until fragrant, about 1½ minutes. Stir into the yogurt and use as a dipping sauce for the fruit.

Preparation time: 10 minutes

Per serving: 82 calories, 1.2 g. fat (12% of calories), 2.2 g. dietary fiber, 23 mg. cholesterol, 203 mg. sodium.

PIZZA IN A FLASH

*H*omemade pizza is more than delicious—it's faster than a speeding delivery truck to make from scratch. For absolutely no fuss, you can buy premade shells that are ready for baking, or you can use flat breads such as Boboli or pita as your base. But you can still have totally homemade pizza in no time flat with this easy crust.

BASIC PIZZA CRUST

MAKES 2 CRUSTS

*U*sing whole-wheat flour gives you an extra measure of dietary fiber that all-white crusts lack.

- 2 *cups warm (about 115°) water*
- 2 *packages quick-rising yeast*
- 4 *cups unbleached flour*
- 3 *cups whole-wheat flour*

In a large bowl, combine the water and yeast. Stir and allow to proof for 5 minutes, or until foamy. Stir in the unbleached flour and mix well with a wooden spoon. Gradually add enough whole-wheat flour to form a soft but kneadable dough.

Turn out onto a lightly floured surface and knead until smooth, about 5 minutes. Divide in half, form each part into a ball, and let rest for 5 minutes.

Coat 2 large baking sheets with no-stick spray. Place 1 ball of dough on each sheet and shape into a 14" circle with a slightly raised edge. (The dough is now ready for your choice of toppings. Bake at about 475° for 10 to 12 minutes.)

Preparation time: 15 minutes

Chef's Note: If you'd like, you may divide the dough into more balls and make smaller pizzas. For individual pies, form 16 balls and shape them into 4" circles.

BROCCOLI PIZZA

SERVES 8

½ recipe for Basic Pizza Crust (opposite page)
1 cup diced onions
1 teaspoon olive oil
1 cup nonfat sour cream
3 cups small broccoli florets, lightly steamed
⅔ cup shredded reduced-fat Cheddar cheese
2 tablespoons grated Parmesan cheese

Prepare the crust as directed.

In a 2-cup glass measure, combine the onions and oil. Cover with vented plastic wrap and microwave on high for 2 minutes, or until the onions are softened. Stir in the sour cream. Spread over the pizza crust, leaving a ½" border. Top with the broccoli. Sprinkle with the Cheddar and Parmesan.

Bake on the bottom shelf of the oven at 475° for 10 to 12 minutes, or until the crust is nicely browned.

Preparation time: 20 minutes
Baking time: 15 minutes

Chef's Note: If you don't have a microwave, sauté the onions in the oil until soft.

Per serving: 233 calories, 1.9 g. fat (7% of calories), 5.1 g. dietary fiber, 1 mg. cholesterol, 62 mg. sodium.

TURKEY AND MUSHROOM PIZZA

SERVES 8

½ recipe for Basic Pizza Crust (opposite page)
1½ cups tomato sauce
1½ cups thinly sliced mushrooms
½ cup shredded turkey pastrami
½ cup diced green peppers
½ teaspoon dried oregano

Prepare the crust as directed.

Spoon the tomato sauce over the crust, leaving a ½" border. Sprinkle with the mushrooms, pastrami, peppers and oregano.

Bake on the bottom shelf of the oven at 475° for 10 to 12 minutes, or until the crust is nicely browned.

Preparation time: 20 minutes
Baking time: 15 minutes

Per serving: 218 calories, 1.3 g. fat (5% of calories), 4.8 g. dietary fiber, 5 mg. cholesterol, 107 mg. sodium.

EASY PEA SALAD

SERVES 8

2   *boxes (10 ounces each) frozen peas, thawed*
½   *cup diced sweet red peppers*
¼   *cup finely chopped scallions*
¼   *cup shredded nonfat mozzarella cheese*
1   *tablespoon minced fresh basil*
½   *cup nonfat mayonnaise*
½   *teaspoon Dijon mustard*
    Lettuce

In a large bowl, mix the peas, peppers, scallions, mozzarella and basil.

In a cup, mix the mayonnaise and mustard. Pour over the salad and mix well. Serve on a bed of the lettuce.

Preparation time: 10 minutes

Chef's Note: For an attractive presentation, spoon the peas into individual "cups" fashioned from the curved leaves of small heads of radicchio, Boston lettuce, butterhead lettuce or kale.

Per serving: 77 calories, 0.3 g. fat (4% of calories), 4.1 g. dietary fiber, 1 mg. cholesterol, 305 mg. sodium.

SUMMER SUNDAES

SERVES 8

2   *large bananas, thinly sliced*
2   *quarts nonfat frozen yogurt*
4   *cups berries or chopped fruit*
¼   *cup sliced almonds*

Divide the bananas among 8 dessert bowls. Top with scoops of the frozen yogurt. Sprinkle with the berries or chopped fruit and almonds.

Preparation time: 10 minutes

Per serving: 176 calories, 2.3 g. fat (11% of calories), 2.7 g. dietary fiber, no cholesterol, 55 mg. sodium.

SOME LIKE IT HOT

*F*or something a little more exotic, try this Indian meal. Start it with a very simple fresh fruit appetizer: thin wedges of cantaloupe, honeydew melon, mango or papaya spritzed with lime juice. Follow with a stewlike main dish that you can prepare ahead. Serve it with spicy rice and a pair of cool side dishes. Round out the meal with a light fruit dessert.

Menu

LIME-SCENTED FRUIT WEDGES
CURRIED LAMB
RICE PILAF WITH INDIAN SPICES
CUCUMBER RAITA
FRESH PINEAPPLE CHUTNEY
FIGS AND DATES WITH WHIPPED YOGURT

CURRIED LAMB

SERVES 8

2 pounds lean leg of lamb, trimmed of all
   visible fat and cut into ¾" cubes

2½ cups defatted beef stock

1½ cups chopped onions

1 cup chopped celery

1½ cups chopped tart apples

2 tablespoons chopped raisins

2 tablespoons curry powder

In a Dutch oven over medium-high heat, brown the lamb in 2 tablespoons stock; add more stock if needed.

Add the onions and celery. Cook, stirring, for 2 minutes more.

Reduce the heat and add the apples, raisins, curry powder and remaining stock. Cover and simmer for 40 minutes, or until the lamb is tender and the sauce is thickened.

Preparation time: 10 minutes
Cooking time: 45 minutes

Per serving: 206 calories, 6.3 g. fat (28% of calories), 1.7 g. dietary fiber, 76 mg. cholesterol, 98 mg. sodium.

RICE PILAF WITH INDIAN SPICES

SERVES 8

2 tablespoons chopped toasted almonds

2 cloves garlic, minced

½ teaspoon red-pepper flakes

¼ teaspoon fennel seeds, crushed

2 teaspoons olive oil

2½ cups defatted chicken stock

2 cups quick-cooking rice

1 carrot, finely diced

1 red pepper, finely diced

1 bay leaf

In a 3-quart saucepan over medium heat, sauté the almonds, garlic, pepper flakes and fennel seeds in the oil for 3 minutes.

Add the stock, rice, carrots, peppers and bay leaf. Bring to a boil. Reduce the heat to medium-low, cover the pan, and simmer for 10 minutes, or until the rice is tender and all the liquid has been absorbed. Fluff the rice with a fork. Remove and discard the bay leaf.

Preparation time: 10 minutes
Cooking time: 15 minutes

Per serving: 93 calories, 2.7 g. fat (28% of calories), 1.7 g. dietary fiber, no cholesterol, 30 mg. sodium.

CUCUMBER RAITA

SERVES 8

2	*teaspoons ground cumin*
4	*cucumbers, peeled and diced*
1	*cup nonfat yogurt*
½	*cup minced fresh coriander*
4	*scallions, finely chopped*
½	*teaspoon ground black pepper*

In a small no-stick frying pan over low heat, warm the cumin, stirring constantly, for 1 minute, or until fragrant.

In a large bowl, mix the cucumbers, yogurt, coriander, scallions and pepper. Sprinkle with the cumin and mix well. Chill until serving time.

Preparation time: 10 minutes plus chilling time

Per serving: 36 calories, 0.4 g. fat (10% of calories), 1.6 g. dietary fiber, trace cholesterol, 26 mg. sodium.

Fresh Pineapple Chutney

SERVES 8

2 small pineapples, peeled, cored and diced
½ cup minced fresh mint
1 green chili pepper, seeded and finely chopped (wear rubber gloves to protect your hands)
2 tablespoons grated fresh ginger
   Juice of 1 lime

In a large bowl, mix the pineapple, mint, peppers, ginger and lime juice. Let stand at room temperature for 30 minutes before serving.

Preparation time: 10 minutes plus marinating time

Chef's Note: For variety, you may replace all or part of the pineapple with diced melons, peaches, apples or mangoes.

Per serving: 62 calories, 0.5 g. fat (7% of calories), 1.6 g. dietary fiber, no cholesterol, 3 mg. sodium.

Figs and Dates with Whipped Yogurt

SERVES 8

2 cups nonfat yogurt
16 fresh figs, halved
12 pitted dates, quartered lengthwise
½ cup apple juice
¼ cup coarsely chopped walnuts
2 tablespoons honey

Line a colander with cheesecloth. Spoon in the yogurt and allow to drain over a bowl for at least 40 minutes. (Longer draining will produce a firmer cheese.)

Meanwhile, in a large bowl, toss together the figs, dates, apple juice and walnuts. Allow to marinate for 30 minutes.

Transfer the yogurt to a medium bowl. With a hand-held electric mixer, whip in the honey.

Spoon the fig mixture into dessert bowls or goblets. Top each serving with a spoonful of the yogurt.

Preparation time: 5 minutes plus draining and marinating time

Chef's Note: If you don't have fresh figs, use 16 dried figs. Place in a 2-quart saucepan, cover with water, and bring to a boil. Remove from the heat and let soak for at least 20 minutes. Drain and halve each lengthwise.

Per serving: 188 calories, 2.8 g. fat (12% of calories), 7.7 g. dietary fiber, 1 mg. cholesterol, 46 mg. sodium.

THE ORIENT EXPRESS

$\mathcal{C}$hinese food is always popular. You can throw together a nifty Oriental meal that's lower in fat than what most take-out establishments offer.

> ## Menu
>
> VEGETABLE ROLLS
> STIR-FRIED BROCCOLI MEDLEY
> SIZZLING BEANS WITH PEANUTS
> FROZEN YOGURT WITH SWEET PEACH SAUCE

VEGETABLE ROLLS

SERVES 8

2   teaspoons oil
⅔   cup shredded carrots
1   cup thinly sliced onions
1   cup julienned scallions
1   cup mung bean sprouts
1   cup sliced mushrooms
8   egg whites, lightly beaten
16   small iceberg lettuce leaves

In a wok or large frying pan over medium-high heat, warm the oil. Add the carrots and onions; stir-fry for 3 minutes. Add the scallions, sprouts and mushrooms; stir-fry for 3 minutes more.

Add the egg whites to the vegetables. Stir slowly until the whites are cooked, about 1 minute.

Divide the vegetables evenly among the lettuce leaves. Loosely roll up the leaves to enclose the vegetables.

Preparation time: 10 minutes
Cooking time: 10 minutes

Chef's Note: You may replace the egg whites with 1 cup fat-free egg substitute. You may also use other types of lettuce, such as Boston and butterhead varieties. For an interesting presentation, use long chives or thin scallion strips to tie up the bundles.

Per serving: 48 calories, 1.3 g. fat (25% of calories), 1.3 g. dietary fiber, no cholesterol, 56 mg. sodium.

STIR-FRIED BROCCOLI MEDLEY

SERVES 8

½   cup pineapple juice
4   cups broccoli florets
4   sweet red peppers, thinly sliced
1   onion, thinly sliced
2   tablespoons oyster sauce
1   tablespoon low-sodium soy sauce
2   cloves garlic, minced
¼   cup crushed pineapple
6   cups hot cooked rice

In a wok or large frying pan over medium-high heat, bring the pineapple juice to a boil. Add the broccoli, peppers and onions. Toss to coat with the juice. Stir-fry for 5 minutes.

Add the oyster sauce, soy sauce and garlic. Stir-fry for 2 minutes. Add the pineapple and heat through.

Serve over the rice.

Preparation time: 10 minutes
Cooking time: 10 minutes

Chef's Note: Oyster sauce is a dark-brown, oyster-based condiment that gives Oriental dishes a rich taste without a hint of its seafood origin. Although it's high in sodium, you need only a small amount to achieve the desired effect.

Per serving: 242 calories, 0.8 g. fat (3% of calories), 3.7 g. dietary fiber, no cholesterol, 241 mg. sodium.

SIZZLING BEANS WITH PEANUTS

SERVES 8

2   pounds green beans
1   tablespoon minced fresh ginger
1   tablespoon low-sodium soy sauce
1   teaspoon peanut oil
1   clove garlic, minced
3   tablespoons chopped roasted peanuts

Steam the beans until just tender, about 4 minutes.

In a cup, combine the ginger, soy sauce, oil and garlic.

While the beans are cooking, heat a large cast-iron frying pan over medium heat until hot, about 4 minutes. Add half of the beans and half of the ginger mixture. Sauté for about 5 minutes. Transfer to a platter and keep warm. Repeat with the remaining beans and ginger mixture. Sprinkle with the peanuts.

Preparation time: 10 minutes
Cooking time: 15 minutes

Per serving: 56 calories, 1.8 g. fat (26% of calories), 2.8 g. dietary fiber, no cholesterol, 100 mg. sodium.

FROZEN YOGURT WITH SWEET PEACH SAUCE

8   peaches, peeled and chopped

2   tablespoons frozen apple juice concentrate,
    thawed

1   tablespoon lemon juice

¼   teaspoon grated nutmeg

2   quarts nonfat frozen vanilla yogurt

In a blender or food processor, puree the peaches, juice concentrate, lemon juice and nutmeg.

Divide the frozen yogurt among 8 dessert bowls or sherbet glasses. Top with the sauce.

Preparation time: 10 minutes

Chef's Note: The easiest way to peel fresh peaches is to drop them into boiling water for about 15 seconds, then rinse with cold water. Use a paring knife to pull the loosened peel free.

Per serving: 259 calories, 0.1 g. fat (<1% of calories), 0.1 g. dietary fiber, no cholesterol, 107 mg. sodium.

CHAPTER 10

A CORNUCOPIA
OF EASY
ACCOMPANIMENTS

ALL THINGS ASIDE

When you're committed to a low-fat diet, side dishes take on new importance. They allow you to extend modest amounts of meat and other protein, so you can keep your diet as lean as possible. But don't fall into the trap of preparing those side dishes with lots of butter, cheese or other fatty flavorings. Turn instead to herbs, spices, full-bodied stock and other no-fat flavorings. And take advantage of cooking methods that safeguard both nutrients and taste, such as microwaving and lightning-quick sautéing. In addition, expand your repertoire of lean, grain-based accompaniments, such as pilafs and stuffings, to satisfy your hunger without sacrificing your waistline.

Vegetable Side Dishes

Microwaving, steaming and stir-frying are not only very quick ways to cook vegetables but also very nutritious ones. Cooking times are so short that nutrients are retained. And because all three methods require either little or no added fat, they keep vegetables light and lean. The following recipes show you how it's done.

Dill Cabbage Wedges

SERVES 4

This makes a wonderful St. Patrick's Day dish, but you needn't wait until then to enjoy it.

1   head (about 1¼ pounds) cabbage
1   small onion, thinly sliced
1   carrot, finely chopped
1   teaspoon dried dill
⅔   cup defatted chicken stock

Snap off any tough outer leaves from the cabbage and slice off the stem. Cut the cabbage in half through the core, then slice each half into quarters, making 8 wedges.

Arrange the wedges in 2 concentric circles in a 9" glass pie plate. (The dish will be pretty full.) Sprinkle with the onions, carrots and dill. Pour on the stock. Cover the plate with vented plastic wrap.

Microwave on high for 6 minutes. Rotate the dish a half turn and microwave on high for 6 minutes, or until the cabbage is tender. Let stand, covered, for about 5 minutes to finish cooking. Drain.

Preparation time: 10 minutes
Cooking time: 15 minutes

Chef's Note: If you don't have a microwave, steam the cabbage and other vegetables until tender, about 20 minutes. Sprinkle with the dill.

Per serving: 46 calories, 0.4 g. fat (7% of calories), 3.4 g. dietary fiber, no cholesterol, 31 mg. sodium.

LEAN AND EASY RATATOUILLE

*R*atatouille is a gardener's dream—it's such an ideal way to use tomatoes, zucchini, peppers and eggplant. Traditional recipes have large amounts of fat and require lots of time over a hot stove. But this microwave method updates the classic dish, slashing calories, fat and time in the process. Although you generally serve ratatouille hot, you can also chill it and serve it as a salad on a bed of lettuce.

1	*medium onion, chopped*
½	*teaspoon olive oil*
1	*small eggplant, peeled and cubed*
2	*small zucchini, cubed*
3	*medium tomatoes, seeded and chopped*
1	*green pepper, chopped*
¼	*cup minced fresh parsley*
3	*tablespoons tomato paste*
2	*cloves garlic, minced*
1	*teaspoon dried basil*
1	*teaspoon dried thyme*
1	*tablespoon white wine vinegar*

Combine the onions and oil in a 3-quart casserole dish. Cover with vented plastic wrap and microwave on high for 1½ minutes, or until the onions are tender.

Stir in the eggplant, zucchini, tomatoes, peppers, parsley, tomato paste, garlic, basil and thyme. Cover again and microwave on high, stirring occasionally, for 15 minutes, or until the vegetables are tender.

Stir in the vinegar. Let stand for 10 minutes.

Preparation time: 15 minutes
Cooking time: 20 minutes

(continued)

Chef's Note: If you don't have a microwave, combine the ingredients in a large pot. Add ½ cup water. Cover and simmer for about 40 minutes. Remove the lid and cook, stirring often, until thick, about 10 minutes more.

Per serving: 82 calories, 1.3 g. fat (14% of calories), 4 g. dietary fiber, no cholesterol, 23 mg. sodium.

GLAZED BRUSSELS SPROUTS AND CHESTNUTS

SERVES 4

icrowaving is an easy and efficient way to cook chestnuts. Just be sure to slash the shells before cooking so that they don't explode.

8   *ounces unshelled chestnuts*
2   *cups small brussels sprouts, trimmed*
1   *cup small white onions, peeled*
½   *cup defatted chicken stock*
2   *tablespoons maple syrup*
2   *teaspoons apple cider vinegar*
½   *teaspoon ground black pepper*

With a sharp knife, cut an ✕ in the flat side of each chestnut shell. Place in a single layer in a 9" glass pie plate. Microwave on high for 2 minutes. Flip the pieces and microwave on high for 1 to 2 minutes, or until the nuts are soft when squeezed. Let stand for 5 minutes, or until cool enough to handle. Remove the shells.

Meanwhile, blanch the brussels sprouts and onions in a large pot of boiling water for 5 minutes. Drain and transfer to a large frying pan.

Add the stock, maple syrup, vinegar and pepper. Cover and cook over medium heat for 5 minutes. Add the chestnuts and cook for 5 minutes, or until the brussels sprouts are just tender. Remove the lid and cook, stirring, until the liquid is reduced to a glaze.

Preparation time: 15 minutes
Cooking time: 15 minutes

Chef's Note: If you don't have a microwave, either bake the slit chestnuts at 375° for about 15 minutes or boil them for about the same amount of time.

Per serving: 125 calories, 1.1 g. fat (8% of calories), 4.9 g. dietary fiber, no cholesterol, 38 mg. sodium.

CRUNCHY SPINACH

SERVES 4

istachios add an unexpected element of flavor to cooked fresh spinach. When preparing spinach, be sure to rinse it well in cold water to remove any sand or grit that might be clinging to the leaves. Shake off excess water, but don't be concerned about drying the leaves. The moisture that stays on them will help speed up the cooking process.

1½   *tablespoons chopped pistachios*
¼   *cup defatted chicken stock*
2   *red onions, thinly sliced*
1   *pound fresh spinach, thick stems removed*
½   *teaspoon grated nutmeg*
1   *teaspoon grated Parmesan cheese*

In a no-stick frying pan over medium-high heat, toast the pistachios for about 2 minutes, or until fragrant and lightly colored. Remove from the pan and set aside.

Heat the stock in the pan and add the onions. Cook for 3 to 5 minutes, or until tender. Add the spinach and nutmeg. Cover and cook until the spinach is limp, about 2 minutes.

Add the pistachios. Toss lightly. Sprinkle with the Parmesan.

Preparation time: 10 minutes
Cooking time: 10 minutes

Per serving: 74 calories, 2.7 g. fat (29% of calories), 4.8 g. dietary fiber, 1 mg. cholesterol, 120 mg. sodium.

PINEAPPLE-STUFFED ACORN SQUASH

*M*icrowaving makes winter squash an everyday vegetable, cutting about 50 minutes off the usual baking time.

2 *medium acorn squash*
1 *cup nonfat cottage cheese*
⅓ *cup well-drained crushed pineapple*
¼ *cup minced fresh parsley*
1 *tablespoon minced scallions*

Cut the squash in half lengthwise; scoop out and discard the seeds. Place, cut side down, in a 7" × 11" baking dish. Microwave on high for 3 minutes. Rearrange the pieces. Microwave on high for 4 minutes, or until easily pierced with a fork. Flip the pieces so that the cut sides are facing up.

In a small bowl, mix the cottage cheese, pineapple, parsley and scallions. Spoon into the squash cavities. If desired, microwave on high for 1 minute to slightly heat the filling.

Preparation time: 10 minutes
Cooking time: 10 minutes

Chef's Note: If you don't have a microwave, coat a baking dish with no-stick spray and place the squash, cut side down, in the dish. Add about ½ cup water. Cover with foil and bake at 375° for 1 hour, or until easily pierced with a fork. Fill with the cottage cheese mixture.

Per serving: 92 calories, 1 g. fat (9% of calories), 4.8 g. dietary fiber, 3 mg. cholesterol, 104 mg. sodium.

SANTA FE CORN

SERVES 4

*S*erve this spicy corn with poached fish, scrambled eggs, grilled chicken or sautéed lean pork. You may also use it as filling for tortillas.

2   *cups corn*
2   *cups peeled, seeded and chopped tomatoes*
1   *medium onion, chopped*
3   *cloves garlic, minced*
1   *teaspoon chili powder*
½   *teaspoon ground cumin*
½   *teaspoon ground coriander*
½   *teaspoon dried oregano*
⅛   *teaspoon hot-pepper sauce*

In a 2-quart saucepan over medium heat, bring the corn, tomatoes, onions, garlic, chili powder, cumin, coriander, oregano and pepper sauce to a boil. Cook, stirring occasionally, for 20 minutes, or until the mixture is thickened.

Preparation time: 5 minutes
Cooking time: 20 minutes

Per serving: 102 calories, 1.4 g. fat (11% of calories), 3.1 g. dietary fiber, no cholesterol, 26 mg. sodium.

STEAMED UP OVER FRESH VEGETABLES

*S*teaming is an ideal way to cook vegetables. It's fast, simple (no fancy equipment) and smart: You retain not only vitamins but also the bright colors and distinctive flavors that characterize all your garden favorites. Best of all, vegetables that aren't overcooked don't *need* fatty sauces to make them appealing.

Use a pot with a tight-fitting lid. Bring about 1 inch of water to a boil in it, then add your vegetables in their steamer basket (whether metal or bamboo). Just make sure the basket sits above the water. Cover the pot and cook for the minimum amount of time listed below. Check for tenderness, and if needed, cook a little longer.

VEGETABLE	FORM	TIME (minutes)
Asparagus	Whole spears	3–5
Beans, green	Whole	5–7
Beans, lima	Shelled	5–7
Broccoli	Medium stalks	7–10
Brussels sprouts	Whole	10–12
Cabbage	Quartered heads	8–10
Carrots	Whole medium	5–7
Cauliflower	Florets	12–15
Corn	Kernels	5–7
Corn	Whole cobs	7–10
Fennel	Quartered heads	10–12
Greens	Whole leaves	3–5
Parsnips	Whole medium	10
Peas	Shelled	3–5
Peas, snap	Whole pods	5
Peas, snow	Whole pods	3
Potatoes	Cut into chunks	7–10
Potatoes	Whole medium	18–20
Squash, summer	Sliced	7
Squash, winter	Cut into large chunks	20–25
Turnips	Quartered	12–15

ORANGE AND POMEGRANATE RELISH

MAKES 2 CUPS

*T*his side dish goes particularly well with roast turkey and makes an interesting alternative to cranberry sauce.

2 *large navel oranges*

1 *pomegranate*

1 *tomato, diced*

2 *tablespoons thinly sliced scallions*

1 *tablespoon minced hot chili peppers (wear rubber gloves to protect your hands)*

1 *tablespoon lime juice*

½ *teaspoon ground cumin*

Peel the oranges, being sure to remove all the bitter white pith. Free each section from its surrounding membranes. Coarsely chop the orange sections. Transfer to a medium bowl.

Break the pomegranate apart to release its seeds. Add the seeds to the bowl.

Stir in the tomatoes, scallions, peppers, lime juice and cumin. Cover and chill.

Preparation time: 15 minutes plus chilling time

Per ¼ cup: 41 calories, 0.2 g. fat (3% of calories), 1.6 g. dietary fiber, no cholesterol, 2 mg. sodium.

MEDITERRANEAN GREEN BEANS

*T*hese beans are extra easy to prepare. For variety, you may turn them into a cold salad. Increase the vinegar to ⅓ cup and add ½ teaspoon olive oil. Chill and serve over shredded lettuce.

1	*pound green beans*
1	*tablespoon red wine vinegar*
1	*teaspoon Dijon mustard*
1	*clove garlic, minced*
½	*teaspoon dried oregano*
¼	*teaspoon ground black pepper*

Steam the beans for 5 minutes, or until just tender.

In a large bowl, whisk together the vinegar, mustard, garlic, oregano and pepper. Add the beans and toss to coat.

Preparation time: 5 minutes
Cooking time: 5 minutes

Per serving: 38 calories, 0.2 g. fat (4% of calories), 3.5 g. dietary fiber, no cholesterol, 23 mg. sodium.

HERB-SCENTED RED ONIONS

*C*ooked onions have a sweet, mellow flavor that complements poultry, fish and any type of meat. This recipe calls for an oven cooking bag, but you may also use a casserole with a tight-fitting lid. (In that case, you may omit the flour.)

> 1 tablespoon unbleached flour
> 4 large red onions, quartered
> 4 plum tomatoes, quartered
> 1 clove garlic, minced
> ½ teaspoon dried basil
> ¼ teaspoon dried thyme
> ¼ cup defatted chicken stock

Place the flour in an oven cooking bag and shake to lightly coat the bag. Add the onions and tomatoes. Sprinkle with the garlic, basil and thyme. Add the stock and close the bag with the plastic tie that comes with it. Place the bag on a plate or in a baking dish. Make several 1" slashes in the top of the bag.

Microwave on high for 3 minutes. Carefully lift the edges of the bag to rearrange the vegetables. Give the plate a half turn. Microwave on high for 2 minutes. Let stand for 5 minutes to finish cooking. Slit open the bag and transfer the vegetables to a serving dish.

Preparation time: 10 minutes
Cooking time: 5 minutes

Per serving: 85 calories, 0.6 g. fat (6% of calories), 3.4 g. dietary fiber, no cholesterol, 16 mg. sodium.

BROCCOLI AND RED PEPPERS

SERVES 4

*M*icrowaving broccoli helps preserve its health-building nutrients and lets you get a really nutritious side dish on the table fast. To turn this recipe into a main course, toss the cooked vegetables with your choice of pasta.

1   *head (about 1¼ pounds) broccoli*
2   *tablespoons water*
1   *teaspoon margarine*
⅓   *cup minced sweet red peppers*
⅓   *cup minced onions*
2   *tablespoons defatted chicken stock*
½   *teaspoon dried thyme*
1   *tablespoon grated Romano cheese*

Chop the broccoli into ¾" pieces. Arrange them in a 9" glass pie plate, with the floret pieces in the middle and the stems around the edge. Sprinkle with the water. Cover with vented plastic wrap and microwave on high for 5 minutes, or until tender. Drain and set aside.

Place the margarine in a large bowl. Microwave on high for 20 seconds, or until melted. Stir in the peppers, onions, stock and thyme. Cover with vented plastic wrap and microwave on high for 3 minutes, or until the vegetables are tender.

Add the broccoli and toss well. Sprinkle with the Romano.

Preparation time: 10 minutes
Cooking time: 10 minutes

Chef's Note: If you don't have a microwave, steam the broccoli until tender. Then lightly sauté the remaining ingredients until tender.

Per serving: 63 calories, 1.9 g. fat (27% of calories), 5.2 g. dietary fiber, 1 mg. cholesterol, 73 mg. sodium.

SAUTÉED CUKES WITH CHIVES

SERVES 4

ou might never have considered cooking cucumbers, but they turn out mild and just slightly crunchy. You'll notice that the percentage of calories from fat in this dish is a little high, but the actual grams of fat is quite low.

3   medium cucumbers
1   teaspoon olive oil
2   tablespoons snipped chives
1   tablespoon minced fresh basil
2   teaspoons lemon juice
¼   teaspoon ground black pepper

Peel the cucumbers and halve lengthwise. Unless the seeds are very small, remove them with the tip of a spoon. Cut the cucumbers into ⅓" slices.

In a large frying pan over medium-high heat, warm the oil for 1 minute. Add the cucumbers and stir-fry for 5 minutes. Sprinkle with the chives, basil, lemon juice and pepper. Toss to coat.

Preparation time: 10 minutes
Cooking time: 5 minutes

Per serving: 41 calories, 1.4 g. fat (28% of calories), 2.3 g. dietary fiber, no cholesterol, 5 mg. sodium.

GINGER-GLAZED CARROTS

SERVES 4

*F*or variety, you may also prepare these carrots with pineapple juice.

- 1 *pound carrots, thinly sliced crosswise*
- ¾ *cup orange juice*
- 2 *teaspoons cornstarch*
- ¼ *teaspoon powdered ginger*
  Pinch of grated nutmeg
  Pinch of ground cinnamon

Steam the carrots for 5 minutes, or until just tender.

In a 2-quart saucepan, mix the orange juice and cornstarch until dissolved. Stirring constantly, bring to a boil over medium heat and continue cooking until thick, about 2 minutes. Stir in the ginger, nutmeg and cinnamon. Add the carrots and stir to coat.

Preparation time: 10 minutes
Cooking time: 10 minutes

Per serving: 75 calories, 0.3 g. fat (4% of calories), 4 g. dietary fiber, no cholesterol, 40 mg. sodium.

GRAINS AND MORE

For really quick side dishes, count on fast-cooking grains and legumes, such as barley, millet and lentils. They'll help you get a healthy dinner on the table in practically no time. The following recipes can be ready in half an hour or less.

BARLEY PILAF

SERVES 4

*T*his satisfying side dish uses quick-cooking barley, which is ready in a fraction of the time needed for regular pearl barley. Serve the pilaf with sautéed chicken breast or pork tenderloin cutlets.

 2 *cups defatted chicken stock*
 1 *cup quick-cooking barley*
 1 *bay leaf*
 1 *teaspoon olive oil*
 1 *cup diced carrots*
 1 *onion, diced*
 ¼ *cup sliced scallions*
 1 *clove garlic, minced*

In a 2-quart saucepan, combine the stock, barley and bay leaf. Bring to a boil. Cover and cook over medium-low heat for 15 minutes, or until the barley is tender and the liquid has been absorbed. Remove and discard the bay leaf. Fluff the barley with a fork and set aside.

Meanwhile, in a large no-stick frying pan over medium heat, warm the oil for 1 minute. Add the carrots, onions, scallions and garlic. Stir-fry for 5 minutes, or until the vegetables are just tender. Add the barley and toss to combine.

Preparation time: 5 minutes
Cooking time: 15 minutes

Per serving: 170 calories, 2.7 g. fat (13% of calories), 5.4 g. dietary fiber, no cholesterol, 52 mg. sodium.

MEXICAN LENTILS AND RICE

SERVES 4

*L*entils cook so quickly that you can serve them often. Here they're paired with rice for a savory accompaniment to poached chicken or fish.

2	*teaspoons olive oil*
1	*cup diced carrots*
1	*cup diced sweet red peppers*
¼	*cup finely chopped onions*
½	*cup rice*
½	*cup lentils*
2	*cups defatted chicken stock*
½	*teaspoon chili powder*
½	*teaspoon ground cumin*
1	*cup peas*

In a 2-quart saucepan over medium-high heat, warm the oil for 30 seconds. Add the carrots, peppers and onions; sauté for 2 minutes. Add the rice and lentils; sauté for 2 minutes.

Add the stock, chili powder and cumin. Bring to a boil. Stir once, cover, and simmer for 12 minutes. Add the peas. Cover and cook for another 5 to 7 minutes, or until the rice is tender and the liquid has been absorbed.

Preparation time: 10 minutes
Cooking time: 25 minutes

Per serving: 253 calories, 3.7 g. fat (13% of calories), 4.2 g. dietary fiber, no cholesterol, 95 mg. sodium.

HEARTY GRAINS IN A HURRY

Grains should be a mainstay in any healthy, low-fat diet. Most have barely any fat of their own, and they can be cooked in ways that keep them very lean. In addition, they're high in the complex carbohydrates that are filling but not fattening.

One drawback to some grains has been the long cooking time they require. But many of these, including barley, corn grits and brown rice, now come in quick varieties. And others, such as bulgur and white rice, have always been fast to prepare.

This easy reference table gives time and liquid guidelines for some commonly available grains that you can incorporate into your everyday meals. Bring the liquid (use water or stock) to a boil and stir in the grain. Then cover the pan tightly, reduce the heat so that the liquid simmers, and cook until all the liquid has been absorbed. Turn off the heat and let the pan stand, covered, for about 5 minutes. Then fluff the grain with a fork to separate the kernels.

GRAIN (1 cup dry)	LIQUID (cups)	TIME (minutes)	YIELD (cups)
Barley, quick	2	10–15	3
Bulgur	2	15–20	2½
Couscous	1½	5	3
Grits, quick	4	5–7	4
Kasha (buckwheat)	2	15–20	3
Millet	2	30	4
Rice, quick brown	1¼	10–15	2
Rice, white	2	20	3

MILLET WITH BROCCOLI

SERVES 6

*M*illet is an oft-neglected grain that's both delicious and easy to prepare. Here it gets a little extra tang from a splash of vinegar.

> 2 *cups defatted chicken stock*
> 1 *cup millet*
> 2 *cups bite-size broccoli florets*
> 1 *onion, thinly sliced*
> 1 *clove garlic, minced*
> ¼ *teaspoon red-pepper flakes*
> 1 *teaspoon olive oil*
> 2 *tablespoons red wine vinegar*
> ¼ *teaspoon ground black pepper*
> 2 *tablespoons grated Parmesan cheese*

In a 2-quart saucepan over high heat, bring the stock to a boil. Stir in the millet. Reduce the heat to medium-low, cover the pan, and cook for 25 minutes, or until the millet is tender and all the liquid has been absorbed. Remove from the heat and fluff with a fork.

Meanwhile, steam the broccoli until just tender, about 5 minutes. Set aside.

In a large no-stick frying pan over medium heat, sauté the onions, garlic and pepper flakes in the oil for 5 minutes. Stir in the broccoli and millet. Sprinkle with the vinegar and pepper; toss well to combine. Sprinkle with the Parmesan.

Preparation time: 10 minutes
Cooking time: 25 minutes

Per serving: 174 calories, 3.4 g. fat (17% of calories), 6.2 g. dietary fiber, 2 mg. cholesterol, 77 mg. sodium.

SOUTHWESTERN CORNBREAD

This cornbread gets added texture from corn kernels and scallions. You can crumble leftovers for use in Spicy Cornbread Stuffing (page 260).

1½	cups yellow cornmeal
1	cup unbleached flour
1	tablespoon baking powder
½	teaspoon turmeric
¼	teaspoon ground allspice
½	cup corn
¼	cup minced scallions
2	tablespoons minced fresh parsley
1½	cups buttermilk
¼	cup honey
¼	cup fat-free egg substitute
2	tablespoons oil

In a large bowl, whisk together the cornmeal, flour, baking powder, turmeric and allspice. Stir in the corn, scallions and parsley.

In a medium bowl, mix the buttermilk, honey, egg and oil. Pour over the dry ingredients. Mix with a rubber spatula until the dry ingredients are moistened; do not overmix.

Coat a 9" × 9" baking dish with no-stick spray. Add the batter and smooth the top with the spatula. Bake at 375° for 25 minutes, or until a cake tester inserted in the middle comes out clean. Serve warm or cold.

Preparation time: 10 minutes
Baking time: 25 minutes

Per serving: 205 calories, 4.4 g. fat (19% of calories), 3.8 g. dietary fiber, 2 mg. cholesterol, 171 mg. sodium.

SPICY CORNBREAD STUFFING

*I*t's always smart to bake the stuffing for poultry separately. That way, it won't soak up any fat from the bird.

2	*stalks celery, minced*
2	*carrots, minced*
1	*onion, minced*
1	*teaspoon olive oil*
4	*cups coarsely crumbled cornbread*
2	*teaspoons red-pepper flakes*
½	*teaspoon dried sage*
½	*teaspoon dried thyme*
¼	*cup fat-free egg substitute*
2–3	*cups defatted chicken stock*

In a large bowl, combine the celery, carrots, onions and oil. Cover with vented plastic wrap and microwave on high for 4 minutes, or until the vegetables are tender.

Add the cornbread, pepper flakes, sage and thyme. Toss to mix well. Add the egg and 2 cups stock. Stir well. If the bread is really dry, add enough of the remaining 1 cup stock to moisten it but not make it soggy.

Coat a 2- or 3-quart casserole with no-stick spray. Add the stuffing. Cover with foil. Bake at 350° for 20 minutes. Remove the foil and bake for 5 minutes to crisp the top.

Preparation time: 15 minutes
Baking time: 25 minutes

Chef's Note: If you don't have a microwave, sauté the vegetables in the oil until tender, about 10 minutes.

Per serving: 106 calories, 2.6 g. fat (21% of calories), 1.8 g. dietary fiber, trace cholesterol, 117 mg. sodium.

CHAPTER 11

DESSERTS
WITH A BIG
FAT
DIFFERENCE

$\mathscr{S}$IMPLE PLEASURES

ow sweet it is! You *can* enjoy fabulous, elegant desserts and still watch your weight, control your cholesterol and protect your heart. Naturally, fresh fruit—at the very peak of its ripeness—is the best dessert going. And we encourage you to make that your everyday dessert. But when your sweet tooth cries out for something more elaborate, you can gussy up these treats without sacrificing their innate goodness. Most of the desserts in this chapter contain lots of fruit. For super-special occasions, try something sinfully delicious, like Chocolate-Ginger Sorbet. And yes, it *is* healthy, thanks to the ingenious use of low-fat ingredients.

261

CHOCOLATE-GINGER SORBET

This simple sorbet has a rich taste and texture, but thanks to cocoa powder—which contains practically no fat—it's actually quite low in fat. Serve it all by itself or over sautéed bananas or poached pears. The recipe calls for fruit concentrate, which is available in health food stores.

1¾   cups skim milk
2   tablespoons grated fresh ginger
½   cup fruit concentrate
⅓   cup cocoa powder
2   tablespoons evaporated skim milk
1   teaspoon vanilla

In a 2-quart saucepan over medium heat, bring the skim milk and ginger almost to the boiling point. Strain into a medium bowl. Stir in the fruit concentrate, cocoa, evaporated skim milk and vanilla. Place in the freezer for 10 minutes, or until cool.

Transfer to the container of an ice-cream maker and freeze according to the manufacturer's directions. To serve, scoop into dessert bowls.

Preparation time: 15 minutes plus chilling time

Per serving: 204 calories, 1 g. fat (5% of calories), trace dietary fiber, 2 mg. cholesterol, 69 mg. sodium.

Pear and Raisin Strudel

This easy-to-assemble strudel is made with phyllo dough, which is available in the freezer section of most supermarkets. Traditional phyllo recipes use lots of butter to make the pastry layers crisp. But this strudel gets the same results—with just a fraction of the fat—by using a light coat of no-stick spray between the layers.

2½   *cups thinly sliced pears*
½   *cup raisins*
⅓   *cup maple syrup*
1   *tablespoon lemon juice*
¼   *teaspoon ground cinnamon*
¼   *teaspoon grated nutmeg*
8   *sheets phyllo dough*

In a large bowl, combine the pears, raisins, maple syrup, lemon juice, cinnamon and nutmeg.

To keep the dough from drying out as you work, unroll it onto a counter and cover with a barely damp towel. Peel off 1 sheet and place it flat on a dry section of the counter.

Spray the top of the sheet lightly with butter-flavored no-stick spray. Cover with a second sheet and brush very lightly with water. Repeat the process, coating alternate sheets with either spray or water, until all 8 sheets have been used.

Spoon the pear mixture onto the dough, positioning it along the lower half of the long side of the rectangle and leaving a 1" border on the sides and bottom. Fold in the sides and lightly coat with the spray. Starting at the bottom, roll the dough to enclose the pear mixture.

Coat a baking sheet with the spray. Transfer the roll, seam side down, to the sheet. Lightly brush the top with water. Bake at 350° for 30 to 35 minutes, or until golden. Serve warm or cold. To make slicing easier, use a serrated knife.

(continued)

Preparation time: 15 minutes
Baking time: 35 minutes

Per serving: 147 calories, 1.8 g. fat (11% of calories), 1.6 g. dietary fiber, no cholesterol, 3 mg. sodium.

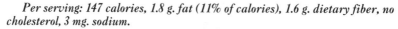

FRESH FRUIT TART

SERVES 8

*T*his dessert also uses phyllo dough for a low-fat alternative to a regular crust. Feel free to vary the fruit according to what's in season.

1½	*cups nonfat vanilla yogurt*
1½	*cups nonfat cottage cheese*
2	*tablespoons honey*
1	*teaspoon vanilla*
4	*sheets phyllo dough*
1½	*cups sliced plums*
½	*cup raspberries*
½	*cup blackberries*
2	*tablespoons all-fruit apricot preserves*

Spoon the yogurt into a yogurt cheese funnel or a sieve lined with cheesecloth. Place over a bowl and set aside to drain for at least 20 minutes.

Meanwhile, in a food processor, puree the cottage cheese, honey and vanilla until smooth, about 3 minutes. Transfer to a medium bowl. Set aside.

To keep the dough from drying out as you work, unroll it onto a counter and cover with a barely damp towel. Drape 1 sheet across a 9" or 10" pie plate. Press it into the plate; fold the edges roughly toward the center, crumpling them slightly to fit. Coat the top with no-stick spray. Repeat with the remaining sheets, spraying each.

Bake at 375° for 5 to 7 minutes, or until golden brown. Let cool for at least 15 minutes.

Fold the drained yogurt into the cottage cheese mixture.

Carefully spread the mixture in the crust, smoothing the surface with a rubber spatula. Arrange the plums, raspberries and blackberries over the surface. Melt the preserves in a small saucepan. Brush over the fruit to glaze it.

Preparation time: 30 minutes
Baking time: 10 minutes

Per serving: 137 calories, 0.9 g. fat (6% of calories), 3.7 g. dietary fiber, 3 mg. cholesterol, 106 mg. sodium.

PEACH TART

SERVES 6

This recipe uses canned sliced peaches, but you may substitute thawed frozen or peeled fresh fruit.

> 1   *can (29 ounces) sliced peaches, drained*
> ¾   *cup rolled oats*
> 1   *cup skim milk*
> ½   *cup fat-free egg substitute*
> 2   *tablespoons honey*
> 1   *teaspoon vanilla*
> ¼   *teaspoon ground cinnamon*

Coat a deep 9" pie plate with no-stick spray. Arrange the peaches in the dish.

In a blender, finely chop the oats. Add the milk, eggs, honey, vanilla and cinnamon. Process until well blended, stopping occasionally to scrape down the sides of the container. Pour over the peaches.

Bake at 350° for 35 to 40 minutes, or until puffed and golden.

Preparation time: 10 minutes
Baking time: 40 minutes

Per serving: 132 calories, 0.7 g. fat (5% of calories), 1.5 g. dietary fiber, 1 mg. cholesterol, 53 mg. sodium.

BLUEBERRY CLAFOUTI

*C*lafouti is a French dessert often made with cherries. But you may substitute other fruit, such as the blueberries used here, pears, other berries or fresh figs.

2½   cups blueberries
1   cup fat-free egg substitute
⅔   cup skim milk
¼   cup honey
¼   cup whole-wheat flour
¼   cup unbleached flour
1   tablespoon oil
½   teaspoon vanilla

Coat a 9" pie plate with no-stick spray. Add the blueberries.

In a blender, process the eggs, milk, honey, whole-wheat flour, unbleached flour, oil and vanilla until smooth, stopping occasionally to scrape down the sides of the container. Pour over the blueberries.

Bake at 400° for 25 to 30 minutes, or until puffed and golden.

Preparation time: 10 minutes
Baking time: 30 minutes

Per serving: 159 calories, 2.7 g. fat (15% of calories), 2.2 g. dietary fiber, 1 mg. cholesterol, 72 mg. sodium.

CHOCOLATE-DIPPED FRUIT

You know, of course, that fresh fruit is the best dessert going. It's naturally sweet, full of fiber and free of fat. But when your sweet tooth cries out for something a little more decadent, you'll be pleased to know that chocolate-dipped strawberries and other fruit *can* fit into a healthy diet.

Unlike those chocolate confections sold in candy shops, your fancy fruit can be virtually fat-free. That's because it uses cocoa powder, which has only a trace of fat, rather than chocolate bars, which are full of fatty cocoa butter.

To do: Heat ½ cup maple syrup in a small saucepan until it reaches 240° on a candy thermometer (the soft-ball stage). In a large bowl, beat 3 egg whites with an electric mixer until stiff but not dry. Gradually beat in the hot syrup, then beat in ¼ cup cocoa powder and ½ teaspoon vanilla. Continue to beat until the mixture is satiny smooth, about 3 minutes. Use to dip whole strawberries, banana chunks, orange sections, pineapple spears, apricot halves, peach slices or even dried fruits (try apricots, peaches, pineapple, prunes and papaya). Eat immediately, fondue style.

PINEAPPLE BLINTZES

MAKES 12

These easy desserts are also good for breakfasts and brunches. If desired, you may lightly sauté the filled blintzes in a no-stick frying pan until mottled gold.

1½	cups nonfat vanilla yogurt
1	cup well-drained crushed pineapple
4	egg whites
2	cups skim milk
2	tablespoons honey
1½	cups whole-wheat flour
½	teaspoon baking powder

Spoon the yogurt into a yogurt cheese funnel or a sieve lined with cheesecloth. Place over a bowl and set aside to drain for 20 minutes. Transfer to a bowl and fold in the pineapple.

Meanwhile, place the egg whites in a medium bowl and whisk until frothy. Whisk in the milk and honey. Add the flour and baking powder; mix well.

Coat a small no-stick frying pan with no-stick spray. Place over medium heat and allow to warm for a few minutes. Add about ¼ cup batter to the pan and tilt the pan in all directions to spread the batter thinly all over the bottom.

Cook for about 1 minute, or until browned on the underside. Carefully flip the blintz and brown the other side for about 30 seconds. Turn the blintz out onto a wire rack. Repeat until you've used all the batter. You'll have about 12 blintzes.

To serve, divide the pineapple filling among the blintzes, spooning it down the center of each. Fold in the sides.

Preparation time: 30 minutes
Cooking time: 15 minutes

Per blintz: 111 calories, 0.4 g. fat (3% of calories), 2.1 g. dietary fiber, 1 mg. cholesterol, 72 mg. sodium.

Cheese Blintzes (page 201)

Chilled Honeydew Soup (page 220) and Chilled Peach Soup (page 100)

Gingerbread Pancakes (page 80)

Light and Luscious Fish Fry (page 211)

Vegetable Rolls (page 237)

Pasta with Zucchini and Fresh Tomatoes (page 151)

Peppered Lamb Loin (page 198) with Honey-Glazed Carrots (page 201) and couscous

California Burgers (page 67) with Summer Potato Salad (page 66) and Banana-Berry Shakes
(page 47)

BERRY CRISP

SERVES 6

*B*erry crisp is a festive dessert that you can vary according to what's in season or even what's available in the frozen-food section of the supermarket (be sure to use unsweetened berries). You can easily prepare this crisp ahead and serve it either cold or warm—reheat a single serving for about 30 seconds in the microwave.

½ *cup rolled oats*
½ *cup whole-wheat pastry flour*
½ *teaspoon ground cinnamon*
¼ *cup maple syrup*
3 *cups mixed fresh or frozen berries*
2 *tablespoons lemon juice*

In a large no-stick frying pan over medium heat, toast the oats by stirring until lightly browned and fragrant, about 5 minutes. Transfer to a medium bowl. Add the flour and cinnamon; toss to combine. Drizzle with the maple syrup and stir with a fork until crumbly.

Coat a 9" pie plate with no-stick spray. Add the berries and lemon juice. Toss to combine. Sprinkle with the crumb mixture. Cover with foil.

Bake at 400° for 20 minutes, or until the berries are bubbly. Remove the foil and bake for about 5 minutes more, or until the topping is lightly browned.

Preparation time: 10 minutes
Baking time: 25 minutes

Per serving: 143 calories, 0.9 g. fat (6% of calories), 5.4 g. dietary fiber, no cholesterol, 4 mg. sodium.

SOUR CHERRY COMPOTE WITH VANILLA SAUCE

SERVES 6

You may use fresh, frozen, canned or dried sour cherries for this quick compote. If you're using the dried cherries, reduce the amount to 1 cup and simmer them in water to cover until plumped. Drain and proceed with the recipe. For variety, you may also serve the compote as a low-fat topping for waffles, pancakes, cooked cereal and yogurt.

Sour Cherry Compote

1	*can (16 ounces) sliced apricots in juice*
2	*cups pitted sour cherries*
2	*tablespoons honey*
1	*tablespoon lemon juice*
½	*teaspoon grated lemon rind*

Vanilla Sauce

2	*tablespoons cornstarch*
2	*cups skim milk*
2	*tablespoons honey*
¼	*cup fat-free egg substitute*
2	*teaspoons vanilla*

To make the sour cherry compote: Drain the apricots, reserving ¼ cup juice. Place the apricots and juice in a 2-quart saucepan. Add the cherries, honey, lemon juice and lemon rind. Bring to a boil over medium heat. Cover and simmer for 5 minutes. Set aside.

To make the vanilla sauce: Place the cornstarch in a 1-quart saucepan. Whisk in a little of the milk to dissolve the cornstarch. Whisk in the honey and remaining milk. Cook over medium heat, stirring constantly, for 5 to 10 minutes, or until the mixture comes to a boil and thickens.

Remove from the heat and whisk in the egg and vanilla. Return to the heat and cook, stirring constantly, for 1 minute. Transfer to a bowl. Serve warm or chilled over the compote.

Preparation time: 10 minutes
Cooking time: 15 minutes

Per serving: 228 calories, 0.6 g. fat (2% of calories), 2.3 g. dietary fiber, 2 mg. cholesterol, 89 mg. sodium.

MANDARIN RICE PUDDING

SERVES 6

*H*ere's an easy rice pudding that gets Far Eastern flair from mandarin oranges and crystallized ginger. For an even more intriguing flavor, start with an aromatic rice, such as basmati.

1   *cup rice*
2   *teaspoons oil*
¼   *teaspoon ground cinnamon*
2   *cups water*
1   *can (15 ounces) evaporated skim milk*
1   *cup drained and chopped mandarin oranges*
2   *tablespoons minced crystallized ginger*
2   *tablespoons toasted almonds*

In a 3-quart saucepan over medium heat, stir the rice and oil until glossy, about 5 minutes. Stir in the cinnamon. Add the water and bring to a boil. Reduce the heat to medium-low, cover the pan, and simmer the rice for 20 minutes, or until all the liquid has been absorbed. Stir in the milk. Cook over medium-low heat, stirring often, for 10 minutes. Stir in the oranges, ginger and almonds. Serve warm or chilled.

Preparation time: 5 minutes
Cooking time: 35 minutes

Per serving: 217 calories, 3.3 g. fat (14% of calories), 0.6 g. dietary fiber, 3 mg. cholesterol, 88 mg. sodium.

APPLE GRATIN

*F*or variety, you may replace the raisins with dried blueberries, cherries or cranberries. Serve the gratin topped with nonfat vanilla or cherry yogurt.

4	*tart apples, peeled, cored and sliced*
½	*cup water*
¼	*cup raisins*
2	*teaspoons lemon juice*
½	*teaspoon ground cinnamon*
½	*teaspoon ground allspice*
1	*cup low-fat granola*

In a large frying pan, combine the apples, water, raisins, lemon juice, cinnamon and allspice. Bring to a boil over medium heat. Cover and cook, stirring occasionally, for 20 minutes, or until the apples are tender. If the water boils away, add a bit more to keep the apples from sticking.

Coat a 9" pie plate with no-stick spray. Add the apple mixture. Sprinkle with the granola. Bake at 350° for 10 minutes.

Preparation time: 10 minutes
Cooking time: 20 minutes
Baking time: 10 minutes

Per serving: 122 calories, 0.9 g. fat (6% of calories), 4 g. dietary fiber, no cholesterol, 21 mg. sodium.

REFRESHING FRUIT ICES

*F*resh-fruit ices are the ultimate coolers during the long, hot summer. Mangoes are tailor-made for this treatment. So are bananas, papayas, pineapples, strawberries, apricots, peaches, melons and kiwis. And you don't need a fancy ice-cream maker to prepare them. Simply peel your fruit, if necessary, and cut it into chunks. Place in a single layer on a tray lined with wax paper and freeze until solid. Then puree the frozen pieces in a food processor.

For a more sherbetlike dessert, add a splash of evaporated skim milk or buttermilk to the puree. Or get a very grown-up flavor by throwing in some candied ginger. Serve your creation in a pretty goblet and sprinkle it with grated citrus rind—whatever flavor best complements the ice.

GRILLED APPLES

SERVES 4

*H*ere's an easy dessert to make when you've got the outdoor grill fired up.

2	*large apples*
¼	*cup white grape juice*
2	*tablespoons lime juice*
2	*teaspoons honey*
1	*teaspoon minced fresh mint*
1	*teaspoon minced fresh ginger*
½	*teaspoon ground coriander*

Peel and core the apples. Cut crosswise into ½" thick rounds. Place in a large bowl. Add the grape juice, lime juice, honey, mint, ginger and coriander. Let marinate for 20 minutes.

Transfer the apple slices to a hot grill; reserve the marinade. Cook, basting occasionally, for 5 minutes per side, or until warmed through and soft but not mushy.

Preparation time: 10 minutes plus marinating time
Cooking time: 10 minutes

Chef's Note: You may also prepare these apples indoors under the broiler. Coat a broiler rack with no-stick spray and arrange the apples in a single layer. Broil about 5" from the heat, occasionally basting with the marinade.

Per serving: 64 calories, 0.3 g. fat (4% of calories), 1.5 g. dietary fiber, no cholesterol, 1 mg. sodium.

SAUTÉ OF SLICED PEARS AND ALMONDS

SERVES 4

 his is a wonderful fall or winter dessert.

4	*firm Bosc or Bartlett pears*
2	*tablespoons lemon juice*
1	*teaspoon oil*
¼	*cup orange juice*
1	*tablespoon maple syrup*
1	*teaspoon grated orange rind*
½	*teaspoon vanilla*
¼	*teaspoon ground cinnamon*
¼	*teaspoon ground cloves*
2	*tablespoons toasted sliced almonds*

Peel and core the pears. Cut into thin lengthwise slices. Place in a large bowl and toss with the lemon juice.

In a large no-stick frying pan over medium-high heat, sauté the pears in the oil for 2 minutes. Cover and cook over low heat, stirring occasionally, for 5 minutes, or until just tender. Remove with a slotted spoon and divide among 4 dessert dishes.

To the pan, add the orange juice, maple syrup, orange rind, vanilla, cinnamon and cloves. Cook over medium-high heat, stirring constantly, until syrupy. Spoon over the pears. Sprinkle with the almonds.

Preparation time: 10 minutes
Cooking time: 10 minutes

Per serving: 138 calories, 3.6 g. fat (24% of calories), 4.2 g. dietary fiber, no cholesterol, 3 mg. sodium.

PINEAPPLE AMBROSIA

SERVES 6

*Y*ou couldn't ask for an easier dessert. And you may vary it according to what's in season or in your pantry. If desired, serve sprinkled with low-fat granola.

16	*ounces nonfat vanilla yogurt*
1	*cup applesauce*
1	*can (8 ounces) crushed pineapple in juice, well drained*
1	*cup blueberries*
1	*banana, thinly sliced*
¼	*cup toasted flaked coconut*
2	*tablespoons toasted slivered almonds*

In a large bowl, whisk together the yogurt and applesauce. Fold in the pineapple, blueberries, bananas, coconut and almonds. Chill.

Preparation time: 10 minutes plus chilling time

Per serving: 161 calories, 3 g. fat (16% of calories), 2.3 g. dietary fiber, 2 mg. cholesterol, 60 mg. sodium.

Spicy Pumpkin Pudding

SERVES 6

*H*ere's a lighter alternative to pumpkin pie for holiday—
or everyday—meals. For an extra-elegant presentation,
serve this pudding in your fanciest crystal goblets.

1	*cup evaporated skim milk*
1	*cup pumpkin puree*
⅓	*cup fat-free egg substitute*
⅓	*cup all-fruit apple butter*
1	*teaspoon vanilla*
½	*teaspoon ground cinnamon*

Pour the milk into a 2-cup glass measure. Microwave on high for
1 minute, or until warm but not boiling.

In a medium bowl, thoroughly whisk together the pumpkin
puree, eggs, apple butter, vanilla and cinnamon. Slowly pour in the
warm milk and mix in well.

Pour the mixture into a 2-quart microwave ring mold. Microwave
on high for a total of 8 minutes, stopping to rotate the pan a quarter
turn every 2 minutes.

Serve warm or refrigerate until thoroughly chilled. (If serving the
pudding chilled, unmold it onto a platter.)

Preparation time: 5 minutes
Cooking time: 10 minutes

*Per serving: 92 calories, 0.4 g. fat (4% of calories), 0.4 g. dietary fiber, no
cholesterol, 71 mg. sodium.*

HAVE A HEART

*G*ot a yen for French coeur à la crème? This classic heart-shaped dessert is traditionally made with cream cheese, sour cream and heavy cream. That's a lot of cream—none of which does *your* heart any good. You can make a luscious look-alike (and taste-alike) from nonfat lemon yogurt.

Line a small coeur à la crème mold, which has holes for easy drainage, with cheesecloth. (You may also use a sieve or other mold with holes.) Spoon in enough yogurt to fill the mold. Place on a small trivet or rack inside a large bowl. Cover with plastic wrap, refrigerate, and allow to drain until very thick, at least 8 hours. Unmold onto a plate.

Serve your heart topped with sliced strawberries; drizzle with warmed honey and sprinkle with thin strips of lemon rind. Or top the dessert with fresh raspberries and a sauce made by pureeing raspberries with a little honey.

RASPBERRY BREAD PUDDING

SERVES 8

*H*ere's an excellent way to use up stale bread. For variety, you may replace the raspberries with blueberries, cherries or chopped peaches. You may also use other types of bread, such as whole-grain or raisin.

1½	*cups skim milk*
¾	*cup fat-free egg substitute*
½	*cup honey*
1	*teaspoon vanilla*
¼	*teaspoon ground cinnamon*
¼	*teaspoon grated nutmeg*
4	*cups oat bread cubes*
2	*cups raspberries*

In a large bowl, whisk together the milk, eggs, honey, vanilla, cinnamon and nutmeg. Add the bread and raspberries.

Coat a 2-quart casserole with no-stick spray. Add the bread mixture. Cover with a lid or vented plastic wrap. Microwave on medium (50% power) for 3 minutes. Stir and microwave on medium for another 3 minutes.

Stir, then microwave on medium for 4 minutes. Give the dish a half turn and microwave on medium for 4 minutes more. Serve warm.

Preparation time: 10 minutes
Cooking time: 15 minutes

Chef's Note: If you don't have a microwave, bake the bread pudding, uncovered, at 350° for 45 to 50 minutes, or until a knife inserted in the center comes out clean.

Per serving: 198 calories, 2.3 g. fat (10% of calories), 2.4 g. dietary fiber, 1 mg. cholesterol, 195 mg. sodium.

CRANBERRY FRUITCAKE

SERVES 10

This moist cake takes only a few minutes to prepare for the oven. As with many other desserts in this chapter, you may vary the fruit. Try substituting pears for the apples and blueberries for the cranberries, for instance.

⅔	*cup whole-wheat flour*
⅔	*cup unbleached flour*
½	*cup rolled oats*
1½	*teaspoons baking soda*
1	*teaspoon powdered ginger*
½	*cup fat-free egg substitute*
½	*cup honey*
⅓	*cup orange juice*
¼	*cup oil*
1	*teaspoon vanilla*
1	*cup cranberries*
¾	*cup shredded apples*

In a large bowl, combine the whole-wheat flour, unbleached flour, oats, baking soda and ginger.

In a medium bowl, whisk together the eggs, honey, orange juice, oil and vanilla. Stir in the cranberries and apples.

Pour the fruit mixture over the dry ingredients. Fold until the dry ingredients are just moistened; do not overmix.

Coat a 9" × 13" baking dish with no-stick spray. Add the batter and spread evenly. Bake at 350° for 20 to 25 minutes, or until browned and firm to the touch. Serve warm or cold.

Preparation time: 15 minutes
Baking time: 25 minutes

Per serving: 192 calories, 6 g. fat (28% of calories), 1.8 g. dietary fiber, no cholesterol, 141 mg. sodium.

OATMEAL-RAISIN COOKIES

*B*ake a batch of these cookies whenever you need a quick treat. They're perfect to take along on picnics or to have on hand for after-school snacks.

½   *cup margarine*
½   *cup honey*
¼   *cup fat-free egg substitute*
1   *teaspoon vanilla extract*
1¼   *cups whole-wheat flour*
½   *teaspoon baking soda*
¼   *teaspoon baking powder*
⅛   *teaspoon ground coriander*
1   *cup rolled oats*
½   *cup raisins*

In a 2-quart saucepan over low heat, melt the margarine. Stir in the honey. Let cool for 5 minutes. Stir in the egg and vanilla.

In a medium bowl, combine the flour, baking soda, baking powder, coriander, oats and raisins. Add the liquid ingredients and stir until just combined.

Coat 2 large baking sheets with no-stick spray. Drop tablespoonfuls of the batter onto the sheets, leaving about 2" between cookies.

Bake 1 sheet at a time at 350° for about 12 minutes, or until golden brown.

Preparation time: 15 minutes
Baking time: 25 minutes

Per cookie: 110 calories, 4.2 g. fat (33% of calories), 1.3 g. dietary fiber, no cholesterol, 76 mg. sodium.

Baked Apple Wedges

SERVES 8

*T*hese fiber-filled oat and apple treats can double as low-fat breakfast bars.

> 2 *cups rolled oats*
> ½ *cup raisins*
> ½ *cup dried apples*
> ½ *cup apple butter*
> 2 *egg whites*

Place the oats, raisins and apples in a food processor. Process with on/off turns until the apples are diced and the ingredients are well combined.

With the motor running, add the apple butter and egg whites. Process for another minute until the mixture forms a dough.

Coat a 9" glass pie plate with no-stick spray. Add the dough and pat it into an even circle. With your finger, make a 1½" round hole in the middle to help the dough cook evenly.

Microwave on high for 4½ minutes, or until cooked through and dry to the touch. Cut into 8 wedges. Serve warm or cold.

Preparation time: 5 minutes
Cooking time: 5 minutes

Chef's Note: If you don't have a microwave, pat the mixture into the pie plate and bake at 350° for 25 to 30 minutes, or until a cake tester inserted in the middle comes out clean.

Per serving: 159 calories, 1.5 g. fat (8% of calories), 2.2 g. dietary fiber, no cholesterol, 20 mg. sodium.

GINGER CARROT BARS

MAKES 12

*C*arrots add some cancer-preventing beta-carotene to these simple bar cookies.

½ *cup orange juice*
⅓ *cup rolled oats*
½ *cup whole-wheat flour*
½ *cup unbleached flour*
1 *teaspoon baking powder*
2 *medium carrots, shredded*
⅓ *cup maple syrup*
¼ *cup fat-free egg substitute*
1 *tablespoon oil*
1 *tablespoon minced fresh ginger*
1 *teaspoon vanilla*

In a small bowl, combine the orange juice and oats. Set aside to soften for 5 minutes.

In a large bowl, stir together the whole-wheat flour, unbleached flour and baking powder.

In a medium bowl, combine the carrots, maple syrup, egg, oil, ginger and vanilla. Stir in the oats. Pour over the flour mixture and combine until all the flour is moistened. Do not overmix.

Coat an 8" × 8" baking pan with no-stick spray. Add the batter. Bake at 375° for 20 minutes, or until a cake tester inserted in the center comes out clean.

Let cool before slicing. Store tightly wrapped in plastic wrap or a cookie tin.

Preparation time: 10 minutes
Baking time: 20 minutes

Per bar: 87 calories, 1.4 g. fat (15% of calories), 1.2 g. dietary fiber, no cholesterol, 41 mg. sodium.

LEMON COFFEECAKE

*L*emon yogurt adds moisture and a pleasant tang to this delicious coffeecake. For variety, you may replace the cranberries with raisins, currants, dried cherries or chopped fresh cherries.

⅔	*cup honey*
⅓	*cup oil*
1	*cup fat-free egg substitute*
1½	*teaspoons lemon extract*
1¾	*cups unbleached flour*
¾	*cup whole-wheat flour*
2½	*teaspoons baking powder*
1	*cup nonfat lemon yogurt*
1	*cup coarsely chopped cranberries*
1	*tablespoon grated lemon rind*

In a large bowl, beat the honey and oil with an electric mixer until creamy. Beat in the eggs and lemon extract.

In a small bowl, combine the unbleached flour, whole-wheat flour and baking powder.

Beginning and ending with the flour mixture, alternately beat the flour mixture (in fourths) and yogurt (in thirds) into the egg mixture. Fold in the cranberries and lemon rind.

Coat a 9-cup Bundt pan with no-stick spray. Add the batter and smooth the top with a rubber spatula. Bake at 325° for 30 to 35 minutes, or until a cake tester inserted in the center comes out clean. Cool in the pan on a wire rack. Invert onto a platter.

Preparation time: 15 minutes
Baking time: 35 minutes

Per serving: 232 calories, 7 g. fat (27% of calories), 1.7 g. dietary fiber, 19 mg. cholesterol, 112 mg. sodium.

Index

Note: Page references in *italic* indicate photographs. **Boldface** references indicate tables.